Dynamic Programming in Java

From Basics to Expert Proficiency

Contents

Introduction

Dynamic programming is a critical algorithmic optimization technique widely used in computer science and beyond. It offers a structured approach to solving complex problems by breaking them down into simpler subproblems, solving each subproblem just once, and storing their solutions. This enables efficient solution retrieval and contributes to significant improvements in computational efficiency.

This book, "Dynamic Programming in Java: From Basics to Expert Proficiency", aims to equip readers with a comprehensive understanding of dynamic programming principles and their application in Java. It provides insight into fundamental and advanced techniques, supported by practical example implementations in Java programming language.

Dynamic programming emerged from the work of Richard Bellman in the 1950s, who articulated the principle of optimality and introduced methods for solving decision processes. Since then, the technique has proven indispensable across a variety of domains, including operations research, bioinformatics, economics, engineering, and artificial intelligence.

The book is organized into ten chapters, addressing the core concepts of dynamic programming and illustrating how these concepts can be implemented and optimized in Java. Each chapter delves into essential topics, providing theoretical explanations complemented by practical coding examples.

The initial chapters introduce the foundational concepts of dynamic programming. We begin by explaining what dynamic programming is, its historical background, and why it is a preferred method over other techniques. Emphasis is placed on the principles of optimality, subproblems, and overlapping subproblems. By grasping these fundamentals, readers can understand the reasons behind dynamic programming's efficacy.

Following this theoretical grounding, we transition to Java-specific implementations. We discuss the development environment setup, Java syntax and features, and basic coding practices required for dynamic programming. The focus is on illustrating how to translate dynamic programming principles into efficient Java code.

Subsequent chapters address more advanced topics. Chapters on memoization and tabulation shed light on different strategies for storing subproblem solutions, highlighting their practical implementations and performance considerations. We illustrate various optimization techniques to enhance algorithm efficiency and scalability.

Moreover, this book covers a range of common problems and solutions tackled effectively via dynamic programming. Problems like the Fibonacci sequence, longest common subsequence, and the knapsack problem are explored in detail, providing step-by-step explanations and Java code samples.

An entire chapter is dedicated to advanced dynamic programming techniques. Readers will learn about state compression, dynamic programming on trees, bitmasking, and other sophisticated methods. These techniques enable the handling of more complex scenarios and larger datasets with elegance and efficiency.

Real-world applications and case studies included in the latter part of the book exemplify dynamic programming's relevance across industries. Examples from e-commerce, cloud computing, healthcare, finance, and artificial intelligence demonstrate the practical impact and versatility of the technique.

By the end of this book, readers will have developed a robust understanding of dynamic programming, armed with the knowledge and skills to apply it effectively in Java. This capability will not only enhance problem-solving proficiency but also provide a valuable toolkit for tackling a wide range of computational challenges.

We encourage readers to actively engage with the provided examples and exercises, fostering a deeper understanding and practical proficiency. Dynamic programming is a powerful tool, and mastering it can markedly elevate one's programming and algorithmic expertise.

Chapter 1

Introduction to Dynamic Programming

Dynamic programming is a method for solving complex problems by breaking them down into simpler subproblems, utilizing the principle of optimality. This chapter provides an overview of dynamic programming, including its history, key principles, and components. It distinguishes dynamic programming from other techniques, emphasizes its benefits, and illustrates fundamental concepts such as subproblems, overlapping subproblems, and optimal substructure. Real-world applications and the Fibonacci sequence are introduced to demonstrate dynamic programming's practical relevance.

1.1 What is Dynamic Programming?

Dynamic Programming (DP) is a powerful optimization technique used to solve complex problems by breaking them down into simpler subproblems. This methodological approach leverages the principle of optimality and utilizes memoization or tabulation to enhance computational efficiency. Unlike other problem-solving strategies, dynamic programming explicitly constructs solutions for subproblems and combines them to address the overall problem.

The essence of dynamic programming can be best illustrated through the fundamental principles it is founded upon: overlapping subproblems and optimal substructure. Both of these attributes distinguish dynamic programming from other approaches like divide-and-conquer or greedy algorithms.

Overlapping Subproblems: In many complex problems, subproblems recur multiple times. Dynamic programming exploits this property by solving each subproblem only once and storing the solution, which can then be reused whenever the subproblem reappears. This approach contrasts with methods like divide-and-conquer, where subproblems are independent and solved multiple times if they recur.

A classic example highlighting overlapping subproblems is the Fibonacci sequence. Consider the naive recursive approach to compute the n-th Fibonacci number, $F(n) = F(n-1) + F(n-2)$, where $F(0) = 0$ and $F(1) = 1$. This recursive method involves redundant calculations which can be efficiently managed using dynamic programming.

```
public class Fibonacci {
    private static long[] memo;

    public static long fibonacci(int n) {
        if (n <= 1) return n;
        if (memo[n] != 0) return memo[n];
        memo[n] = fibonacci(n - 1) + fibonacci(n - 2);
        return memo[n];
    }

    public static void main(String[] args) {
        int n = 50; // Example input
        memo = new long[n + 1];
        System.out.println("Fibonacci number " + n + " is: " + fibonacci(n));
    }
}
```

In the above Java implementation, we utilized an array memo to store intermediate results, thereby ensuring that each subproblem $F(k)$ is solved only once. This optimization dramatically decreases the time complexity from exponential $O(2^n)$ to linear $O(n)$.

Optimal Substructure: Dynamic programming also relies on the problem having an optimal substructure. This property means that the optimal solution to the overall problem can be composed of optimal solutions to its subproblems. Recognizing and utilizing optimal substructure allows dynamic programming to ensure that the solution is globally optimal.

A typical example of optimal substructure is the shortest path problem in graph theory, where the shortest path from a node to the destination node consists of the shortest paths from intermediate nodes. Consider using dynamic programming to solve the shortest path in a directed acyclic graph (DAG) using the following Java code:

```
import java.util.*;

public class ShortestPathDAG {
    private static final int INF = Integer.MAX_VALUE;

    static class Edge {
        int source, dest, weight;
        Edge(int source, int dest, int weight) {
            this.source = source;
            this.dest = dest;
            this.weight = weight;
        }
    }

    public static void shortestPath(List<Edge>[] graph, int source, int totalNodes) {
        int[] dist = new int[totalNodes];
        Arrays.fill(dist, INF);
        dist[source] = 0;

        Stack<Integer> stack = topologicalSort(graph, totalNodes);

        while (!stack.isEmpty()) {
            int u = stack.pop();
            if (dist[u] != INF) {
                for (Edge edge : graph[u]) {
                    if (dist[u] + edge.weight < dist[edge.dest]) {
                        dist[edge.dest] = dist[u] + edge.weight;
                    }
                }
            }
        }

        System.out.println("Shortest distances from node " + source + ":");
        for (int i = 0; i < dist.length; i++) {
            System.out.println("To node " + i + " = " + (dist[i] == INF ? "Inf" : dist[i
                ]));
        }
    }

    private static Stack<Integer> topologicalSort(List<Edge>[] graph, int totalNodes)
        {
        boolean[] visited = new boolean[totalNodes];
        Stack<Integer> stack = new Stack<>();
        for (int i = 0; i < totalNodes; i++) {
            if (!visited[i]) {
                topologicalSortUtil(i, visited, stack, graph);
            }
        }
        return stack;
    }

    private static void topologicalSortUtil(int v, boolean[] visited, Stack<Integer> stack
        , List<Edge>[] graph) {
        visited[v] = true;
        for (Edge edge : graph[v]) {
            if (!visited[edge.dest]) {
                topologicalSortUtil(edge.dest, visited, stack, graph);
            }
        }
```

```
        stack.push(v);
    }

    public static void main(String[] args) {
        int totalNodes = 6;
        List<Edge>[] graph = new List[totalNodes];
        for (int i = 0; i < totalNodes; i++) {
            graph[i] = new ArrayList<>();
        }

        graph[0].add(new Edge(0, 1, 5));
        graph[0].add(new Edge(0, 2, 3));
        graph[1].add(new Edge(1, 3, 6));
        graph[1].add(new Edge(1, 2, 2));
        graph[2].add(new Edge(2, 4, 4));
        graph[2].add(new Edge(2, 5, 2));
        graph[2].add(new Edge(2, 3, 7));
        graph[3].add(new Edge(3, 4, -1));
        graph[4].add(new Edge(4, 5, -2));

        int source = 1;
        shortestPath(graph, source, totalNodes);
    }
}
```

The algorithm above ensures that each node and edge are processed only once, thanks to the optimal substructure property, ensuring the paths computed are indeed the shortest.

Dynamic programming straddles the spectrum between brute-force and highly specialized algorithms. It systematically examines all possible solutions and stores computed values to avoid redundant calculations, thus striking an efficient balance. For problems exhibiting overlapping subproblems and optimal substructure, dynamic programming emerges as the method of choice, offering significant computational savings and simplicity.

1.2 History and Origins

Dynamic programming (DP), as a formal algorithmic method, traces its origins to the pioneering work of Richard Bellman in the 1950s. Bellman's motivation for developing dynamic programming emerged from his work on multi-stage decision processes while he was at the RAND Corporation. It is essential to understand the historical context in which dynamic programming was developed to appreciate its significance and widespread adoption in both theoretical and practical computations.

In the early 1950s, optimization problems were predominantly solved using linear programming techniques that lacked efficiency for more complex, multi-stage problems. Traditional methods often involved enumerative approaches, which became computationally infeasible as the size of the problem grew. Bellman recognized the potential to address these limitations by breaking down larger problems into smaller, manageable subproblems, solving each subproblem once, and remembering their solutions.

Bellman's paradigm shift was to move away from these cumbersome methods by leveraging the principle of optimality. This principle states that an optimal solution to the problem contains optimal solutions to its subproblems, explicitly formalized by Bellman in his seminal work in 1954. His contributions led to the formulation of the Bellman equation, the foundational recurrence relation characterizing optimal policies in dynamic programming.

The term "dynamic programming" itself, as Bellman noted, was chosen strategically to avoid emphasizing the mathematical rigor and to instead focus on the notion of "planning" and "optimization" over time. This terminology choice helped in securing research funding by downplaying the mathematical complexity and foregrounding the practical implications.

Bellman's book, *Dynamic Programming*, published in 1957, cemented the theoretical foundation of DP and spread its methodologies across various fields. Initially, the adoption of dynamic programming was limited due to the computational constraints of that era. However, with advances in computer technology, DP has gained considerable traction, becoming an indispensable tool in operations research, economics, bioinformatics, artificial intelligence, and more.

During the 1960s and 1970s, dynamic programming was applied extensively to solve problems in economics, thanks to its adaptability in handling sequential decision-making processes. Economists utilized DP to model decision problems in finance, resource allocation, and macroeconomic planning.

In parallel, the field of control theory began to incorporate dynamic programming techniques, particularly after the publication of Bellman's *Adaptive Control Processes: A Guided Tour* in 1961. The application of DP to determine optimal control policies further demonstrated its versatility and power in handling complex, real-world problems.

A significant breakthrough occurred with the advent of the Floyd-Warshall algorithm in 1962, showcasing the power of dynamic programming in solving shortest path problems in weighted graphs. This algorithm's elegance in reducing computational complexity underscored DP's potential in graph theory and network analysis, areas crucial for computer science and communication networks.

The versatility of dynamic programming was also emphasized by its successful application in solving the Knapsack problem, demonstrating its ability to tackle combinatorial optimization problems. These contributions laid the groundwork for DP algorithms to be adapted and utilized in various fields, further enriching the landscape of computational problem-solving techniques.

As computer power grew exponentially over subsequent decades, the practical application of dynamic programming expanded into numerous domains. From sequence alignment in bioinformatics to reinforcement learning in artificial intelligence, the principles of dynamic programming continue to provide robust solutions to problems characterized by optimal substructure and overlapping subproblems.

The history and origins of dynamic programming highlight the forward-thinking nature of Bellman's contributions and the adaptability of DP techniques across diverse disciplines. Bellman's vision to simplify the complex by breaking it down into simpler components remains a cornerstone of algorithmic thinking, illustrating the timeless relevance and enduring legacy of dynamic programming.

1.3 Dynamic Programming vs. Other Techniques

Dynamic programming (DP) distinguishes itself from other algorithmic techniques such as divide and conquer, greedy algorithms, and brute-force methods through its unique approach to solving problems by leveraging past computations to optimize performance. Understanding these differences is crucial for selecting the appropriate method to solve a given problem. We will explore how DP compares with other techniques on key parameters, including problem decomposition, optimality, time complexity, and space complexity.

Divide and Conquer algorithms, like merge sort and quicksort, decompose the problem into independent subproblems, which are then solved recursively. The solutions to these subproblems are combined to solve the original problem. Merge sort, for example, splits the array into halves, sorts each half, and merges the sorted halves to obtain the sorted array. The crucial distinction here is the independence of subproblems. Dividing an instance into independent subproblems facilitates parallelism, but it often involves redundant computations, leading to suboptimal performance for certain classes of problems.

Dynamic programming optimizes by solving each subproblem just once and storing the results in a table (memoization). It exploits overlapping subproblems, a characteristic not amenable to divide and conquer. Consider the Fibonacci sequence:

```
public class FibonacciDP {
    public static long fibonacci(int n) {
        long[] fib = new long[n + 1];
        fib[0] = 0;
        fib[1] = 1;
        for (int i = 2; i <= n; i++) {
            fib[i] = fib[i - 1] + fib[i - 2];
        }
        return fib[n];
    }
}
```

Executing the code:

```
FibonacciDP.fibonacci(10)
55
```

The computed values are stored in the fib array to avoid redundant computation and retrieve results in constant time. This results in a linear time complexity $O(n)$, compared to the exponential time complexity $O(2^n)$ of naive recursive approaches.

Greedy algorithms build up a solution piece by piece, always choosing the next piece that offers the most immediate benefit. They are efficient and can yield globally optimal solutions for certain problems, such as Huffman coding or Dijkstra's algorithm for shortest paths. However, they can fail for problems requiring more globally optimal evaluation. Consider the coin change problem: choosing the largest denomination coin first works when denominations are standard (1, 5, 10, 25), but not if some denominations are missing or nonstandard.

Dynamic programming, in contrast, systematically explores all combinations to ensure the global optimum is found. For instance, in the coin change problem, DP evaluates all potential ways to make change by combining subproblems' solutions. Here is an example:

```
public class CoinChangeDP {
    public static int minCoins(int[] coins, int amount) {
        int[] dp = new int[amount + 1];
        Arrays.fill(dp, Integer.MAX_VALUE);
        dp[0] = 0;
        for (int i = 1; i <= amount; i++) {
```

```
            for (int coin : coins) {
                if (i >= coin && dp[i - coin] != Integer.MAX_VALUE) {
                    dp[i] = Math.min(dp[i], dp[i - coin] + 1);
                }
            }
        }
        return dp[amount] == Integer.MAX_VALUE ? -1 : dp[amount];
    }
}
```

Executing the code:

```
CoinChangeDP.minCoins(new int[] {1, 2, 5}, 11)
3
```

The result shows the minimum number of coins (three coins: 5, 5, and 1) required to make the amount. DP ensures an optimal solution through comprehensive evaluation, albeit typically at the cost of higher space complexity, as it maintains a table of previously computed results.

Brute-force methods systematically enumerate all possible candidates and verify each one to determine the best solution. They are straightforward and applicable to a broad range of tasks but are generally impractical due to their high time complexity. For instance, a brute-force solution to the travelling salesman problem (TSP) would evaluate all possible tours, resulting in factorial time complexity $O(n!)$.

Dynamic programming, through methods like the Held-Karp algorithm, significantly reduces this time complexity for the TSP to $O(n^2 \cdot 2^n)$ by storing intermediate distances and avoiding redundant computations. This efficiency gain makes DP much more feasible than brute-force for combinatorial problems when optimal substructure and overlapping subproblems are present.

In summary, while each technique has its merits and specific use cases, dynamic programming stands out in scenarios where problems exhibit optimal substructure and overlapping subproblems. The advantage brought by avoiding redundant calculations and storing intermediate results often translates to substantial improvements in time and space complexity, making DP a robust and versatile algorithmic strategy.

1.4 Why Use Dynamic Programming?

Dynamic programming (DP) is a highly powerful technique employed to solve a wide class of computational problems. It is particularly useful in scenarios requiring optimization and efficiency. Here, the importance and reasons for using dynamic programming are elaborated upon, covering its advantages, applications, and impact on problem-solving.

Dynamic programming excels over other techniques such as divide-and-conquer and greedy algorithms primarily due to its ability to handle overlapping subproblems and optimal substructures efficiently. The divide-and-conquer method, while useful, often solves the same subproblems multiple times, leading to redundant computations. Dynamic programming, on the other hand, stores the results of these subproblems in a table (also referred to as memoization), avoiding the recomputation and hence optimizing the overall process.

Consider the class of optimization problems. An optimization problem can be solved using dynamic programming if it can be broken down into simpler subproblems. In such scenarios, each subproblem must have a solution that can contribute to the solution of the larger problem, and the global solution must be formed optimally. This characteristic is known as the principle of optimality.

Efficiency and Time Complexity

Dynamic programming significantly improves computational efficiency by transforming exponential-time recursive problems into polynomial-time solutions. For instance, the Fibonacci sequence, commonly presented as:

$$F(n) = \begin{cases} 0 & \text{if } n = 0 \\ 1 & \text{if } n = 1 \\ F(n-1) + F(n-2) & \text{if } n > 1 \end{cases}$$

A naive recursive implementation would entail a time complexity of $O(2^n)$ due to repetitively computing the same values.

```
public class Fibonacci {

    public static long naiveFibonacci(int n) {
        if (n <= 1) return n;
        return naiveFibonacci(n - 1) + naiveFibonacci(n - 2);
    }

    public static void main(String[] args) {
        int n = 40;
        System.out.println(naiveFibonacci(n));
    }
}
```

Executing this code with a parameter such as 40 would result in an impractically lengthy computation. However, employing dynamic programming achieves the same result in $O(n)$ time by storing intermediate results, as shown:

```
public class Fibonacci {

    public static long dpFibonacci(int n) {
        if (n <= 1) return n;
        long[] fib = new long[n + 1];
        fib[0] = 0;
        fib[1] = 1;
        for (int i = 2; i <= n; i++) {
            fib[i] = fib[i - 1] + fib[i - 2];
        }
        return fib[n];
    }

    public static void main(String[] args) {
        int n = 40;
        System.out.println(dpFibonacci(n));
    }
}
```

The conversion from recursive to iterative substantially improves performance, demonstrating a significant reduction in time complexity from exponential to linear. This illustration encapsulates why dynamic programming is favored in complex problem domains.

Optimal Solutions and Problem Solving

Dynamic programming guarantees obtaining optimal solutions, making it indispensable for problems involving decision-making, resource allocation, and optimization. Take for example the Knapsack problem, which can either be solved using a polynomial-time dynamic programming algorithm or an exhaustive search, with the latter being computationally infeasible for large inputs. By systematically solving subproblems and combining their solutions, dynamic programming determines the most efficient and optimal allocation of resources, essential for many scientific, engineering, and economic applications.

```
public class Knapsack {

    public static int dpKnapsack(int W, int[] wt, int[] val, int n) {
        int[][] K = new int[n + 1][W + 1];

        for (int i = 0; i <= n; i++) {
            for (int w = 0; w <= W; w++) {
                if (i == 0 || w == 0) {
                    K[i][w] = 0;
                } else if (wt[i - 1] <= w) {
                    K[i][w] = Math.max(val[i - 1] + K[i - 1][w - wt[i - 1]], K[i - 1][w]);
```

```
            } else {
                K[i][w] = K[i - 1][w];
            }
        }
    }
    return K[n][W];
}

public static void main(String[] args) {
    int val[] = new int[]{60, 100, 120};
    int wt[] = new int[]{10, 20, 30};
    int W = 50;
    int n = val.length;
    System.out.println(dpKnapsack(W, wt, val, n));
}
}
```

Dynamic programming transforms problems with overlapping subproblems, ensuring each subproblem is solved once and its solution is stored for future reference. This logic of reusing precomputed subproblem solutions saves computational resources and time, making it an essential technique in various fields from network optimization to operational research.

Ultimately, dynamic programming's capability to provide optimal solutions efficiently stands as the primary reason for its widespread adoption in solving complex problems across numerous domains. It brings about a balance of computational efficiency and optimal results, vital for problem-solving in theoretical and practical applications.

1.5 Basic Principles of Dynamic Programming

Dynamic programming is predicated on a few fundamental principles that underpin its effectiveness and versatility in tackling complex computational problems. These principles include optimal substructure, overlapping subproblems, memoization, and tabulation. Understanding these principles is vital for designing and implementing efficient dynamic programming solutions.

Optimal Substructure: Optimal substructure implies that an optimal solution to the problem contains optimal solutions to its subproblems. Practically, this means that to solve a problem, one can recursively solve its subproblems first and combine their solutions to form the solution to the original problem. Formally, if O_n is the optimal solution to a problem of size n, and $P(n)$ represents the problem, then O_n can be derived as:

$$O_n = f(O_{n-1}, O_{n-2}, \ldots, O_1, O_0)$$

for some function f.

Consider the shortest path problem in graph theory as an example. If the shortest path from node A to node C passes through node B, then the optimal solution from $A \to C$ consists of the optimal solution from $A \to B$ and the optimal solution from $B \to C$.

Overlapping Subproblems: Dynamic programming problems exhibit overlapping subproblems, meaning the same subproblems are solved multiple times. In contrast to divide-and-conquer algorithms (which approach non-overlapping subproblems), dynamic programming recursively solves and stores solutions to these overlapping subproblems, thereby avoiding redundant computations. This storage of computed solutions is what principally leads to the efficiency gains of dynamic programming algorithms.

For instance, in the calculation of the Fibonacci sequence, the computation of $F(n) = F(n-1) + F(n-2)$ involves repeatedly computing $F(n-1)$ and $F(n-2)$. By storing the results of already computed values, a dynamic programming approach can reduce the exponential time complexity to linear time.

Memoization: Memoization is a top-down approach to dynamic programming where solutions to subproblems are cached as they are computed for the first time. When a solution to a subproblem is requested, it can be retrieved from the cache instead of being recomputed. This caching mechanism significantly reduces redundant calculations and improves efficiency.

In Java, memoization can be implemented using arrays or hash maps. Consider the following illustrative code for memoizing Fibonacci numbers:

```
import java.util.HashMap;

public class Fibonacci {
    private HashMap<Integer, Integer> memo = new HashMap<>();

    public int fib(int n) {
        if (memo.containsKey(n)) {
            return memo.get(n);
        }
        if (n <= 1) {
            return n;
        }
        int result = fib(n - 1) + fib(n - 2);
        memo.put(n, result);
        return result;
```

```
    }
}
```

At each step, the function checks if the Fibonacci value for the given n is already computed and stored in the memo map. If it is, the function returns the stored value to avoid recomputing it.

Tabulation: Tabulation is a bottom-up approach where an array or a table is created to store the results of subproblems. This approach starts solving the smallest subproblem and uses these solutions to iteratively solve larger subproblems. This can lead to an iterative solution that is often more space-efficient than a recursive solution.

Below is an example of using tabulation to compute Fibonacci numbers in Java:

```
public class Fibonacci {
    public int fib(int n) {
        if (n <= 1) return n;
        int[] fibArray = new int[n + 1];
        fibArray[0] = 0;
        fibArray[1] = 1;
        for (int i = 2; i <= n; i++) {
            fibArray[i] = fibArray[i - 1] + fibArray[i - 2];
        }
        return fibArray[n];
    }
}
```

In this code, an array fibArray is used to store Fibonacci values from 0 to n. The values are computed iteratively, leveraging the fact that each value depends only on the previous two values.

Understanding and applying these principles are crucial to effectively designing dynamic programming algorithms. These principles enable the transformation of exponential time complexity problems into polynomial or linear time complexity through strategic storage and reuse of subproblem solutions. Thus, dynamic programming harnesses the power of optimal substructure and overlapping subproblems to deliver elegant and efficient computing solutions.

1.6 Components of a Dynamic Programming Solution

Dynamic programming solutions are characterized by several distinct components that systematically develop optimal solutions for complex problems. Understanding these components is critical for both constructing and analyzing dynamic programming algorithms. The primary constituents of a dynamic programming solution include the recurrence relation, the memoization or tabulation strategy, the initialization process, and state transition diagrams.

Recurrence Relation: At the heart of a dynamic programming solution lies the recurrence relation. This mathematical expression relates a problem of size n to smaller subproblems, typically of size $n-1$, $n-2$, and so on. A recurrence relation is typically derived from the problem's inherent properties and dictates how subproblems combine to form the solution to the original problem.

For instance, consider the Fibonacci sequence where $F(n) = F(n-1) + F(n-2)$, with base cases $F(0) = 0$ and $F(1) = 1$. The recurrence relation here explicitly defines how each term in the sequence is formed by summing the two preceding terms. More generally, a typical recurrence relation takes the form:

$$T(n) = f(T(n-1), T(n-2), \ldots, T(n-k))$$

where f is a function that combines the solutions of subproblems of size $n-1$, $n-2$, up to $n-k$.

Memoization vs. Tabulation: The choice between memoization and tabulation is pivotal in dynamic programming. Memoization is a top-down approach involving recursion and caching. It stores the results of expensive function calls and reuses them when the same inputs occur again. This strategy avoids redundant computations by caching the solutions of subproblems, making it particularly useful for problems with substantial overlapping subproblems.

In Java, memoization can be implemented using data structures like arrays or hash maps to store intermediate results:

```
import java.util.HashMap;

public class Fibonacci {
    private HashMap<Integer, Integer> memo;

    public Fibonacci() {
        memo = new HashMap<>();
    }

    public int fib(int n) {
        if (n <= 1) return n;
        if (memo.containsKey(n)) return memo.get(n);

        int result = fib(n - 1) + fib(n - 2);
```

```
        memo.put(n, result);
        return result;
    }

    public static void main(String[] args) {
        Fibonacci fibonacci = new Fibonacci();
        System.out.println(fibonacci.fib(10)); // Output: 55
    }
}
```

Tabulation, on the other hand, is a bottom-up approach that builds a table in an iterative manner. In this approach, we start from the base case and gradually build up the solution to the original problem. This method often uses arrays to store the results of subproblems and fill them iteratively based on the recurrence relation.

Here is how the Fibonacci sequence can be computed using tabulation in Java:

```
public class FibonacciTabulation {

    public static int fib(int n) {
        if (n <= 1) return n;

        int[] dp = new int[n + 1];
        dp[0] = 0;
        dp[1] = 1;

        for (int i = 2; i <= n; i++) {
            dp[i] = dp[i - 1] + dp[i - 2];
        }

        return dp[n];
    }

    public static void main(String[] args) {
        System.out.println(fib(10)); // Output: 55
    }
}
```

Initialization: Initialization of the dynamic programming table (or cache) is another crucial component. This involves setting up the base cases which are the simplest, smallest instances of the problem and their trivial solutions. For the Fibonacci sequence example, we initialize the base cases with $F(0) = 0$ and $F(1) = 1$, as shown in the tabulation example above. Proper initialization ensures that subsequent computations have a correct starting point.

State Transition Diagrams: State transition diagrams are graphical representations of the dynamic programming process. These diagrams illustrate how states (subproblems) transition to one another based on the recurrence relation. Each node in the diagram represents a state, and the directed edges show the transition from one state to another.

Consider a simple state transition diagram for the Fibonacci sequence:

$$F(0) \longrightarrow F(1) \longrightarrow F(2) \longrightarrow F(3) \longrightarrow F(4)$$

This diagram visually encapsulates the subproblem dependencies and how the solution progresses through these states. State transition diagrams can be particularly helpful in understanding and designing dynamic programming solutions, especially for complex problems with numerous states and transitions.

Together, these components form the backbone of any dynamic programming approach. By rigorously defining the recurrence relation, choosing between memoization and tabulation, initializing appropriately, and utilizing state transition diagrams, one can systematically solve a wide array of problems using dynamic programming techniques.

1.7 Common Terminology and Notations

Understanding the common terminology and notations used in dynamic programming (DP) is crucial for effectively grasping the concepts and implementing algorithms. This section will describe frequently used terms and symbols in DP, establishing a foundation for the subsequent sections.

Dynamic programming involves breaking problems into subproblems, solving each subproblem, and using these solutions to build up answers to larger subproblems. Several key terms and notations facilitate this process.

Subproblem: A subproblem is a smaller instance of the original problem. The idea is to solve each subproblem once and store its solution in a table, thereby avoiding the redundant computation in overlapping subproblems. For instance, in computing the Fibonacci sequence, each Fibonacci number $F(n)$ can be considered a subproblem.

State: In dynamic programming, a state represents a subproblem defined by one or more parameters. The value of the state is the solution to the corresponding subproblem. For example, in the Fibonacci sequence, the state can be represented by the integer n, where the value of the state is $F(n)$.

Transition: A transition defines how to move from one state to another. It typically involves combining the solutions of smaller subproblems to solve a larger subproblem. In the case of the Fibonacci sequence, the transition is defined by the recurrence relation:

$$F(n) = F(n-1) + F(n-2)$$

Memoization: Memoization is a technique used to store the results of subproblems to avoid redundant calculations. In dynamic programming, this is commonly implemented using a table. For instance:

```
int[] memo = new int[n + 1];
Arrays.fill(memo, -1);
```

Tabulation: Tabulation is an iterative approach where solutions to subproblems are computed and stored in a table, starting from the base case and moving towards the desired solution. This is typically done in a bottom-up manner. Consider the bottom-up approach for the Fibonacci sequence:

```
int[] dp = new int[n + 1];
dp[0] = 0;
dp[1] = 1;
for (int i = 2; i <= n; i++) {
    dp[i] = dp[i - 1] + dp[i - 2];
}
```

Optimal Substructure: This property implies that the solution to a problem can be constructed from optimal solutions of its subproblems. If a problem has an optimal substructure, it is possible to apply dynamic programming. The Fibonacci sequence demonstrates optimal substructure, as each term is formed from the sum of the two preceding terms.

Overlapping Subproblems: This property suggests that the problem can be broken down into subproblems, which are solved multiple times. Dynamic programming exploits overlapping subproblems by storing solutions to subproblems and reusing these solutions, thus reducing computation. For example, calculating $F(n-1)$ and $F(n-2)$ for the Fibonacci sequence repeatedly without storing intermediate results would be inefficient.

State Space: State space refers to the set of all possible states for a given problem. It encompasses all the potential subproblems that need to be solved. The state space for the Fibonacci sequence includes all $F(i)$ where $0 \leq i \leq n$.

Recurrence Relation: A recurrence relation defines the relationship between the solutions of subproblems and can be viewed as the backbone of dynamic programming. It provides a formula to compute the state value based on other state values. For instance, the recurrence relation for the Fibonacci sequence is:

$$F(n) = \begin{cases} 0 & \text{if } n = 0 \\ 1 & \text{if } n = 1 \\ F(n-1) + F(n-2) & \text{if } n > 1 \end{cases}$$

Base Case: The base case is the simplest, smallest instance of the problem which can be solved directly. In the recurrence relation, it halts the recursion. For the Fibonacci sequence, the base cases are $F(0) = 0$ and $F(1) = 1$.

Top-Down Approach: This approach involves breaking the problem into smaller subproblems and solving each recursively. It is typically combined with memoization to store and reuse the results of subproblems. Below is a Java implementation using top-down approach for Fibonacci sequence:

```
int fib(int n, int[] memo) {
    if (n == 0) return 0;
    if (n == 1) return 1;
    if (memo[n] != -1) return memo[n];
    memo[n] = fib(n-1) + memo[n-2];
    return memo[n];
}
```

Bottom-Up Approach: In contrast to the top-down approach, the bottom-up approach starts with the smallest subproblems and iteratively solves them, storing their solutions in a table. The earlier code snippet illustrating the bottom-up method for Fibonacci is an example of this approach.

Both top-down and bottom-up approaches can be used to craft dynamic programming solutions effectively. Understanding these terms and notations is essential for designing, analyzing, and implementing dynamic programming algorithms proficiently.

1.8 The Role of Subproblems and Overlapping Subproblems

Dynamic programming (DP) is predicated on the systematic approach of breaking down problems into simpler components, specifically subproblems. Within this framework, two fundamental concepts are pivotal: subproblems and overlapping subproblems. Understanding these concepts is crucial for grasping the essence of dynamic programming.

Subproblems are essentially smaller versions of the main problem that need to be solved to address the larger problem. They form the basis for constructing a solution incrementally. Take for instance the well-known Fibonacci sequence, which can be defined recursively as follows:

$$F(n) = \begin{cases} 0 & \text{if } n = 0, \\ 1 & \text{if } n = 1, \\ F(n-1) + F(n-2) & \text{if } n > 1. \end{cases}$$

In this case, $\mathrm{F}(2)$ depends on $\mathrm{F}(1)$ and $\mathrm{F}(0)$, $\mathrm{F}(3)$ depends on $\mathrm{F}(2)$ and $\mathrm{F}(1)$, and so forth. Each Fibonacci number requires the solutions of two smaller subproblems: calculating the preceding two Fibonacci numbers. Notably, as we progress through the sequence, the same subproblems—such as $\mathrm{F}(1)$ and $\mathrm{F}(0)$—recur multiple times.

This recurrent necessity to solve the same subproblems multiple times brings us to overlapping subproblems. Overlapping subproblems refer to a scenario where the recursive approach leads to redundant computations of the same subproblems. For instance, if we compute $\mathrm{F}(5)$, we need $\mathrm{F}(4)$ and $\mathrm{F}(3)$; to compute $\mathrm{F}(4)$, we need $\mathrm{F}(3)$ and $\mathrm{F}(2)$. Both $\mathrm{F}(3)$ and $\mathrm{F}(2)$ are repeatedly solved, leading to inefficiency.

To illustrate this concept with code, consider the following naive recursive implementation of the Fibonacci sequence:

```
public class Fibonacci {
    public static int fib(int n) {
        if (n <= 1) {
            return n;
        }
        return fib(n - 1) + fib(n - 2);
    }

    public static void main(String[] args) {
        int n = 10;
        System.out.println("Fibonacci number at position " + n + " is: " + fib(n));
```

```
    }
}
```

When executed, the program yields:

```
Fibonacci number at position 10 is: 55
```

While straightforward, this approach is inefficient due to overlapping subproblems. Each call to fib generates two additional calls, leading to an exponential number of duplicate computations.

Dynamic programming optimizes such scenarios by storing the results of subproblems—either in a bottom-up manner (iterative approach) or top-down manner (memoization approach). This minimizes redundant calculations, improving efficiency.

Bottom-up dynamic programming involves solving the smallest subproblems first and progressively building up to the original problem. Here's an iterative version of the Fibonacci sequence:

```
public class Fibonacci {
    public static int fib(int n) {
        if (n <= 1) {
            return n;
        }
        int[] fibArray = new int[n + 1];
        fibArray[0] = 0;
        fibArray[1] = 1;
        for (int i = 2; i <= n; i++) {
            fibArray[i] = fibArray[i - 1] + fibArray[i - 2];
        }
        return fibArray[n];
    }

    public static void main(String[] args) {
        int n = 10;
        System.out.println("Fibonacci number at position " + n + " is: " + fib(n));
    }
}
```

Upon execution, we achieve the same result, but significantly more efficiently:

```
Fibonacci number at position 10 is: 55
```

Memoization, an alternative approach, involves storing the results of subproblems to avoid redundant computation. A memoized solution for the Fibonacci sequence is shown below:

```
import java.util.HashMap;

public class Fibonacci {
    private static HashMap<Integer, Integer> memo = new HashMap<>();

    public static int fib(int n) {
```

```
        if (n <= 1) {
            return n;
        }
        if (memo.containsKey(n)) {
            return memo.get(n);
        }
        int result = fib(n - 1) + fib(n - 2);
        memo.put(n, result);
        return result;
    }

    public static void main(String[] args) {
        int n = 10;
        System.out.println("Fibonacci number at position " + n + " is: " + fib(n));
    }
}
```

This memoized version also results in:

```
Fibonacci number at position 10 is: 55
```

The HashMap `memo` acts as a cache, storing already computed Fibonacci numbers, which prevents redundant calculations of subproblems.

Understanding subproblems and overlapping subproblems helps frame issues efficiently solvable using dynamic programming. Identifying these foundational elements within a problem is the first step toward crafting a dynamic programming solution.

1.9 The Importance of Optimal Substructure

Optimal substructure is a fundamental characteristic of problems that can be effectively solved using dynamic programming. The principle asserts that an optimal solution to the problem contains optimal solutions to its subproblems. Therefore, understanding and identifying optimal substructure is crucial for applying dynamic programming techniques.

In formal terms, a problem exhibits optimal substructure if the solution to a given instance of the problem can be constructed efficiently from optimal solutions to its sub-instances. This means that if you can break down a problem into smaller, manageable subproblems and solve each subproblem optimally, you can then combine these solutions to address the overall problem optimally.

Consider the classic problem of finding the shortest path in a graph. The shortest path problem between two vertices in a graph illustrates the importance of optimal substructure. Suppose we want to find the shortest path from vertex A to vertex D. If there is an intermediate vertex B on this path, the optimal solution from A to D will include the shortest path from A to B and the shortest path from B to D. Formally, if $P(A, D)$ denotes the shortest path from A to D, and B is an intermediate vertex on this path, then:

$$P(A, D) = P(A, B) + P(B, D)$$

This relationship showcases that the subpaths $P(A, B)$ and $P(B, D)$ within the overall path $P(A, D)$ are also optimal.

The optimal substructure property is not limited to shortest path problems. Many optimization problems possess this characteristic. For example, in the context of the Fibonacci sequence, the computation of any Fibonacci number $F(n)$ is based on the sum of the two preceding Fibonacci numbers $F(n-1)$ and $F(n-2)$. Given that $F(n-1)$ and $F(n-2)$ are computed optimally, their sum will give us the optimal result for $F(n)$. Mathematically, this can be expressed as:

$$F(n) = F(n-1) + F(n-2)$$

To further elucidate, consider the Knapsack Problem, another quintessential example in dynamic programming. Given a set of items, each with a weight and a value, the problem seeks to maximize the total value in a knapsack of fixed capacity. If one solves the subproblem of finding the optimal subset of items for a reduced capacity and one less item, one can construct the solution to the larger problem by considering whether or not to include the item left out in the subproblem. The dynamic programming approach for the 0/1 Knapsack Problem relies profoundly on this optimal substructure property.

To summarize, recognizing optimal substructure in problems allows for the decomposition of a complex problem into simpler subproblems, solving each subproblem optimally, and then combining these solutions to solve the overall problem. This approach is the essence of dynamic programming. Below is a simple Java implementation example of the Fibonacci sequence to illustrate how recognizing the optimal substructure makes dynamic programming highly efficient:

```
public class FibonacciDP {
    public static int fibonacci(int n) {
        if (n <= 1) return n;
        int[] fib = new int[n+1];
        fib[0] = 0;
```

```
        fib[1] = 1;
        for (int i = 2; i <= n; i++) {
            fib[i] = fib[i-1] + fib[i-2];
        }
        return fib[n];
    }

    public static void main(String[] args) {
        int n = 10;
        System.out.println("Fibonacci number " + n + " is " + fibonacci(n));
    }
}
```

Executing the above code yields:

```
Fibonacci number 10 is 55
```

This code demonstrates how the optimal substructure property of the Fibonacci sequence allows us to build a solution from the bottom up, ensuring each subproblem is solved optimally, leading to an efficient overall solution.

Identifying and leveraging optimal substructure is a crucial step in designing a dynamic programming solution, making it indispensable for efficiently solving a wide range of complex problems in computer science. Understanding this concept deeply enhances one's ability to approach and decompose problems methodically, thereby applying dynamic programming techniques effectively.

1.10 Introduction to the Fibonacci Sequence

The Fibonacci sequence is a classic example often used to introduce the concepts and applications of dynamic programming due to its simplicity and the clear illustration of overlapping subproblems and optimal substructure.

The Fibonacci sequence is defined as a series of numbers where each number is the sum of the two preceding ones, typically starting with 0 and 1. Mathematically, it can be expressed as:

$$F(n) = \begin{cases} 0 & \text{if } n = 0 \\ 1 & \text{if } n = 1 \\ F(n-1) + F(n-2) & \text{if } n > 1 \end{cases}$$

To illustrate the power of dynamic programming, we'll explore the naive recursive solution, identify its inefficiencies, and then introduce the memoized and bottom-up approaches which significantly optimize the computation.

Naive Recursive Solution

The naive recursive solution directly follows the mathematical definition, where each Fibonacci number is computed by recursive calls to compute its two predecessors. The corresponding Java implementation can be written as follows:

```
public class Fibonacci {
    public static int fibonacci(int n) {
        if (n <= 1) {
            return n;
        }
        return fibonacci(n - 1) + fibonacci(n - 2);
    }

    public static void main(String[] args) {
        System.out.println(fibonacci(10)); // Outputs: 55
    }
}
```

Executing this code for larger values of n reveals its inefficiency due to redundant computations, as shown in the output.

```
55
```

Analysis of Inefficiency

The naive recursive approach has an exponential time complexity of $O(2^n)$ as it recalculates the same subproblems multiple times. For instance, to compute $F(5)$, it redundantly computes $F(4)$, $F(3)$, and so forth. This inefficiency becomes apparent when visualizing the recursion tree, where each node represents a function call.

Memoized Approach

To mitigate this inefficiency, we can use memoization, an optimization technique where we store the results of expensive function calls and reuse them when the same inputs occur again. This transforms the exponential time complexity into linear time complexity $O(n)$.

The Java implementation of the memoized Fibonacci sequence is as follows:

```
import java.util.HashMap;
import java.util.Map;

public class MemoizedFibonacci {
    private static Map<Integer, Integer> memo = new HashMap<>();

    public static int fibonacci(int n) {
        if (n <= 1) {
```

```
            return n;
        }
        if (memo.containsKey(n)) {
            return memo.get(n);
        }
        int result = fibonacci(n - 1) + fibonacci(n - 2);
        memo.put(n, result);
        return result;
    }

    public static void main(String[] args) {
        System.out.println(fibonacci(10)); // Outputs: 55
    }
}
```

In this approach, the computed values of Fibonacci numbers are stored in the memoization map, eliminating redundant calculations and drastically improving performance.

Bottom-Up Approach

An alternative to memoization is the bottom-up approach, which builds the solution iteratively from the base cases up to the desired value. This method uses an array to store the Fibonacci numbers as they are computed.

Here is the Java implementation of the bottom-up approach:

```
public class BottomUpFibonacci {
    public static int fibonacci(int n) {
        if (n <= 1) {
            return n;
        }
        int[] fib = new int[n + 1];
        fib[0] = 0;
        fib[1] = 1;
        for (int i = 2; i <= n; i++) {
            fib[i] = fib[i - 1] + fib[i - 2];
        }
        return fib[n];
    }

    public static void main(String[] args) {
        System.out.println(fibonacci(10)); // Outputs: 55
    }
}
```

Here, instead of making recursive calls, the algorithm iteratively fills an array from $F(0)$ to $F(n)$, thus achieving an optimal dynamic programming solution with linear time complexity $O(n)$ and linear space complexity $O(n)$.

Space Optimization in Bottom-Up Approach

Further optimization is possible by reducing the space complexity. Noting that the calculation of any $F(n)$ only requires the last two computed values, we can optimize the space to constant $O(1)$ by maintaining only two variables instead of an array.

The optimized version is shown below:

```
public class SpaceOptimizedFibonacci {
    public static int fibonacci(int n) {
        if (n <= 1) {
            return n;
        }
        int prev2 = 0;
        int prev1 = 1;
        for (int i = 2; i <= n; i++) {
            int current = prev2 + prev1;
            prev2 = prev1;
            prev1 = current;
        }
        return prev1;
    }

    public static void main(String[] args) {
        System.out.println(fibonacci(10)); // Outputs: 55
    }
}
```

This code optimizes both time and space efficiently, making the computation of Fibonacci numbers both fast and lightweight.

The Fibonacci sequence provides a foundational example for understanding dynamic programming. It illustrates the key principles of solving problems by breaking them down into subproblems, avoiding redundant calculations, and optimizing both time and space complexities effectively. This basic understanding can be applied to more complex problems, thereby broadening the scope of dynamic programming applications in computational problem-solving.

1.11 Real-World Applications of Dynamic Programming

Dynamic programming (DP) is not just a theoretical construct; it is a tool with significant practical applications across various domains. By leveraging the principles of breaking complex problems into simpler subproblems, reusing solutions to overlapping subproblems, and optimizing recursively, DP has found applications in computer science, operations research, economics, bioinformatics, artificial intelligence, and more. This section explores several prominent real-world applications where dynamic programming techniques are indispensable.

1. Shortest Path Problems:

In computer networks and graph theory, dynamic programming plays a crucial role in finding the shortest path between nodes. One of the most well-known algorithms, Dijkstra's algorithm, although not a pure dynamic programming approach, is similar and often compared with the Bellman-Ford algorithm, which is a dynamic programming solution. The Bellman-Ford algorithm computes shortest paths from a single source vertex to all other vertices, even in the presence of negative weight edges.

```
public class BellmanFord {
    static final int INF = Integer.MAX_VALUE;

    static void bellmanFord(int graph[][], int V, int E, int src) {
        int[] dist = new int[V];
        for (int i = 0; i < V; ++i)
            dist[i] = INF;
        dist[src] = 0;

        for (int i = 1; i < V; ++i) {
            for (int j = 0; j < E; ++j) {
                int u = graph[j][0];
                int v = graph[j][1];
                int weight = graph[j][2];
                if (dist[u] != INF && dist[u] + weight < dist[v])
                    dist[v] = dist[u] + weight;
            }
        }

        for (int j = 0; j < E; ++j) {
            int u = graph[j][0];
            int v = graph[j][1];
            int weight = graph[j][2];
            if (dist[u] != INF && dist[u] + weight < dist[v])
                System.out.println("Graph contains negative weight cycle.");
        }

        printArr(dist, V);
    }

    static void printArr(int dist[], int V) {
        System.out.println("Vertex Distance from Source");
        for (int i = 0; i < V; ++i)
            System.out.println(i + "\t\t" + dist[i]);
    }

    public static void main(String[] args) {
        int V = 5;
        int E = 8;

        int graph[][] = {
            { 0, 1, -1 }, { 0, 2, 4 }, { 1, 2, 3 },
            { 1, 3, 2 }, { 1, 4, 2 }, { 3, 2, 5 },
            { 3, 1, 1 }, { 4, 3, -3 }
        };

        bellmanFord(graph, V, E, 0);
    }
```

```
}
```

This code snippet demonstrates the Bellman-Ford algorithm, effectively calculating shortest paths.

2. Sequence Alignment in Bioinformatics:

In bioinformatics, dynamic programming is widely used for sequence alignment tasks. Sequence alignment involves arranging sequences of DNA, RNA, or protein to identify regions of similarity. The Needleman-Wunsch algorithm for global alignment and the Smith-Waterman algorithm for local alignment are classic examples.

```
public class NeedlemanWunsch {
    static int match = 1;
    static int mismatch = -1;
    static int gap = -2;

    public static int getScore(char a, char b) {
        if (a == b)
            return match;
        else
            return mismatch;
    }

    public static void needlemanWunsch(String seq1, String seq2) {
        int n = seq1.length();
        int m = seq2.length();
        int[][] score = new int[n + 1][m + 1];

        for (int i = 0; i <= n; i++)
            score[i][0] = i * gap;
        for (int j = 0; j <= m; j++)
            score[0][j] = j * gap;

        for (int i = 1; i <= n; i++) {
            for (int j = 1; j <= m; j++) {
                int scoreDiag = score[i - 1][j - 1] + getScore(seq1.charAt(i - 1), seq2.
                    charAt(j - 1));
                int scoreUp = score[i - 1][j] + gap;
                int scoreLeft = score[i][j - 1] + gap;
                score[i][j] = Math.max(scoreDiag, Math.max(scoreUp, scoreLeft));
            }
        }

        System.out.println("Optimal alignment score: " + score[n][m]);
    }

    public static void main(String[] args) {
        String seq1 = "GATTACA";
        String seq2 = "GCATGCU";
        needlemanWunsch(seq1, seq2);
    }
}
```

This implementation of the Needleman-Wunsch algorithm illustrates how dynamic programming can optimize the alignment of two sequences to find the highest similarity score.

3. Inventory Management:

Dynamic programming models assist businesses in optimizing inventory management by determining the best strategy for ordering and holding products. The Economic Order Quantity (EOQ) model and the Wagner-Whitin algorithm are common methods employed. The Wagner-Whitin algorithm, for example, helps solve the lot-sizing problem in inventory management.

4. Optimal Matrix Chain Multiplication:

In computing matrix products, determining the optimal order of matrix multiplication can significantly reduce computation time. The dynamic programming approach evaluates all probable parenthesizations and computes the minimal number of multiplications.

```
public class MatrixChainMultiplication {
    public static int matrixChainOrder(int p[], int n) {
        int m[][] = new int[n][n];

        for (int i = 1; i < n; i++)
            m[i][i] = 0;

        for (int L = 2; L < n; L++) {
            for (int i = 1; i < n - L + 1; i++) {
                int j = i + L - 1;
                m[i][j] = Integer.MAX_VALUE;
                for (int k = i; k <= j - 1; k++) {
                    int q = m[i][k] + m[k + 1][j] + p[i - 1] * p[k] * p[j];
                    if (q < m[i][j])
                        m[i][j] = q;
                }
            }
        }
        return m[1][n - 1];
    }

    public static void main(String[] args) {
        int arr[] = { 1, 2, 3, 4 };
        int size = arr.length;
        System.out.println("Minimum number of multiplications is " +
                matrixChainOrder(arr, size));
    }
}
```

Applying dynamic programming to matrix chain multiplication determines the most efficient matrix order, minimizing computational overhead.

5. Portfolio Optimization in Finance:

In finance, dynamic programming can solve portfolio optimization problems, where the objective is to maximize returns while minimizing risk.

By evaluating different investment combinations, dynamic programming models help identify optimal investment strategies, balancing expected returns against potential risks.

6. Resource Allocation and Knapsack Problems:

Resource allocation and knapsack problems are classic optimization problems solvable by dynamic programming. The 0/1 knapsack problem, for instance, aims to maximize the total value of items in a knapsack without exceeding its capacity.

```
public class Knapsack {
    static int knapSack(int W, int wt[], int val[], int n) {
        int K[][] = new int[n + 1][W + 1];

        for (int i = 0; i <= n; i++) {
            for (int w = 0; w <= W; w++) {
                if (i == 0 || w == 0)
                    K[i][w] = 0;
                else if (wt[i - 1] <= w)
                    K[i][w] = Math.max(val[i - 1] + K[i - 1][w - wt[i - 1]], K[i - 1][w]);
                else
                    K[i][w] = K[i - 1][w];
            }
        }

        return K[n][W];
    }

    public static void main(String args[]) {
        int val[] = new int[] { 60, 100, 120 };
        int wt[] = new int[] { 10, 20, 30 };
        int W = 50;
        int n = val.length;
        System.out.println(knapSack(W, wt, val, n));
    }
}
```

Implementing the 0/1 knapsack problem using dynamic programming optimizes the inclusion of items based on their weights and values.

7. Speech Recognition:

In artificial intelligence, dynamic programming is used in speech recognition systems. The Viterbi algorithm, for instance, finds the most likely sequence of hidden states, aiding in recognizing spoken words and phrases. The Hidden Markov Model (HMM) framework leverages DP to decode the speech signal.

Through these examples, it is apparent that dynamic programming's versatility and efficiency make it an essential tool in solving a wide array of complex real-world problems. By breaking down large problems into manageable components and reusing prior computations, dynamic programming often provides optimal solutions in computationally feasible time.

1.12 Summary and Key Takeaways

Dynamic programming (DP) is a pivotal algorithmic technique aimed at solving optimization problems by breaking them down into simpler, overlapping subproblems, each of which adheres to the principle of optimality. This chapter has systematically introduced various facets of dynamic programming, elucidating its core principles and relevance in computational problem solving.

The foundational element of dynamic programming is the method of decomposing complex problems into smaller, manageable subproblems. This approach capitalizes on the **optimal substructure** property, where the optimal solution to a problem can be constructed efficiently from the optimal solutions of its subproblems. We have also explored the **overlapping subproblems** property, which implies that a recursive algorithm would re-compute the same subproblems multiple times without memoization or a tabular approach.

The historical context established dynamic programming's inception with Richard Bellman's pioneering work in the 1950s, situating it within a framework that emphasizes efficiency and optimization. Bellman's insights into mathematical optimization and computational feasibility have laid the groundwork for the adoption and evolution of dynamic programming in various fields.

Dynamic programming distinguishes itself from other algorithmic strategies such as **Divide and Conquer** and **Greedy Algorithms**. While Divide and Conquer also decomposes problems into subproblems, it does not typically reuse solutions to overlapping subproblems. Greedy Algorithms, on the other hand, build up a solution piece by piece, always choosing the next piece that offers the most immediate benefit, without necessarily considering the global optimum. In contrast, DP ensures an optimal solution by evaluating multiple possibilities and storing the best results.

We discussed the **benefits of using dynamic programming**, emphasizing its ability to transform exponential time complexity problems into polynomial time complexity solutions. This makes DP especially powerful in scenarios where naive approaches would be computationally infeasible.

The **basic principles** of dynamic programming involve breaking down problems into subproblems, solving each subproblem only once, and storing their solutions—typically in a table—to avoid redundant computations. This tabular method is a common implementation approach for DP, also known as **bottom-up dynamic programming**. Alternatively, **top-down dynamic programming**, or memoization, solves problems recursively but stores previously computed results.

Several key **components of a dynamic programming solution** were identified, including:

- The identification and formulation of subproblems.
- The establishment of a recursive relationship that connects the subproblems.
- The use of a data structure, often an array or matrix, to store solutions to subproblems.
- The construction of the final solution based on the stored results.

Common terminology and notations in dynamic programming were clarified, such as the use of T to denote the cost function, S for subproblems, and OPT representing the optimal solution.

Examining the **role of subproblems and overlapping subproblems**, we noted their critical importance in reducing the solution space. Algorithms such as those solving the Fibonacci sequence or knapsack problem demonstrate how results of smaller subproblems can be reused to build the result for larger problems.

The principle of **optimal substructure** was explored in depth, highlighting its necessity for a problem to be amenable to dynamic programming. A problem demonstrates optimal substructure if an optimal solution to the problem contains within it optimal solutions to its subproblems.

Through the introduction to the **Fibonacci sequence**, an iconic example of a problem suited to dynamic programming, both naive and efficient implementations were compared. The initial recursive approach to solving Fibonacci numbers, while straightforward, exhibits exponential time complexity. In contrast, a dynamic programming approach leverages memoization or tabulation, reducing the time complexity significantly.

```
public class FibonacciDP {
```

```
    public static long fibonacci(int n) {
        long[] dp = new long[n + 1];
        dp[0] = 0;
        dp[1] = 1;
        for (int i = 2; i <= n; i++) {
            dp[i] = dp[i - 1] + dp[i - 2];
        }
        return dp[n];
    }

    public static void main(String[] args) {
        int n = 50;
        System.out.println("Fibonacci number at position " + n + " is " + fibonacci(n))
            ;
    }
}
```

The program's output demonstrates the efficiency of dynamic programming for the Fibonacci sequence:

```
Fibonacci number at position 50 is 12586269025
```

Finally, the chapter illuminated **real-world applications** of dynamic programming, showing its versatility and utility in fields such as bioinformatics (sequence alignment), operations research, economics, and artificial intelligence (reinforcement learning).

DP's capability to handle combinatorial optimization problems makes it a crucial tool in both theoretical and applied computing domains. Students and practitioners should now possess a solid understanding of dynamic programming's theoretical underpinnings and practical implementations, prepared to tackle complex problems with enhanced computational efficiency.

Chapter 2

Dynamic Programming Fundamentals

This chapter delves into the core principles of dynamic programming, introducing the principle of optimality, the process of breaking down problems into subproblems, and recognizing overlapping subproblems. It covers essential components such as state variables, transition relations, and base cases. Additionally, the chapter explains the formulation of dynamic programming recurrences and contrasts top-down and bottom-up approaches, including memoization and tabulation techniques, while providing an analysis of time and space complexity.

2.1 The Principle of Optimality

The principle of optimality is a fundamental concept in dynamic programming that asserts that any optimal solution to a problem can be decomposed into optimal solutions of its subproblems. This concept is central to the dynamic programming paradigm as it justifies the recursive approach to solving problems by breaking them down into smaller, more manageable components.

To understand the principle of optimality in depth, consider a problem P that can be divided into subproblems P_1, P_2, ..., P_n. The principle of optimality states that if the overall solution to P is optimal, then the solutions to P_1, P_2, ..., P_n must also be optimal. In mathematical terms, if S is the optimal solution for problem P, and S_1, S_2, ..., S_n are the segments of S corresponding to the subproblems, then S_1, S_2, ..., S_n are optimal solutions for P_1, P_2, ..., P_n respectively.

Consider a classic problem such as the shortest-path problem in a weighted graph. If vertex v lies on the shortest path from vertex u to vertex w, then the shortest path from u to v and from v to w are themselves the shortest paths. This manifests the principle of optimality: the shortest path from u to w consists of the shortest paths between the intermediate vertices.

Formally, let us consider a minimization problem where $f(\cdot)$ is an objective function to be minimized. Suppose P is divided into subproblems P_1 and P_2. Let X be the set of valid solutions for P, and X_1, X_2 be the sets of valid solutions for P_1 and P_2 respectively, where each solution in X can be regarded as a combination of solutions from X_1 and X_2. The principle of optimality asserts that:

If $x^* \in X$ is optimal for P, then $x_1^* \in X_1$ and $x_2^* \in X_2$ (where $x^* = (x_1^*, x_2^*)$) are

In practice, adherence to the principle of optimality enables the recursive breakdown of problems, facilitating dynamic programming approaches. Let us illustrate this with an example—the Fibonacci sequence.

The recursive definition of the Fibonacci sequence is:

$$F(n) = \begin{cases} 0 & \text{if } n = 0 \\ 1 & \text{if } n = 1 \\ F(n-1) + F(n-2) & \text{if } n > 1 \end{cases}$$

The principle of optimality applies as to compute $F(n)$, we need the optimal solutions $F(n-1)$ and $F(n-2)$. Hence, the solution $F(n)$ can be built by combining these smaller subproblem solutions, each of which is optimal by definition.

The implementation of Fibonacci sequence using dynamic programming, specifically with memoization, is as follows:

```
public class Fibonacci {
    private static HashMap<Integer, Integer> memo = new HashMap<>();

    public static int fibonacci(int n) {
```

```
        if (n <= 1) return n;

        if (memo.containsKey(n)) {
            return memo.get(n);
        }

        int result = fibonacci(n - 1) + fibonacci(n - 2);
        memo.put(n, result);

        return result;
    }

    public static void main(String[] args) {
        int n = 10;
        System.out.println("Fibonacci of " + n + " is " + fibonacci(n));
    }
}
```

The output of the above Java program for $n = 10$:

```
Fibonacci of 10 is 55
```

In the code, we utilize memoization to store intermediate results so they can be reused, ensuring each subproblem is solved optimally and efficiently. This adherence to the principle of optimality ensures that the overall computation is both correct and optimized for performance.

Without the principle of optimality, solving optimization problems using dynamic programming would not be feasible since the optimal solution could not be guaranteed through a series of smaller, optimal subproblem solutions. Thus, the principle of optimality is not only a theoretical cornerstone but also a practical enabler in the application of dynamic programming algorithms.

2.2 Breaking Down Problems into Subproblems

Breaking down problems into subproblems is a critical concept in dynamic programming (DP). This methodology allows for the transformation of a complex problem into simpler, more manageable components. By resolving these smaller subproblems, one can then combine their solutions to address the original problem comprehensively and efficiently.

To understand this process, consider a problem P that can be divided into subproblems $P_1, P_2, \ldots, P_n$. Each subproblem should ideally be a simpler instance of the original problem. The key is to ensure that solving these smaller subproblems will facilitate solving the larger problem due to the property of optimal substructure, which was previously discussed under the principle of optimality.

1. Decomposition

Effective decomposition requires identifying the minimal subproblems that capture the essence of the original problem. This involves breaking the problem down recursively. For example, to compute the nth Fibonacci number, one might express it in terms of the $(n-1)$th and $(n-2)$th Fibonacci numbers:

$$F(n) = F(n-1) + F(n-2)$$

Here, solving for $F(n-1)$ and $F(n-2)$ are smaller subproblems compared to solving directly for $F(n)$.

2. Subproblem Interdependency

The interdependency between subproblems must be understood to optimize computation. If subproblems share sub-subproblems, this overlap should be recognized to avoid redundant computations. For instance, consider $F(n)$:

$$F(n-1) = F(n-2) + F(n-3)$$
$$F(n-2) = F(n-3) + F(n-4)$$

Clearly, $F(n-3)$ is computed multiple times. An efficient DP solution caches such results to prevent re-computation, which we'll cover in depth in later sections.

```
import java.util.HashMap;

public class Fibonacci {
    private HashMap<Integer, Integer> memo = new HashMap<>();

    public int fib(int n) {
        if (n <= 1) return n;
        if (memo.containsKey(n)) return memo.get(n);

        int result = fib(n-1) + fib(n-2);
        memo.put(n, result);
        return result;
    }
}
```

3. Systematic Approach

A systematic approach to breaking down problems into subproblems involves the following steps:

- Identify the base case(s): The simplest instances of the problem, which are solved directly.

- Define the state: Determine what parameters describe the subproblems.
- Derive transition relations: Formulate the relationship between the state and the subproblems.

Taking the example of the Fibonacci sequence, the base cases are:

$$F(0) = 0$$
$$F(1) = 1$$

The state is represented by the integer n, and the transition relation is given by:

$$F(n) = F(n-1) + F(n-2)$$

4. Examples Across Domains

The principles behind breaking down problems into subproblems are applicable across various domains:

- **String Operations**: For example, calculating the minimum edit distance between two strings can be broken down into comparing smaller substrings.
- **Optimization Problems**: Problems like the Knapsack problem decompose based on including or excluding an item.
- **Graph Algorithms**: Shortest path algorithms such as Floyd-Warshall break down the problem by considering paths through intermediate nodes.

5. Complexity Considerations

The complexity of breaking down problems into subproblems is essential for evaluating the efficiency of the DP approach. Naïve solutions typically exhibit exponential time complexity due to redundant subproblem calculations. DP techniques such as memoization and tabulation optimize this by storing and reusing computed values, effectively reducing the time complexity to polynomial levels in many cases.

Using the mentioned Fibonacci example, the naive recursive approach exhibits exponential time complexity $O(2^n)$. In contrast, the memoized approach runs in linear time $O(n)$, thanks to avoiding redundant computations by caching results.

The careful decomposition of problems into subproblems is foundational to mastering dynamic programming. Through appropriate state definition, identification of base cases, and derivation of transition relations, complex problems become solvable in an efficient and structured manner.

2.3 Understanding Overlapping Subproblems

In the paradigm of dynamic programming, one of the most critical aspects to be comprehended is the concept of overlapping subproblems. Overlapping subproblems refer to the scenario where the same subproblems are solved multiple times in a naive recursive solution. Recognizing and leveraging overlapping subproblems can significantly optimize the solution for complex problems.

To illustrate overlapping subproblems, consider the classic example of computing the Fibonacci sequence. The Fibonacci sequence $F(n)$ is defined as:

$$F(n) = \begin{cases} 0 & \text{if } n = 0 \\ 1 & \text{if } n = 1 \\ F(n-1) + F(n-2) & \text{if } n > 1 \end{cases}$$

A naive recursive solution for computing the n-th Fibonacci number can be represented as follows:

```
public static int fibonacci(int n) {
    if (n <= 1) return n;
    return fibonacci(n - 1) + fibonacci(n - 2);
}
```

Upon examining the recursive calls generated by this method, we can notice significant redundancy. For instance, computing $F(5)$ results in the following recursive calls:

```
fibonacci(5)
|- fibonacci(4)
|  |-fibonacci(3)
|  | |-fibonacci(2)
|  | | |-fibonacci(1) -> 1
|  | | |-fibonacci(0) -> 0
|  | |-fibonacci(1) -> 1
|  |-fibonacci(2)
|    |-fibonacci(1) -> 1
|    |-fibonacci(0) -> 0
|- fibonacci(3)
   |-fibonacci(2)
   | |-fibonacci(1) -> 1
   | |-fibonacci(0) -> 0
   |-fibonacci(1) -> 1
```

From this call structure, it is evident that the function $fibonacci(2)$ is computed multiple times. This repetitive computation signifies the presence of overlapping subproblems.

By caching the results of the subproblem solutions, we can avoid this redundancy. This caching technique is referred to as memoization when implemented in a top-down recursive manner. Here, we store the results of subproblems in a data structure (e.g., an array or hashmap) and reuse them when needed. The optimized version of the Fibonacci function using memoization is as follows:

```
public class FibonacciMemoization {
    private int[] memo;

    public FibonacciMemoization(int n) {
        memo = new int[n + 1];
        Arrays.fill(memo, -1);
    }

    public int fibonacci(int n) {
        if (memo[n] != -1) return memo[n];
        if (n <= 1) return n;
        memo[n] = fibonacci(n - 1) + fibonacci(n - 2);
        return memo[n];
    }
}
```

Here, the memoization array memo records the results of the subproblems, ensuring each subproblem is solved only once.

Alternatively, we can address overlapping subproblems using a bottom-up approach. This technique is known as tabulation, where we solve each subproblem iteratively and store their results in a table (usually an array) before solving larger problems. The tabulated solution for the Fibonacci sequence would look like this:

```
public int fibonacciTabulation(int n) {
    if (n <= 1) return n;
    int[] dp = new int[n + 1];
    dp[0] = 0;
```

```
    dp[1] = 1;
    for (int i = 2; i <= n; i++) {
        dp[i] = dp[i - 1] + dp[i - 2];
    }
    return dp[n];
}
```

In this implementation, we create a dp array where $\mathrm{dp[i]}$ represents the i-th Fibonacci number. By filling the table iteratively, we ensure each subproblem is computed exactly once, eliminating redundancy.

Understanding overlapping subproblems is vital for optimizing dynamic programming solutions because it allows us to focus on reducing redundant computations. This concept not only enhances performance but also lays the groundwork for advanced dynamic programming strategies to tackle more complex problems efficiently. By effectively recognizing and exploiting overlapping subproblems, we can transform exponential-time recursive solutions into polynomial-time dynamic programming solutions.

2.4 Recursive Solutions in Dynamic Programming

The crux of dynamic programming revolves around solving problems recursively, where the problem is divided into simpler subproblems. Dynamic programming distinguishes itself from mere recursion by systematically storing solutions to subproblems to avoid redundant computations. This section will explore the methodology of leveraging recursive solutions in dynamic programming, elucidating the transition from a recursive format to an optimized dynamic programming approach.

Consider a classic example, the Fibonacci sequence, where each term is the sum of the preceding two terms. In its naive recursive form, the Fibonacci sequence can be defined mathematically as:

$$F(n) = \begin{cases} 0 & \text{if } n = 0 \\ 1 & \text{if } n = 1 \\ F(n-1) + F(n-2) & \text{if } n > 1 \end{cases}$$

This definition quickly translates to a recursive Java method as:

```
public int fib(int n) {
    if (n == 0) return 0;
```

```
    if (n == 1) return 1;
    return fib(n-1) + fib(n-2);
}
```

The above approach, while straightforward, is inefficient because it recalculates Fibonacci numbers multiple times. The time complexity of this naive approach is $O(2^n)$, derived from the exponential growth of recursive calls. To optimize, we identify overlapping subproblems and utilize memoization—caching the results of expensive function calls.

Implementing Memoization in Recursive Solutions

Memoization involves storing the results of expensive function calls and reusing the cached result when the same inputs occur again. This effectively transforms the exponential time complexity into polynomial time. Utilizing an auxiliary data structure like an array or a hash map, we can store intermediate results.

An enhanced version of the Fibonacci method using memoization in Java can be implemented as follows:

```
import java.util.HashMap;
import java.util.Map;

public class Fibonacci {
    private Map<Integer, Integer> memo;

    public Fibonacci() {
        memo = new HashMap<>();
    }

    public int fib(int n) {
        if (n == 0) return 0;
        if (n == 1) return 1;

        if (memo.containsKey(n)) {
            return memo.get(n);
        }

        int result = fib(n-1) + fib(n-2);
        memo.put(n, result);

        return result;
    }
}
```

Analyzing the Memoized Solution

Transformation through memoization significantly optimizes the computation. Here, we reduce redundancy by storing the results of each subproblem. The foregoing example's time complexity, using memoization, is reduced to $O(n)$, since each state is solved only once.

General Approach to Recursive Solutions in Dynamic Program-

ming

1. **Base Case Identification**: Establish the simplest case(s) that can be solved directly. These form the foundation of the recursive solution.

2. **Recursive Relation**: Define the problem in terms of its subproblems. This steps forward as the recursive relation which decomposes the problem into subproblems.

3. **Memoization Structure**: Utilize a data structure, typically an array or map, to record results of subproblems. This helps avoid recomputation.

4. **Transition to Iteration or Tabulation**: Often, a recursive solution can be further optimized by converting it into an iterative solution using a table (array) to store computed values, which leads to the tabulation method discussed later.

Leveraging Java for Complex Recursive Solutions

Dynamic programming can be extended beyond simple problems like the Fibonacci sequence. Consider the problem of finding the nth value in the Catalan series, which has applications in combinatorial mathematics. The recursive definition is:

$$C_n = \begin{cases} 1 & \text{if } n = 0 \\ \sum_{i=0}^{n-1} C_i \cdot C_{n-i-1} & \text{if } n > 0 \end{cases}$$

A straightforward recursive approach in Java might look like:

```
public int catalan(int n) {
    if (n == 0) return 1;

    int result = 0;
    for (int i = 0; i < n; i++) {
        result += catalan(i) * catalan(n - 1 - i);
    }
    return result;
}
```

Catalan Number Calculation Using Memoization

Transforming the naive recursive approach with memoization to avoid redundant calculations is done similarly to our Fibonacci example:

```
import java.util.HashMap;
import java.util.Map;

public class Catalan {
    private Map<Integer, Integer> memo;

    public Catalan() {
```

```
        memo = new HashMap<>();
    }

    public int catalan(int n) {
        if (n == 0) return 1;

        if (memo.containsKey(n)) {
            return memo.get(n);
        }

        int result = 0;
        for (int i = 0; i < n; i++) {
            result += catalan(i) * catalan(n - 1 - i);
        }
        memo.put(n, result);

        return result;
    }
}
```

By incorporating memoization, we enhance performance significantly and ensure each subproblem is calculated only once, thus making our recursive solution optimal. For large-scale problems, transitioning to an iterative or tabulation solution will bring further efficiencies, ensuring robustness against the limitations of recursive stack depth and promoting reduced time complexity.

2.5 Identifying State and State Variables

In dynamic programming, successfully identifying the state and the corresponding state variables is essential to solving complex problems efficiently. The state represents a snapshot of the computation at any given recursive stage, encompassing sufficient information to continue the computation to the final solution. The state variables are the dimensions or elements that define this state.

A proper grasp of identifying the state and state variables can significantly streamline the design of dynamic programming algorithms. This process often hinges on understanding the fundamental properties and constraints of the problem at hand.

State: In dynamic programming, the state can be conceptualized as a configuration that encapsulates all relevant information for reaching an optimal solution from a given stage. For instance, in the classic Knapsack problem, the state might comprise remaining capacity in the knapsack and the set of items considered so far.

State Variables: State variables are dimensions that characterize the state. They are responsible for differentiating various scenarios or stages of a problem. Continuing with the Knapsack problem, the state variables might include the index of the current item and the remaining capacity of the knapsack. These two variables are sufficient to describe any subproblem uniquely.

To illustrate this further, consider the following formal breakdown: - Let i represent the index of the current item being processed. - Let w denote the remaining capacity of the knapsack.

Together, (i, w) form the state variables that define the state for the dynamic programming solution of the Knapsack problem.

```
class Knapsack {
    private int[] weights;
    private int[] values;
    private int[][] dp;

    public Knapsack(int[] weights, int[] values, int capacity) {
        this.weights = weights;
        this.values = values;
        this.dp = new int[weights.length + 1][capacity + 1];
    }

    public int getMaxValue() {
        for (int i = 0; i <= weights.length; i++) {
            for (int w = 0; w <= dp[0].length; w++) {
                if (i == 0 || w == 0) {
                    dp[i][w] = 0;
                } else if (weights[i - 1] <= w) {
                    dp[i][w] = Math.max(dp[i - 1][w], dp[i - 1][w - weights[i - 1]] + values[
                        i - 1]);
                } else {
                    dp[i][w] = dp[i - 1][w];
                }
            }
        }
        return dp[weights.length][dp[0].length - 1];
    }
}
```

The two-dimensional array dp demonstrates where the states are stored. Each entry $\mathrm{dp}[i][w]$ corresponds to a state described by the variables i and w.

When identifying state variables, consider the following steps:

1. **Identify the Decision Point:** Determine the stages at which decisions are made. In the Longest Common Subsequence (LCS) problem, the decision is whether to match characters from both strings.

2. **Determine the Influencing Parameters:** Identify the parameters that impact the decisions. For LCS, these are the indices of the characters being compared in both strings.

```
class LCS {
    private String s1;
    private String s2;
    private int[][] dp;

    public LCS(String s1, String s2) {
        this.s1 = s1;
        this.s2 = s2;
        this.dp = new int[s1.length() + 1][s2.length() + 1];
    }

    public int getLCSLength() {
        int m = s1.length();
        int n = s2.length();
        for (int i = 1; i <= m; i++) {
            for (int j = 1; j <= n; j++) {
                if (s1.charAt(i - 1) == s2.charAt(j - 1)) {
                    dp[i][j] = dp[i - 1][j - 1] + 1;
                } else {
                    dp[i][j] = Math.max(dp[i - 1][j], dp[i][j - 1]);
                }
            }
        }
        return dp[m][n];
    }
}
```

Here, the state variables (i, j) represent indices in strings $s1$ and $s2$ respectively, and the dp array stores the states.

3. **Define Base Case:** Establish the initial state where no decisions are left, providing a termination point for the recursive formulation.

4. **Design State Transition:** Formulate the rules by which one state transitions to another. These rules are generally expressed as recurrence relations.

Accurately identifying state and state variables enables the tabulated representation of the problem, which is manipulated systematically to derive the optimal solution.

2.6 Defining Transition Relations

In dynamic programming, transition relations play a pivotal role in the formulation and execution of algorithms. A transition relation defines how the solution to a problem can be constructed incrementally from the solutions to its sub-problems. By specifying the transition relations, we provide a clear pathway through which the problem's optimal solution can evolve. To elucidate the essence of transition relations, we will delve into their construction, their impact on the overall algorithm design, and demonstrate with concrete examples.

Transition relations essentially express the dependencies between the states of a dynamic programming problem. Consider that we have already defined the state variables and the corresponding state space. Transition relations map the states at time or step t to one or more preceding states (typically at time or steps $t-1$, $t-2$, etc.). Formally, if $dp[i]$ represents the state at the i-th position or step, a transition relation may look like:

$$dp[i] = \text{function of } \{dp[j] \mid j < i\}$$

The formulation of transition relations typically involves the following steps:

1. **Identify Dependencies:** Determine which subproblems directly influence the current problem state. This step requires understanding the problem constraints and how optimal sub-solutions combine to form larger solutions.

2. **Construct Transition Functions:** Develop mathematical functions or relations that describe how to transition from one state to another. This often involves leveraging known sub-problem solutions.

3. **Inspect for Overlaps and Redundancies:** Verify that the transitions do not result in overlapping computations and ensure each state transition is accounted for efficiently.

Consider the classic example of the Fibonacci sequence, where each term $F(n)$ is the sum of the two preceding ones, usually starting from 0 and 1. The state variable $F(n)$ at position n can be defined by the transition relation:

$$F(n) = F(n-1) + F(n-2)$$

Assuming base cases $F(0) = 0$ and $F(1) = 1$, we can recursively compute any term in the sequence. The above relation clearly outlines the dependency of $F(n)$ on its two preceding terms.

To further concretize this with a Java implementation:

```
public int fibonacci(int n) {
    if (n <= 1)
        return n;
    int[] dp = new int[n + 1]; // State space array
    dp[0] = 0; // Base case
```

```
    dp[1] = 1; // Base case

    // Transition relation
    for (int i = 2; i <= n; i++) {
        dp[i] = dp[i-1] + dp[i-2];
    }
    return dp[n]; // Final state
}
```

When executed, the above code for computing $F(n)$ results in:

F(0) = 0, F(1) = 1, F(2) = 1, F(3) = 2, F(4) = 3, F(5) = 5, ...

The transition relation defined in this example ($F(n) = F(n-1)+F(n-2)$) adheres to the principles of breaking down the problem into smaller subproblems.

The same notion of defining transition relations extends to more complex problems like the Knapsack problem, Longest Common Subsequence (LCS), and the Edit Distance problem.

For instance, the LCS problem involves comparing two sequences to find the longest subsequence present in both. If $dp[i][j]$ denotes the length of the LCS of the first i characters of the first sequence and the first j characters of the second sequence, the transition relations can be expressed as:

$$dp[i][j] = \begin{cases} dp[i-1][j-1]+1 & \text{if } X[i-1] = Y[j-1] \\ \text{max}(dp[i-1][j], dp[i][j-1]) & \text{if } X[i-1] \neq Y[j-1] \end{cases}$$

With base cases $dp[0][j] = 0$ for all j and $dp[i][0] = 0$ for all i.

A Java implementation for LCS transition relations looks like:

```
public int longestCommonSubsequence(String X, String Y) {
    int m = X.length();
    int n = Y.length();
    int[][] dp = new int[m+1][n+1];

    for (int i = 1; i <= m; i++) {
        for (int j = 1; j <= n; j++) {
            if (X.charAt(i-1) == Y.charAt(j-1)) {
                dp[i][j] = dp[i-1][j-1] + 1;
            } else {
                dp[i][j] = Math.max(dp[i-1][j], dp[i][j-1]);
            }
        }
    }
    return dp[m][n];
}
```

For sequences $X = "ABCBDAB"$ and $Y = "BDCAB"$, the output is:

4

This indicates that the length of the longest common subsequence is 4.

Defining precise and efficient transition relations is crucial to harnessing the power of dynamic programming, ensuring that every computation step is optimally utilized.

2.7 Understanding the Base Case

In dynamic programming, understanding the base case is essential for defining the solution accurately and ensuring the algorithm terminates correctly. The base case serves as the simplest instance of the problem, which can be solved directly without any further recursion or iterative computation. Identifying and appropriately defining base cases can dramatically affect the efficacy and correctness of the dynamic programming solution.

In any dynamic programming problem, a recurrence relation is defined. This relation recursively breaks down the original problem into subproblems. While these relations define how larger instances of problems can be constructed from smaller ones, the base case specifies the smallest instances, which provide the exit conditions for the recursion. Without a correctly defined base case, the recursive process may result in infinite loops or incorrect calculations.

Consider the classic problem of computing Fibonacci numbers. The Fibonacci sequence is defined as:

$$F(n) = F(n-1) + F(n-2)$$

For this recurrence relation to be useful, we need base cases that specify the outcomes for the smallest values of n. Typically, we define the base cases for $n = 0$ and $n = 1$:

$$F(0) = 0 \quad (2.1)$$
$$F(1) = 1 \quad (2.2)$$

These base cases act as the stopping criteria for the recursion, allowing the solution to construct larger Fibonacci numbers from these known values.

Let's look at the Java implementation of the Fibonacci sequence using dynamic programming with memoization. Consider the following code:

```
import java.util.HashMap;

public class Fibonacci {
    private HashMap<Integer, Integer> memo = new HashMap<>();

    public int fibonacci(int n) {
        if (n == 0) return 0;
        if (n == 1) return 1;

        if (memo.containsKey(n)) {
            return memo.get(n);
        }

        int result = fibonacci(n - 1) + fibonacci(n - 2);
        memo.put(n, result);

        return result;
    }

    public static void main(String[] args) {
        Fibonacci fib = new Fibonacci();
        System.out.println(fib.fibonacci(10)); // Output: 55
    }
}
```

In this code, the base cases for $n = 0$ and $n = 1$ are explicitly defined and directly return the values 0 and 1, respectively. This prevents further recursive calls when n equals 0 or 1, ensuring that the overarching recursion gradually builds up results from these fundamental cases.

Understanding the base case is not limited to simple numeric sequences. It is equally crucial in more complex problems. For instance, consider the problem of finding the longest common subsequence of two strings. Given two sequences, X and Y, the recurrence relation for the length of the longest common subsequence LCS can be defined as:

$$LCS(X[1..m], Y[1..n]) = \begin{cases} 0 & \text{if } m = 0 \text{ or } n = 0 \\ LCS(X[1..m-1], Y[1..n-1]) + 1 & \text{if } X[m] = Y[n] \\ \max(LCS(X[1..m-1], Y[1..n]), & \\ LCS(X[1..m], Y[1..n-1])) & \text{if } X[m] \neq Y[n] \end{cases}$$

Here, the base case occurs when either m or n is 0, which results in an LCS length of 0 because an empty sequence has no common elements with any other sequence.

The Java implementation for the longest common subsequence might look like this:

```
public class LCS {
    public int lcs(String s1, String s2) {
        int m = s1.length();
        int n = s2.length();

        int[][] dp = new int[m+1][n+1];

        for (int i = 0; i <= m; i++) {
            for (int j = 0; j <= n; j++) {
                if (i == 0 || j == 0) {
                    dp[i][j] = 0; // Base case
                } else if (s1.charAt(i-1) == s2.charAt(j-1)) {
                    dp[i][j] = dp[i-1][j-1] + 1;
                } else {
                    dp[i][j] = Math.max(dp[i-1][j], dp[i][j-1]);
                }
            }
        }
        return dp[m][n];
    }

    public static void main(String[] args) {
        LCS lcs = new LCS();
        System.out.println(lcs.lcs("AGGTAB", "GXTXAYB")); // Output: 4
    }
}
```

In this implementation, the base case $dp[i][j] = 0$ for $i = 0$ or $j = 0$ reflects the definition that the longest common subsequence of any sequence with an empty sequence is 0.

Thus, correctly identifying and implementing the base case is crucial for ensuring that a dynamic programming solution accurately and efficiently solves the problem at hand. This approach enables the algorithm to build up from these foundational solutions, ensuring termination and correctness in any complex recursive structure.

2.8 Formulating Dynamic Programming Recurrences

Formulating dynamic programming recurrences is a methodical process that involves expressing the solution to a problem as a combination of solutions to its subproblems. This structuring is achieved through the development of recurrence relations, which are mathematical equations or inequalities that describe the relationships between the values of the solution for different input sizes.

The first step in formulating a dynamic programming recurrence involves identifying the subproblems central to the overall problem. These subproblems are typically smaller instances of the original problem. Given our objective to minimize or maximize a certain value, we express this value in terms of smaller subproblems that can be more effortlessly managed and solved.

Let us consider a few key concepts:

State Variables: State variables are the set of parameters that define the subproblems. Choosing the right state variables is crucial, as they provide a precise description of the subproblem in the context of dynamic programming. A state, often denoted as dp or using a specific symbol like f, is typically a function of these state variables. For example, in the classic knapsack problem, the state might be defined by two variables: the remaining capacity of the knapsack and the set of items considered so far.

Recurrence Relation: The recurrence relation defines the solution to a given subproblem in terms of the solutions to smaller subproblems. It typically takes the form of a function involving previously computed values, which ensures that by solving the smaller subproblems and storing their results, we can efficiently solve the original problem. For example, in a Fibonacci sequence, the recurrence relation is $f(n) = f(n-1) + f(n-2)$.

Base Case: The base case initializes the state variables. It represents the smallest subproblem(s) that can be solved without further decomposition. The base case typically arises naturally from the problem itself. Continuing with the Fibonacci sequence example, the base cases are defined as $f(0) = 0$ and $f(1) = 1$.

To elucidate these concepts, consider the problem of computing the minimum cost to reach the last cell in a matrix starting from the first cell, with movement allowed only to the right or downward. Here is how we develop the recurrence relation step by step:

1. **Defining the State Variables:** Define $dp[i][j]$ as the minimum cost to reach cell (i, j). This definition encapsulates the state of the problem at cell (i, j) and allows for the breaking down into subproblems.

2. **Developing the Recurrence Relation:** To determine the value of $dp[i][j]$, consider the two possible cells from which it could have been reached:

1. The cell directly above: $(i-1, j)$
2. The cell directly to the left: $(i, j-1)$

The recurrence relation can thus be expressed as:

$$dp[i][j] = \text{cost}[i][j] + \min(dp[i-1][j], dp[i][j-1])$$

Here, $\text{cost}[i][j]$ represents the cost of entering cell (i, j).

3. **Establishing the Base Case:** The base case for this problem involves the starting point at $(0, 0)$:

$$dp[0][0] = \text{cost}[0][0]$$

For the cells in the first row $dp[0][j]$ and the first column $dp[i][0]$:

$$dp[0][j] = dp[0][j-1] + \text{cost}[0][j] \quad \text{for all } j$$
$$dp[i][0] = dp[i-1][0] + \text{cost}[i][0] \quad \text{for all } i$$

```
public class MinCostPath {
    static int minCost(int cost[][], int m, int n) {
        int dp[][] = new int[m+1][n+1];

        dp[0][0] = cost[0][0];

        for (int i = 1; i <= m; i++)
            dp[i][0] = dp[i-1][0] + cost[i][0];

        for (int j = 1; j <= n; j++)
            dp[0][j] = dp[0][j-1] + cost[0][j];

        for (int i = 1; i <= m; i++) {
            for (int j = 1; j <= n; j++) {
                dp[i][j] = cost[i][j] + Math.min(dp[i-1][j], dp[i][j-1]);
            }
        }

        return dp[m][n];
    }

    public static void main(String args[]) {
        int cost[][] = { {1, 2, 3},
                         {4, 8, 2},
                         {1, 5, 3} };
        System.out.println("Minimum cost to reach (2,2) = " + minCost(cost, 2, 2));
    }
}
```

```
Minimum cost to reach (2,2) = 8
```

Formulating these relations requires a comprehensive understanding of the problem's structure, which dictates how subproblems combine to build up the solution to the original problem. Once the recurrence is correctly formulated, the next steps include implementing the recursion either through memoization (top-down approach) or tabulation (bottom-up approach), solving the problem efficiently without redundant computations.

2.9 Top-Down vs. Bottom-Up Approaches

In dynamic programming, two primary strategies are employed to solve problems: the top-down approach and the bottom-up approach. Both techniques aim to tackle complex problems by breaking them down into manageable subproblems and solving these subproblems to build up to a solution for the original problem. The distinction lies in the order in which subproblems are addressed and the specific implementation techniques associated with each approach.

The top-down approach, often implemented with memoization, begins by solving the original problem, recursively breaking it down into smaller subproblems until reaching the simplest forms, known as base cases. Whenever a solution for a subproblem is computed, it is stored in a data structure (e.g., an array or a hash map) to avoid redundant calculations in subsequent calls. This technique is optimal for problems that exhibit overlapping subproblems.

Consider the following Java code implementing a top-down approach with memoization:

```
import java.util.HashMap;

public class Fibonacci {
    private HashMap<Integer, Integer> memo;

    public Fibonacci() {
        memo = new HashMap<>();
    }

    public int fib(int n) {
        if (n <= 1) {
            return n;
        }
        if (memo.containsKey(n)) {
            return memo.get(n);
        }
        int result = fib(n - 1) + fib(n - 2);
        memo.put(n, result);
        return result;
    }

    public static void main(String[] args) {
        Fibonacci fibonacci = new Fibonacci();
        System.out.println(fibonacci.fib(10)); // Output: 55
    }
}
```

The above code demonstrates that the Fibonacci sequence is computed using a top-down approach where each call to the fib method checks if the result for the subproblem has been computed before. If so, it retrieves the result from the memo map, significantly reducing the execution time compared to a naive recursive solution.

On the other hand, the bottom-up approach systematically solves all subproblems, starting from the simplest base cases and iteratively combining them to tackle more complex subproblems until reaching the original problem. This strategy can be more efficient in both time and space since it eliminates the overhead of recursive function calls and utilizes a simple iteration mechanism to fill up a table (often implemented as an array).

Here is the bottom-up approach implemented in Java for the Fibonacci sequence:

```
public class Fibonacci {
    public int fib(int n) {
        if (n <= 1) {
            return n;
        }
        int[] dp = new int[n + 1];
        dp[0] = 0;
        dp[1] = 1;

        for (int i = 2; i <= n; i++) {
            dp[i] = dp[i - 1] + dp[i - 2];
        }

        return dp[n];
    }

    public static void main(String[] args) {
        Fibonacci fibonacci = new Fibonacci();
        System.out.println(fibonacci.fib(10)); // Output: 55
    }
}
```

In this bottom-up implementation, the function iterates from the base cases (0 and 1) up to the desired value of n, storing intermediate results in an array and avoiding redundant calculations found in the top-down approach.

To elucidate the computational differences:

- **Top-Down with Memoization:** This approach uses a depth-first strategy to break problems into subproblems. Each unique subproblem is solved once and stored for future reference, resulting in reduced recomputational overhead. The memoized approach is straightforward to implement for problems naturally expressed in a recursive manner. However, it may still use considerable stack space for deep recursions unless tail recursion optimization is applicable.

- **Bottom-Up with Tabulation:** This method employs an iterative strategy to solve problems from the ground up. Starting with the base cases, it iteratively computes the solutions to progressively larger subproblems using previously computed results. The iterative nature of this approach ensures that it is less prone to stack overflow issues encountered in deep recursion. However, it may involve more explicit management of intermediate results and may require careful indexing in the tabulation table.

Understanding these two approaches and recognizing when to apply each is crucial for mastering dynamic programming. Problems that fit naturally into a recursive structure and benefit from an explicit memoization map are best addressed with a top-down approach. Conversely, problems wherein a straightforward iterative process can yield results efficiently are more suited to the bottom-up approach. Balancing these techniques and their respective trade-offs is key to efficient algorithm design in dynamic programming.

2.10 Memoization Techniques

Memoization is a crucial technique in dynamic programming aimed at optimizing the efficiency of recursive algorithms by storing computed results of subproblems. This approach ensures that each subproblem is solved only once, thus avoiding redundant calculations that can lead to excessive computational wastage.

To implement memoization, one typically employs a data structure, such as an array or a hashmap, to cache the results of function calls. This cached result then serves for future calls with the same parameters, returning the stored value immediately instead of recomputing it. This technique can significantly reduce the time complexity of algorithms that exhibit overlapping subproblems.

Consider the quintessential example of the Fibonacci sequence, which is defined as follows:

$$F(n) = \begin{cases} 0 & \text{if } n = 0 \\ 1 & \text{if } n = 1 \\ F(n-1) + F(n-2) & \text{if } n > 1 \end{cases}$$

The naive recursive implementation has an exponential time complexity, specifically $O(2^n)$, due to the redundant calculations of the same subproblems. The following is the naive implementation in Java:

```
public class Fibonacci {
    public int fib(int n) {
        if (n <= 1) {
            return n;
        }
        return fib(n - 1) + fib(n - 2);
    }
}
```

By observing the call tree of this recursive function, one can identify the overlapping subproblems. To optimize this, we introduce memoization:

```
import java.util.HashMap;

public class Fibonacci {
    private HashMap<Integer, Integer> memo = new HashMap<>();

    public int fib(int n) {
        if (n <= 1) {
            return n;
        }
        if (memo.containsKey(n)) {
            return memo.get(n);
        }
        int result = fib(n - 1) + fib(n - 2);
        memo.put(n, result);
        return result;
    }
}
```

In this implementation, the HashMap memo is used to store the results of previously computed Fibonacci numbers. Before performing the recursive computation, the function fib checks whether the result for the current value of n exists in the hashmap. If present, it directly returns the cached result, thus skipping redundant calculations.

$\text{fib}(30) = 832040$

Memoization may also be implemented using arrays, which can be more space-efficient than hashmaps for certain types of problems, particularly when the range of possible subproblem indices is known and bounded. Below is an implementation of the Fibonacci sequence using an array for memoization:

```
public class Fibonacci {
    public int fib(int n) {
        int[] memo = new int[n + 1];
        return fib(n, memo);
    }

    private int fib(int n, int[] memo) {
        if (n <= 1) {
            return n;
```

```
        }
        if (memo[n] != 0) {
            return memo[n];
        }
        memo[n] = fib(n - 1, memo) + fib(n - 2, memo);
        return memo[n];
    }
}
```

In this version, an integer array memo is passed along with the recursive calls. This array initially contains zeroes. When a Fibonacci number is calculated, it is saved in the memo array. If a value different from zero (indicating a previously computed value) is encountered, it is returned immediately.

```
fib(30) = 832040
```

When employing memoization, the time complexity is reduced from $O(2^n)$ to $O(n)$, as each subproblem is solved only once and the solution is reused in $O(1)$ time.

Analyzing the space complexity, memoization requires $O(n)$ additional space to store the results of the subproblems. In the case of the Fibonacci sequence, both the array and hashmap implementations adhere to this space complexity.

Memoization is not restricted to simple problems like the Fibonacci sequence; it can be applied to more complex scenarios involving multiple state variables. For instance, consider solving the problem of finding the minimum cost path in a grid. Each cell in the grid has a cost, and the goal is to move from the top-left corner to the bottom-right corner with the minimum cumulative cost. Cells can only be traversed to the right or downwards.

The memoized solution to this problem involves computing the cost for each cell and storing these results for future reference.

```
public class MinCostPath {
    private int[][] memo;

    public int minCost(int[][] cost, int m, int n) {
        memo = new int[m + 1][n + 1];
        for (int[] row : memo) {
            Arrays.fill(row, -1);
        }
        return minCost(cost, m, n);
    }

    private int minCost(int[][] cost, int m, int n) {
        if (m < 0 || n < 0) {
            return Integer.MAX_VALUE;
        } else if (m == 0 && n == 0) {
            return cost[0][0];
```

```
        } else if (memo[m][n] != -1) {
            return memo[m][n];
        } else {
            memo[m][n] = cost[m][n] + Math.min(minCost(cost, m - 1, n), minCost(cost,
                    m, n - 1));
            return memo[m][n];
        }
    }
}
```

This implementation uses a 2D array as a memoization table to store the minimum costs of reaching each cell. The function minCost initializes the memo array with -1 to indicate uncomputed cells. As the recursive function computes the minimum cost path, it populates the memo table, avoiding unnecessary recalculations.

Understanding and implementing memoization techniques allows programmers to transform inefficient recursive solutions into efficient ones, ensuring that dynamic programming solutions leverage the full potential of computational resources. Memoization is a fundamental strategy in dynamic programming that is widely applicable across various domains and problem-solving scenarios.

2.11 Tabulation Techniques

Tabulation is a bottom-up, iterative dynamic programming approach that systematically fills in a table of results until the solution to the original problem is obtained. This method requires identifying the state variables and the transition relations and then using them to populate a table, generally referred to as a DP table.

Tabulation starts by iteratively solving smaller subproblems, storing their results, and using these results to build up to the solution of the larger problem. Unlike the top-down approach which uses recursion and memoization, the tabulation approach is non-recursive. Let's delve into the step-by-step process of the tabulation technique.

- **Initialization**: The DP table needs to be initialized in a way that encapsulates the base cases of the dynamic programming recurrence.
- **Filling the DP Table**: Using the pre-identified transition relations, iteratively fill the DP table from the base cases upwards.
- **Extracting the Solution**: Once the DP table is completely filled,

the final solution to the problem is typically found in a predetermined table cell, often at the end of the table.

Consider the example of the Fibonacci sequence to illustrate the tabulation technique. The Fibonacci sequence is defined as:

$$F(n) = \begin{cases} 0 & \text{if } n = 0 \\ 1 & \text{if } n = 1 \\ F(n-1) + F(n-2) & \text{if } n > 1 \end{cases}$$

Using tabulation, we aim to fill up a table, DP, where each entry $DP[i]$ holds the value of $F(i)$. Here are the detailed steps:

Initialization:

```
int n; // n is the target Fibonacci number index
int DP[n + 1]; // Array to hold the Fibonacci numbers up to n
DP[0] = 0; // Base case: F(0) = 0
DP[1] = 1; // Base case: F(1) = 1
```

Filling the DP Table:

```
for (int i = 2; i <= n; i++) {
    DP[i] = DP[i - 1] + DP[i - 2];
}
```

Extracting the Solution:

```
int nthFibonacci = DP[n];
```

This example fills the DP table iteratively from $DP[0]$ and $DP[1]$, working upwards to $DP[n]$. The time complexity of this approach is $O(n)$, and the space complexity is also $O(n)$.

For a more complex example, let's consider the problem of finding the minimum cost path in a grid. Given a grid represented as a 2D array cost, where cost[i][j] represents the cost to move to cell (i, j), the goal is to find the minimum cost to reach cell (m, n) from cell $(0, 0)$. Only moves to the right and down are allowed.

Dynamic Programming Recurrence: The cost to reach any cell (i, j) is:

$$DP[i][j] = \text{cost}[i][j] + \text{min}(DP[i-1][j], DP[i][j-1])$$

Initialization:

```
int m, n; // dimensions of the grid
int DP[m+1][n+1];
```

```
// Base case: starting cell
DP[0][0] = cost[0][0];

// Initialize the first row
for (int j = 1; j <= n; j++) {
    DP[0][j] = DP[0][j - 1] + cost[0][j];
}

// Initialize the first column
for (int i = 1; i <= m; i++) {
    DP[i][0] = DP[i - 1][0] + cost[i][0];
}
```

Filling the DP Table:

```
for (int i = 1; i <= m; i++) {
    for (int j = 1; j <= n; j++) {
        DP[i][j] = cost[i][j] + min(DP[i-1][j], DP[i][j-1]);
    }
}
```

Extracting the Solution:

```
int minCost = DP[m][n];
```

In this example, the DP table is initialized with the base cases for the first row and first column. The double loop iterates through each cell, computing the minimum cost to reach that cell by considering the cost of moving from either the left or above, following the established recurrence relation. The final solution is the value in $DP[m][n]$.

The time complexity of this solution is $O(m \times n)$, and the space complexity is also $O(m \times n)$. This highlights the efficiency of the tabulation method in solving problems with deterministic transitions between states.

It is also possible to further optimize the space complexity of some tabulation-based solutions by noticing patterns in the DP table access patterns. For example, in the Fibonacci sequence case, we only need the last two computed values to determine the next value, which allows us to reduce the space complexity from $O(n)$ to $O(1)$.

```
int Fibonacci(int n) {
    if (n <= 1) return n;
    int prev = 0, curr = 1;
    for (int i = 2; i <= n; i++) {
        int next = prev + curr;
        prev = curr;
        curr = next;
    }
    return curr;
}
```

Verbatim output:

```
Result of Fibonacci(10): 55
```

In this optimized version, instead of maintaining an entire array of Fibonacci numbers, only two variables are maintained to capture the necessary previous values. This results in a space complexity of $O(1)$.

Thus, the tabulation technique serves as a powerful tool in dynamic programming, providing a structured and efficient way to derive solutions by filling out a table iteratively, with the additional possibility of optimizing space when applicable.

2.12 Analyzing Time and Space Complexity

Analyzing the time and space complexity of dynamic programming algorithms is crucial for understanding their efficiency and limitations. This analysis helps in determining whether an algorithm is feasible for large inputs and ensuring that the resources used are within acceptable bounds.

The time complexity of a dynamic programming solution is typically defined by the number of subproblems solved and the time taken per subproblem. Let n denote the size of the input. The space complexity, on the other hand, is determined by the amount of memory required to store the intermediate results. To perform a thorough analysis, we need to examine both the dimensions of the state space and the operations required to compute the value of each state.

Given a dynamic programming problem, let's represent the number of unique states that need to be computed as states(n). Additionally, let the time complexity for computing each state from previously computed states be $T_{\text{state}}(n)$. Therefore, the overall time complexity $T(n)$ can be expressed as:

$$T(n) = \text{states}(n) \cdot T_{\text{state}}(n)$$

Example 1: Fibonacci Numbers

To elucidate this concept, consider the classic problem of computing the n-th Fibonacci number using dynamic programming. The recurrence relation for Fibonacci numbers is defined as:

$$F(n) = F(n-1) + F(n-2)$$

with base cases $F(0) = 0$ and $F(1) = 1$. To implement this using a bottom-up dynamic programming approach, the algorithm iteratively computes the values from the smallest subproblems up to the original problem.

```
public class FibonacciDP {
    public static int computeFibonacci(int n) {
        if (n <= 1) return n;
        int[] fib = new int[n + 1];
        fib[0] = 0;
        fib[1] = 1;
        for (int i = 2; i <= n; i++) {
            fib[i] = fib[i - 1] + fib[i - 2];
        }
        return fib[n];
    }
}
```

The dynamic programming table 'fib' has a size of $n+1$, requiring $O(n)$ space. Each state $fib[i]$ is computed in $O(1)$ time, given the values of $fib[i-1]$ and $fib[i-2]$. Thus, the time complexity for this algorithm is $O(n)$.

Example 2: Longest Common Subsequence

For a more intricate example, consider the Longest Common Subsequence (LCS) problem, which is defined as follows: given two sequences X and Y of lengths m and n, find the length of their longest common subsequence. The LCS problem can be solved by defining a 2-dimensional DP table where:

$$\text{LCS}(i,j) = \begin{cases} 0, & \text{if } i = 0 \text{ or } j = 0 \\ \text{LCS}(i-1, j-1) + 1, & \text{if } X[i-1] = Y[j-1] \\ \max(\text{LCS}(i-1, j), \text{LCS}(i, j-1)), & \text{otherwise} \end{cases}$$

The implementation is as follows:

```
public class LongestCommonSubsequence {
    public static int computeLCS(String X, String Y) {
        int m = X.length();
        int n = Y.length();
        int[][] lcs = new int[m+1][n+1];

        for (int i = 0; i <= m; i++) {
```

```
            for (int j = 0; j <= n; j++) {
                if (i == 0 || j == 0) {
                    lcs[i][j] = 0;
                } else if (X.charAt(i-1) == Y.charAt(j-1)) {
                    lcs[i][j] = lcs[i-1][j-1] + 1;
                } else {
                    lcs[i][j] = Math.max(lcs[i-1][j], lcs[i][j-1]);
                }
            }
        }
        return lcs[m][n];
    }
}
```

The DP table here has dimensions $(m+1) \times (n+1)$, thus the space complexity is $O(m \cdot n)$. Each state is computed in $O(1)$ time based on the values of adjacent states. Consequently, the time complexity is also $O(m \cdot n)$.

Example 3: Knapsack Problem

Another classical problem is the 0/1 Knapsack problem. Given n items, each with a weight w_i and value v_i, determine the maximum value that can be achieved within a given weight capacity W. The state can be defined as:

$$\text{DP}(i, w) = \begin{cases} 0, & \text{if } i = 0 \text{ or } w = 0 \\ \text{DP}(i-1, w), & \text{if } w_i > w \\ \max(\text{DP}(i-1, w), v_i + \text{DP}(i-1, w-w_i)), & \text{otherwise} \end{cases}$$

The implementation is:

```
public class KnapsackDP {
    public static int knapsack(int W, int[] weights, int[] values, int n) {
        int[][] dp = new int[n + 1][W + 1];

        for (int i = 0; i <= n; i++) {
            for (int w = 0; w <= W; w++) {
                if (i == 0 || w == 0) {
                    dp[i][w] = 0;
                } else if (weights[i - 1] <= w) {
                    dp[i][w] = Math.max(values[i - 1] + dp[i - 1][w - weights[i - 1]], dp[i -
                        1][w]);
                } else {
                    dp[i][w] = dp[i - 1][w];
                }
            }
        }
        return dp[n][W];
    }
}
```

The DP table has dimensions $(n + 1) \times (W + 1)$, leading to a space complexity of $O(n \cdot W)$. Each state is evaluated in constant time $O(1)$. Therefore, the time complexity for the 0/1 Knapsack problem is $O(n \cdot W)$.

Understanding both time and space complexities provides a comprehensive view of dynamic programming solutions, enabling one to gauge their practicality and efficiency accurately.

Chapter 3

Optimizing Algorithms with Dynamic Programming

This chapter focuses on optimizing algorithms using dynamic programming. It discusses the importance of choosing the right data structures and provides strategies for reducing time and space complexity. The chapter guides readers through transforming naive solutions into optimized dynamic programming implementations, minimizing overhead, avoiding redundant computations, and incorporating space-efficient, in-place algorithms. A case study on optimizing the knapsack problem illustrates practical applications of these optimization techniques.

3.1 Introduction to Algorithm Optimization

Algorithm optimization aims to enhance the efficiency of algorithms, focusing on reducing both time complexity and space complexity. Understanding the principles and strategies related to improving algorithms is crucial for developing efficient and scalable software solutions.

Firstly, the performance of an algorithm is largely determined by its time complexity, a measure of the number of operations required as the input size grows. For example, given a function $f(n)$ describing the number of steps needed by an algorithm with an input of size n, the primary goal is to make $f(n)$ as small as possible. Common time complexities include constant time $O(1)$, logarithmic time $O(\log n)$, linear time $O(n)$, linearithmic time $O(n \log n)$, quadratic time $O(n^2)$, and exponential time $O(2^n)$.

In addition to time complexity, space complexity assesses the amount of memory required by an algorithm as the input size increases. Similar to time complexity, space complexity is described using Big-O notation, denoted as $O(g(n))$. Here, the goal is to minimize the memory footprint, especially in environments with constrained resources.

Dynamic programming (DP) is a powerful optimization technique used to solve problems by breaking them down into simpler sub-problems and storing the results of these sub-problems to avoid redundant computations.

```
public class Fibonacci {
    public static int naiveFibonacci(int n) {
        if (n <= 1) {
            return n;
        }
        return naiveFibonacci(n - 1) + naiveFibonacci(n - 2);
    }
}
```

The above example demonstrates a naive recursive approach to computing Fibonacci numbers. Despite its simplicity, this method has an exponential time complexity, $O(2^n)$, due to the redundant calculations of the same sub-problems.

To optimize, we can apply dynamic programming, solving the problem using either a top-down approach with memoization or a bottom-up approach with tabulation. Memoization involves storing the results of expensive function calls and reusing these stored results when the same inputs occur again. The conversion to a top-down DP implementation involves adding a cache to remembering already computed results:

```
import java.util.HashMap;
import java.util.Map;

public class Fibonacci {
    private static Map<Integer, Integer> memo = new HashMap<>();

    public static int dpFibonacci(int n) {
        if (n <= 1) {
            return n;
        }

        if (memo.containsKey(n)) {
            return memo.get(n);
        }
```

```
        int result = dpFibonacci(n - 1) + dpFibonacci(n - 2);
        memo.put(n, result);

        return result;
    }
}
```

By storing and reusing previously computed values, the time complexity is reduced to linear time $O(n)$, a significant improvement. Another way to achieve optimization is through the bottom-up approach, building the solution iteratively and using a table to store intermediate results, which avoids overhead introduced by recursive calls.

```
public class Fibonacci {
    public static int bottomUpFibonacci(int n) {
        if (n <= 1) {
            return n;
        }

        int[] dp = new int[n + 1];
        dp[0] = 0;
        dp[1] = 1;

        for (int i = 2; i <= n; i++) {
            dp[i] = dp[i - 1] + dp[i - 2];
        }

        return dp[n];
    }
}
```

In this bottom-up approach, the space complexity is $O(n)$ to store the entire DP table. However, it is possible to further optimize the space complexity. Since only the last two computed values are needed at any point, an in-place algorithm can reduce the space complexity to $O(1)$.

```
public class Fibonacci {
    public static int inPlaceFibonacci(int n) {
        if (n <= 1) {
            return n;
        }

        int prev1 = 0, prev2 = 1;
        for (int i = 2; i <= n; i++) {
            int current = prev1 + prev2;
            prev1 = prev2;
            prev2 = current;
        }

        return prev2;
    }
}
```

This in-place implementation is highly space-efficient, with a space complexity of $O(1)$, while maintaining a time complexity of $O(n)$. Such transformations exemplify the power of dynamic programming in algorithm optimization, allowing for significant improvements in both time and space complexities.

3.2 Understanding the Need for Optimization

The performance of algorithms is a critical aspect in computer science, especially in applications where resources such as time and memory are constrained. The need for optimization arises from the desire to make algorithms more efficient, typically by reducing their time and space complexity. This section addresses the fundamental reasons why optimization is imperative and lays the groundwork for the subsequent techniques introduced in this chapter.

Efficient algorithms are essential for several reasons: computational resource constraints, scalability requirements, and the necessity for real-time responsiveness in certain critical applications. Large-scale data, such as those encountered in big data analytics, machine learning, and real-time processing systems, exacerbates the need for optimized algorithms. An algorithm that performs acceptably with a small dataset might become infeasible when applied to significantly larger datasets.

Consider an algorithm with a time complexity of $O(n^2)$. For a dataset with $n = 100$, this algorithm performs $10,000$ operations, which might be manageable. However, if the dataset size increases to $n = 1,000$, the number of operations balloons to $1,000,000$. This quadratic growth can quickly render the algorithm impractical as data scales. Algorithm optimization aims to find solutions that grow less rapidly with n, such as reducing an $O(n^2)$ algorithm to $O(n \log n)$, thereby making it more scalable.

Memory constraints also drive the need for optimization. An algorithm with high space complexity can exhaust available memory, resulting in crashes or significantly degraded performance. This situation is particularly critical in environments with limited memory resources, such as embedded systems or mobile applications. Space-efficient algorithms ensure the judicious use of memory, enabling applications to run smoothly and effectively even in constrained environments.

Dynamic programming (DP) is a systematic optimization technique employed to eliminate redundancy and inefficiencies seen in naive algorithms. A classic example is the Fibonacci sequence. A naive recursive implementation exhibits exponential time complexity, as it recalculates the same subproblems multiple times.

```
public class Fibonacci {
    public static int naiveFibonacci(int n) {
        if (n <= 1) return n;
        return naiveFibonacci(n - 1) + naiveFibonacci(n - 2);
    }

    public static void main(String[] args) {
        System.out.println(naiveFibonacci(10)); // Outputs: 55
    }
}
```

This naive recursive approach recalculates $Fibonacci(n-2)$ and $Fibonacci(n-1)$ multiple times. For instance, $Fibonacci(4)$ is computed as follows:

$$Fibonacci(4) = Fibonacci(3) + Fibonacci(2)$$

Expanding $Fibonacci(3)$:

$$\begin{aligned} Fibonacci(3) &= Fibonacci(2) + Fibonacci(1) \\ &= (Fibonacci(1) + Fibonacci(0)) + Fibonacci(1) \end{aligned}$$

This expands further into multiple recalculations, showing inefficiency. Introducing a memoization technique transforms the algorithm into a more efficient version by storing intermediate results.

```
import java.util.HashMap;
import java.util.Map;

public class Fibonacci {
    private static Map<Integer, Integer> memo = new HashMap<>();

    public static int memoizedFibonacci(int n) {
        if (n <= 1) return n;
        if (!memo.containsKey(n)) {
            memo.put(n, memoizedFibonacci(n - 1) + memoizedFibonacci(n - 2));
        }
        return memo.get(n);
    }

    public static void main(String[] args) {
        System.out.println(memoizedFibonacci(10)); // Outputs: 55
    }
}
```

Memoization reduces the time complexity from $O(2^n)$ to $O(n)$ by ensuring each distinct subproblem is computed once. This transformation exemplifies the power of dynamic programming in optimizing recursive algorithms. The need to avoid redundant computations and the adoption of more efficient data structures underpin the rationale for optimization.

Storage efficiency is equally vital. In scenarios where space is limited, such as IoT devices or systems with stringent memory bandwidth, minimizing the memory footprint is crucial. Dynamic programming techniques offer solutions like in-place algorithms that achieve space efficiency without compromising time complexity.

To illustrate, the traditional dynamic programming solution to the knapsack problem uses a two-dimensional array, consuming a significant amount of memory. An optimized approach would use a one-dimensional array, achieving the same functional result with reduced space complexity.

Overall, understanding the need for optimization involves recognizing the implications of computational resource constraints, scalability, and space efficiency. Optimization transforms algorithms from theoretical constructs to practical tools capable of addressing real-world problems efficiently and effectively. This understanding is the cornerstone upon which dynamic programming builds to provide robust solutions.

3.3 Choosing the Right Data Structures

The efficacy of an algorithm is often heavily influenced by the appropriate selection of data structures. In dynamic programming, the choice of data structures not only affects time complexity but also impacts space complexity and the overall efficiency of the solution. This section delves into the considerations and strategies for selecting the most suitable data structures for dynamic programming implementations, enhancing both clarity and performance.

The primary objective of dynamic programming (DP) is to break a problem down into simpler subproblems, solve each subproblem once, and store their solutions. This process typically employs data structures designed for efficient lookup and storage of intermediate results. Commonly used data structures in dynamic programming include arrays, hash tables, and memoization tables.

Arrays

Arrays are the simplest form of data structure and are often the default choice in dynamic programming solutions, especially when the problem's subproblems are indexed by integers ranging over a contiguous domain. Arrays provide $\mathcal{O}(1)$ time complexity for both access and update operations, making them highly efficient for storing DP states.

```
public int fibonacci(int n) {
    if (n <= 1) return n;
    int[] dp = new int[n + 1];
    dp[0] = 0;
    dp[1] = 1;
    for (int i = 2; i <= n; i++) {
        dp[i] = dp[i - 1] + dp[i - 2];
    }
    return dp[n];
}
```

In the above example, an array is used to store the Fibonacci numbers up to n. The use of an array ensures constant-time access and efficient updating of the Fibonacci values.

Hash Tables

In cases where the subproblem space is sparse or non-contiguous, hash tables provide a flexible alternative. Hash tables offer average case $\mathcal{O}(1)$ time complexity for lookup and insertion operations, making them suitable for problems where subproblem indices are not sequentially ordered or are dynamically generated.

```
public int uniquePathsWithObstacles(int[][] obstacleGrid) {
    int m = obstacleGrid.length;
    int n = obstacleGrid[0].length;
    Map<String, Integer> dp = new HashMap<>();
    return paths(obstacleGrid, m - 1, n - 1, dp);
}

private int paths(int[][] grid, int i, int j, Map<String, Integer> dp) {
    if (i < 0 || j < 0 || grid[i][j] == 1) return 0;
    if (i == 0 && j == 0) return 1;
    String key = i + "," + j;
    if (dp.containsKey(key)) return dp.get(key);
    int result = paths(grid, i - 1, j, dp) + paths(grid, i, j - 1, dp);
    dp.put(key, result);
    return result;
}
```

In this example, a hash table is used to store the number of unique paths in a grid with obstacles. The hash table is keyed by a string combination of the cell's coordinates, accommodating non-contiguous subproblem indices.

Memoization Tables

Memoization tables are similar to hash tables but are specifically designed for caching results of expensive function calls to avoid redundant computations. Unlike arrays, memoization tables can handle complex keys, such as tuples or objects, making them versatile for a broader range of DP problems.

```
public int numTrees(int n) {
    return countTrees(1, n, new HashMap<>());
}

private int countTrees(int start, int end, Map<String, Integer> memo) {
    if (start > end) return 1;
    String key = start + "," + end;
    if (memo.containsKey(key)) return memo.get(key);
    int total = 0;
    for (int root = start; root <= end; root++) {
        int leftTrees = countTrees(start, root - 1, memo);
        int rightTrees = countTrees(root + 1, end, memo);
        total += leftTrees * rightTrees;
    }
    memo.put(key, total);
    return total;
}
```

The example demonstrates the use of a memoization table to count the number of unique Binary Search Trees (BSTs) that can be formed with n nodes. The key for the memoization table is a string representing the range of tree nodes considered, allowing efficient caching and retrieval of subproblem solutions.

Choosing the correct data structure often involves evaluating the nature and structure of the problem's subproblems, the complexity of accessing and updating intermediate results, and the overhead associated with managing the data structure itself. Structured experimentation and profiling can guide the decision towards the most performant and scalable data structure, facilitating optimal dynamic programming implementations.

3.4 Strategies for Reducing Time Complexity

Reducing the time complexity of an algorithm is crucial for enhancing its efficiency, particularly when dealing with large datasets or computationally intensive tasks. In this section, we will explore methods to optimize an algorithm's execution time, focusing on relevant techniques that are often applied in dynamic programming.

1. Memoization

Memoization is a technique utilized to store the results of expensive function calls and reuse them when the same inputs occur again. This reduces the number of calculations required by avoiding redundant computation. Consider the classical recursive approach to calculate the Fibonacci sequence, which can be optimized with memoization.

```
import java.util.HashMap;

public class FibonacciMemoization {
    private HashMap<Integer, Integer> memo = new HashMap<>();

    public int fib(int n) {
        if (n <= 1) return n;
        if (memo.containsKey(n)) return memo.get(n);

        int result = fib(n - 1) + fib(n - 2);
        memo.put(n, result);
        return result;
    }

    public static void main(String[] args) {
        FibonacciMemoization fm = new FibonacciMemoization();
        System.out.println(fm.fib(10)); // Output: 55
    }
}
```

In the example above, the 'fib' method checks if the result for a given 'n' is already computed (memoized). If so, it returns the precomputed value, effectively reducing the typical exponential time complexity to linear time complexity $O(n)$.

2. Tabulation

Tabulation, often referred to as the bottom-up approach, involves solving subproblems iteratively and storing the results in an array (or table). This avoids the overhead of recursive calls by iterating through subproblems. The Fibonacci sequence can also be solved using tabulation:

```
public class FibonacciTabulation {
```

```
    public int fib(int n) {
        if (n <= 1) return n;

        int[] fibTable = new int[n + 1];
        fibTable[0] = 0;
        fibTable[1] = 1;

        for (int i = 2; i <= n; i++) {
            fibTable[i] = fibTable[i - 1] + fibTable[i - 2];
        }

        return fibTable[n];
    }

    public static void main(String[] args) {
        FibonacciTabulation ft = new FibonacciTabulation();
        System.out.println(ft.fib(10)); // Output: 55
    }
}
```

Using tabulation, each subproblem is solved only once, yielding a time complexity of $O(n)$ just like memoization.

3. Efficient Sorting and Searching

Efficient sorting and searching algorithms can substantially reduce time complexity. For instance, using quicksort or mergesort reduces the time complexity from $O(n^2)$ in bubble sort to $O(n \log n)$. Similarly, using binary search reduces the complexity from $O(n)$ in linear search to $O(\log n)$, as demonstrated below.

```
import java.util.Arrays;

public class BinarySearchExample {

    public static int binarySearch(int[] arr, int target) {
        int left = 0, right = arr.length - 1;

        while (left <= right) {
            int mid = left + (right - left) / 2;
            if (arr[mid] == target) return mid;
            if (arr[mid] < target) left = mid + 1;
            else right = mid - 1;
        }

        return -1; // Target not found
    }

    public static void main(String[] args) {
        int[] arr = {1, 3, 5, 7, 9, 11};
        Arrays.sort(arr); // Ensure the array is sorted
        int index = binarySearch(arr, 7); // Output: 3
        System.out.println(index);
    }
}
```

3

4. Divide and Conquer

The divide and conquer strategy entails breaking a problem into smaller subproblems, solving each subproblem recursively, and combining their solutions. Merge sort and quicksort are classical examples. Consider merge sort:

```
import java.util.Arrays;

public class MergeSort {

    public static void mergeSort(int[] arr, int left, int right) {
        if (left < right) {
            int middle = (left + right) / 2;
            mergeSort(arr, left, middle);
            mergeSort(arr, middle + 1, right);
            merge(arr, left, middle, right);
        }
    }

    public static void merge(int[] arr, int left, int middle, int right) {
        int[] leftArray = Arrays.copyOfRange(arr, left, middle + 1);
        int[] rightArray = Arrays.copyOfRange(arr, middle + 1, right + 1);

        int i = 0, j = 0, k = left;

        while (i < leftArray.length && j < rightArray.length) {
            if (leftArray[i] <= rightArray[j]) {
                arr[k++] = leftArray[i++];
            } else {
                arr[k++] = rightArray[j++];
            }
        }

        while (i < leftArray.length) {
            arr[k++] = leftArray[i++];
        }

        while (j < rightArray.length) {
            arr[k++] = rightArray[j++];
        }
    }

    public static void main(String[] args) {
        int[] arr = {12, 11, 13, 5, 6, 7};
        mergeSort(arr, 0, arr.length - 1);
        System.out.println(Arrays.toString(arr)); // Output: [5, 6, 7, 11, 12, 13]
    }
}
```

```
[5, 6, 7, 11, 12, 13]
```

5. Pruning Search Spaces

Pruning reduces the search space, making algorithms more efficient. Techniques like branch-and-bound and alpha-beta pruning (used in game trees) help eliminate parts of the solution space that do not need to be explored. For example, solving the 15-puzzle problem can benefit from pruning strategies to avoid unnecessary state explorations.

In dynamic programming, recognizing subproblems that need not be recomputed aids in trimming down the potential states. Implementing a technique as seen in memoization or utilizing cutoff thresholds in recursive calls are instances of pruning.

3.5 Strategies for Reducing Space Complexity

Reducing space complexity in dynamic programming is crucial for developing efficient algorithms, particularly when dealing with large datasets or limited memory resources. Techniques for space optimization revolve around judiciously reusing memory and minimizing the storage of unnecessary data. This section will explore several strategies to reduce space complexity, including state compression, iterative computation, and in-place updates.

State Compression

State compression is a technique aimed at reducing the memory footprint of dynamic programming tables by leveraging the problem's inherent properties. It involves collapsing multiple states into a single representative state or a reduced form. For instance, consider a problem where we need only a few previous states to compute the current state. Instead of storing all previous states, we can compress the space by holding only the necessary subset.

In problems like the Fibonacci sequence or knapsack problem, where only the last few states are required, we can significantly optimize space. For example, the space complexity of a naive Fibonacci implementation is $O(n)$. However, by maintaining only the last two numbers in the sequence, we can reduce the space complexity to $O(1)$.

```
public int fibonacci(int n) {
    if (n <= 1) return n;
    int a = 0, b = 1, c;
    for (int i = 2; i <= n; i++) {
        c = a + b;
        a = b;
        b = c;
    }
    return b;
}
```

Iterative Computation

Iterative computation replaces recursion with iteration, often leading to a reduction in space complexity. Recursive algorithms typically use a call stack that grows with the number of recursive calls, resulting in $O(n)$ additional space complexity. By converting the recursive process into an iterative one and using loops, we confine our space complexity to $O(1)$.

Consider the dynamic programming solution to find the minimum path sum in a triangle. The recursive approach uses $O(n^2)$ space due to memoization. However, we can convert it into an iterative algorithm with a space complexity of $O(n)$, or even $O(1)$, by updating the path sums in-place.

```
public int minimumTotal(List<List<Integer>> triangle) {
    int[] dp = new int[triangle.size()];
    for (int i = 0; i < triangle.get(triangle.size() - 1).size(); i++) {
        dp[i] = triangle.get(triangle.size() - 1).get(i);
    }
    for (int i = triangle.size() - 2; i >= 0; i--) {
        for (int j = 0; j < triangle.get(i).size(); j++) {
            dp[j] = triangle.get(i).get(j) + Math.min(dp[j], dp[j + 1]);
        }
    }
    return dp[0];
}
```

In-Place Updates

In-place updates are another effective strategy for reducing space complexity. They involve modifying the existing data structures without using extra space. This technique is particularly useful in matrix-based problems such as those found in dynamic programming algorithms.

A classic example is the Two-Dimensional Longest Common Subsequence (LCS) problem, which typically requires $O(m \times n)$ space. By recognizing that we only need information from previous row computations, we can reduce the space complexity to $O(\min(m, n))$ through in-place updates.

```
public int longestCommonSubsequence(String text1, String text2) {
    int m = text1.length();
    int n = text2.length();
    if (m < n) {
        return longestCommonSubsequence(text2, text1);
    }
    int[] dp = new int[n + 1];
    for (int i = 1; i <= m; i++) {
        int prev = 0;
        for (int j = 1; j <= n; j++) {
            int temp = dp[j];
            if (text1.charAt(i - 1) == text2.charAt(j - 1)) {
                dp[j] = prev + 1;
            } else {
```

```
                dp[j] = Math.max(dp[j], dp[j - 1]);
            }
            prev = temp;
        }
    }
    return dp[n];
}
```

Focused application of state compression, iterative computation, and in-place updates can significantly reduce space complexity in dynamic programming algorithms. Understanding the problem structure and identifying opportunities to optimize memory usage are key to implementing efficient solutions.

3.6 From Brute Force to Dynamic Programming

Transitioning from brute force approaches to dynamic programming is fundamental for optimizing algorithms, particularly in tackling complex computational problems. Brute force methods, while simple to implement, are often impractical for large inputs due to their exponential time complexities. Dynamic programming (DP) offers an efficient solution by breaking problems down into overlapping subproblems, storing results, and reusing these results to minimize redundant computations.

To illustrate the transformation from brute force to dynamic programming, we will consider the classic Fibonacci sequence calculation. The brute force method employs a straightforward recursive approach:

```
public class Fibonacci {
    public static int fibonacci(int n) {
        if (n <= 1) return n;
        return fibonacci(n - 1) + fibonacci(n - 2);
    }

    public static void main(String[] args) {
        System.out.println(fibonacci(10)); // Output: 55
    }
}
```

This naive implementation has an exponential time complexity of $O(2^n)$, as it redundantly recalculates Fibonacci numbers multiple times. To optimize this, we can use dynamic programming techniques such as memoization and tabulation.

Memoization involves storing the results of expensive function calls and reusing these results when the same inputs occur again. Here's how memoization can be applied to the Fibonacci sequence:

```
import java.util.HashMap;
import java.util.Map;

public class FibonacciMemo {
    private static Map<Integer, Integer> memo = new HashMap<>();

    public static int fibonacci(int n) {
        if (n <= 1) return n;
        if (memo.containsKey(n)) return memo.get(n);

        int result = fibonacci(n - 1) + fibonacci(n - 2);
        memo.put(n, result);
        return result;
    }

    public static void main(String[] args) {
        System.out.println(fibonacci(10)); // Output: 55
    }
}
```

By storing intermediate results, this method reduces the time complexity to $O(n)$, with space complexity $O(n)$ for storing the memoized values.

Tabulation employs an iterative approach, building up a table (array) from the base case to the desired result, thereby avoiding recursion. Here is the tabulation method for Fibonacci sequence calculation:

```
public class FibonacciTabulation {
    public static int fibonacci(int n) {
        if (n <= 1) return n;

        int[] fib = new int[n + 1];
        fib[0] = 0;
        fib[1] = 1;

        for (int i = 2; i <= n; i++) {
            fib[i] = fib[i - 1] + fib[i - 2];
        }
        return fib[n];
    }

    public static void main(String[] args) {
        System.out.println(fibonacci(10)); // Output: 55
    }
}
```

This method also achieves a time complexity of $O(n)$ with a space complexity of $O(n)$. However, by using iterative computation, it avoids the stack overflow issues that can arise with deep recursion on large inputs.

Taking another example, consider the problem of finding the minimum number of coins needed to make a given amount with a set of denominations. The brute force approach would involve trying out all combinations, leading to an exponential number of possibilities. With dynamic programming, we can optimize this problem efficiently.

Brute force solution:

```
public class CoinChangeBruteForce {
    public static int coinChange(int[] coins, int amount) {
        if (amount == 0) return 0;
        int res = amount + 1;

        for (int coin : coins) {
            if (amount - coin >= 0) {
                int subRes = coinChange(coins, amount - coin);
                if (subRes != amount + 1) {
                    res = Math.min(res, subRes + 1);
                }
            }
        }
        return res;
    }

    public static void main(String[] args) {
        int[] coins = {1, 2, 5};
        int amount = 11;
        System.out.println(coinChange(coins, amount)); // Output: 3
    }
}
```

Dynamic programming solution:

```
public class CoinChangeDP {
    public static int coinChange(int[] coins, int amount) {
        int[] dp = new int[amount + 1];
        Arrays.fill(dp, amount + 1);
        dp[0] = 0;

        for (int i = 1; i <= amount; i++) {
            for (int coin : coins) {
                if (i - coin >= 0) {
                    dp[i] = Math.min(dp[i], dp[i - coin] + 1);
                }
            }
        }
        return dp[amount] > amount ? -1 : dp[amount];
    }

    public static void main(String[] args) {
        int[] coins = {1, 2, 5};
        int amount = 11;
        System.out.println(coinChange(coins, amount)); // Output: 3
    }
}
```

This dynamic programming approach drastically reduces the time complexity to $O(n \times k)$, where n is the amount and k is the number of different coins, and the space complexity remains $O(n)$.

Through these examples, the progression from brute force to dynamic programming demonstrates the substantial gains in efficiency. Dynamic programming is an indispensable toolkit for solving computational problems that feature overlapping subproblems and optimal substructure.

3.7 Transforming Naive Solutions

The initial step toward optimizing an algorithm often involves transforming a naive, brute-force approach into a more structured and efficient solution using dynamic programming (DP). To facilitate comprehension, this section delineates the systematic transformation of naive solutions into optimized dynamic programming implementations, anchoring the discussion with applicable examples.

Consider the problem of calculating the n-th Fibonacci number, traditionally approached with a naive recursive implementation:

```
public static int naiveFibonacci(int n) {
    if (n <= 1) {
        return n;
    }
    return naiveFibonacci(n - 1) + naiveFibonacci(n - 2);
}
```

This method exhibits an exponential time complexity of $\mathcal{O}(2^n)$ due to the overlap in subproblems, specifically recalculating the same Fibonacci values multiple times. To enhance efficiency, we can apply the principle of memoization, a core technique in dynamic programming.

```
public static int memoizedFibonacci(int n) {
    int[] memo = new int[n + 1];
    Arrays.fill(memo, -1);
    return memoizedFibonacciHelper(n, memo);
}

private static int memoizedFibonacciHelper(int n, int[] memo) {
    if (n <= 1) {
        return n;
    }
    if (memo[n] != -1) {
        return memo[n];
    }
    memo[n] = memoizedFibonacciHelper(n - 1) + memoizedFibonacciHelper(n - 2);
    return memo[n];
}
```

In the above implementation, an auxiliary array memo stores the intermediate results of Fibonacci calculations to prevent redundant computations. By doing so, the time complexity is drastically reduced to $\mathcal{O}(n)$, with additional $\mathcal{O}(n)$ space overhead.

Moving further, we can transform our memoized approach into a tabulation (bottom-up) method, which uses an iterative approach to fill the table:

```
public static int tabulatedFibonacci(int n) {
    if (n <= 1) {
        return n;
    }
    int[] dp = new int[n + 1];
    dp[0] = 0;
    dp[1] = 1;
    for (int i = 2; i <= n; i++) {
        dp[i] = dp[i - 1] + dp[i - 2];
    }
    return dp[n];
}
```

This approach leverages a table dp to store Fibonacci numbers in a bottom-up manner, retaining the $\mathcal{O}(n)$ time complexity but also maintaining $\mathcal{O}(n)$ space complexity.

For scenarios where space optimization is crucial, we can further transform the iterative DP approach into an in-place DP solution, reducing the space complexity to $\mathcal{O}(1)$:

```
public static int spaceOptimizedFibonacci(int n) {
    if (n <= 1) {
        return n;
    }
    int a = 0, b = 1;
    for (int i = 2; i <= n; i++) {
        int c = a + b;
        a = b;
        b = c;
    }
    return b;
}
```

In this approach, only two variables (a and b) are used to store the previous two Fibonacci numbers, achieving space efficiency without sacrificing time performance.

Each transformation from naive to fully optimized dynamic programming solution underpins the strategic use of memoization, tabulation, and in-place state representation. Grasping these transformations illuminates the systematic methodology to refine algorithms, enabling not only computational efficiency but also deeper algorithmic insight.

The next logical progression in dynamic programming is to extend these principles to complex problem domains, as observed in combinatorial or optimization problems where dynamic programming shines by mitigating redundant computations and managing state transitions effectively. An exemplary problem to illustrate this is the optimization of the knapsack problem, as discussed in later sections.

3.8 Optimizing Recursive Solutions

To optimize recursive solutions using dynamic programming, it is critical to understand the inefficiencies inherent in naive recursive implementations. A brute force recursive approach often recalculates the same subproblems multiple times, leading to an exponential time complexity. Transforming these naive solutions into optimized ones typically involves either memoization or a bottom-up dynamic programming approach.

Memoization

Memoization is a technique where intermediate results are stored to avoid redundant computations. This process involves creating a data structure, usually a hash table or an array, to save the results of subproblems as they are computed. When the recursive function is called, it first checks this data structure to see if the result is already available. If it is, the function returns the precomputed result, thus saving computation time. This technique effectively converts the recursive solution from exponential time complexity to polynomial time complexity.

The implementation of memoization can be illustrated with the Fibonacci sequence example. Without memoization, the time complexity of the naive recursive Fibonacci function is $O(2^n)$. However, by storing previously computed Fibonacci numbers, we can reduce the time complexity to $O(n)$.

```
import java.util.HashMap;

public class MemoizedFibonacci {
    private HashMap<Integer, Long> memo;

    public MemoizedFibonacci() {
        this.memo = new HashMap<>();
    }

    public long fibonacci(int n) {
        if (n <= 1) {
            return n;
        }
        if (memo.containsKey(n)) {
            return memo.get(n);
        }
        long result = fibonacci(n - 1) + fibonacci(n - 2);
        memo.put(n, result);
```

```
        return result;
    }

    public static void main(String[] args) {
        MemoizedFibonacci mf = new MemoizedFibonacci();
        System.out.println("Fibonacci of 10: " + mf.fibonacci(10));
    }
}
```

In the provided implementation, the HashMap memo stores the results of the Fibonacci calculations. The fibonacci method checks whether the result for n is already in the memo before computing it. This significantly reduces the number of recursive calls.

Bottom-Up Dynamic Programming

Bottom-up dynamic programming eliminates the need for recursion altogether by solving all subproblems iteratively, starting with the smallest. This approach uses an iterative process to fill up a table (array or vector) with computed values. Each value is built upon the previously computed values, eventually leading to the solution of the original problem.

Let's illustrate this with the same Fibonacci sequence problem. In the bottom-up approach, we iteratively compute each Fibonacci number and store it in an array.

```
public class BottomUpFibonacci {
    public long fibonacci(int n) {
        if (n <= 1) {
            return n;
        }
        long[] fib = new long[n + 1];
        fib[0] = 0;
        fib[1] = 1;

        for (int i = 2; i <= n; i++) {
            fib[i] = fib[i - 1] + fib[i - 2];
        }
        return fib[n];
    }

    public static void main(String[] args) {
        BottomUpFibonacci buf = new BottomUpFibonacci();
        System.out.println("Fibonacci of 10: " + buf.fibonacci(10));
    }
}
```

In this implementation, the array fib is used to store the computed Fibonacci numbers. The loop iteratively fills the array by summing the previous two numbers, thus avoiding redundant computations entirely. The time complexity remains $O(n)$, but this approach also boasts a space complexity of $O(n)$.

Optimizations in State Space Reduction

Beyond these fundamental techniques, optimizing recursive solutions often involves additional strategies that reduce the state space or the size of the data structures required. For some problems, storing only a subset of the intermediate results is sufficient. For example, the Fibonacci sequence can be further optimized in space by maintaining only the last two Fibonacci numbers at any time, reducing the space complexity to $O(1)$.

```
public class SpaceEfficientFibonacci {
    public long fibonacci(int n) {
        if (n <= 1) {
            return n;
        }
        long a = 0, b = 1;
        for (int i = 2; i <= n; i++) {
            long temp = a + b;
            a = b;
            b = temp;
        }
        return b;
    }

    public static void main(String[] args) {
        SpaceEfficientFibonacci sef = new SpaceEfficientFibonacci();
        System.out.println("Fibonacci of 10: " + sef.fibonacci(10));
    }
}
```

This code maintains only two variables, a and b, to hold the last two Fibonacci numbers, thus achieving the desired reduction in space complexity while retaining the $O(n)$ time complexity.

By converting recursive solutions into their dynamic programming counterparts, we effectively eliminate overlapping subproblem computations and reduce the overall complexity of our algorithms. Whether using memoization, a bottom-up approach, or optimizing for space, the core principle remains the same: Efficiently solve and store subproblems to save computation time.

3.9 Minimizing Overhead in DP Algorithms

Minimizing overhead in dynamic programming (DP) algorithms is crucial for enhancing performance and efficiency. Overhead can stem from various sources, including excessive memory allocation, redundant operations, and unnecessary computational steps. This section elucidates methods to mitigate such overhead, thereby optimizing the execution of DP algorithms.

A prevalent source of overhead in DP solutions is the repeated recomputation of values that have already been computed. Memoization is a fundamental technique to address this, wherein computed values are stored in an auxiliary data structure, typically an array or a hash table, for future reuse. Consider the following pseudocode for the Fibonacci sequence using naive recursion:

```
public int naiveFibonacci(int n) {
    if (n <= 1) return n;
    return naiveFibonacci(n - 1) + naiveFibonacci(n - 2);
}
```

This naive recursive implementation has an exponential time complexity, $O(2^n)$, due to redundant calculations. By implementing memoization, we can store intermediate results and avoid recomputation, drastically reducing time complexity:

```
public class MemoizedFibonacci {
    private int[] memo;

    public MemoizedFibonacci(int n) {
        memo = new int[n + 1];
        Arrays.fill(memo, -1);
    }

    public int fib(int n) {
        if (n <= 1) return n;
        if (memo[n] != -1) return memo[n];
        memo[n] = fib(n - 1) + fib(n - 2);
        return memo[n];
    }
}
```

In this optimized version, the time complexity is reduced to $O(n)$, reflecting the benefit of memoization. However, this solution still allocates memory upfront, which may contribute to overhead in scenarios with limited resources.

Another method to mitigate overhead employs bottom-up dynamic programming, where computations are performed iteratively rather than recursively. This approach initializes a base case and builds up the solution by systematically solving subproblems. The iterative version of the Fibonacci sequence avoids both the overhead of recursive calls and excessive memory usage:

```
public int bottomUpFibonacci(int n) {
    if (n <= 1) return n;
    int[] fib = new int[n + 1];
    fib[0] = 0;
    fib[1] = 1;
    for (int i = 2; i <= n; i++) {
```

```
        fib[i] = fib[i - 1] + fib[i - 2];
    }
    return fib[n];
}
```

The iterative approach maintains $O(n)$ time complexity while reducing the function call overhead inherent in recursion. Further optimization can be achieved by using variables to store intermediate values, thus minimizing memory usage:

```
public int optimizedFibonacci(int n) {
    if (n <= 1) return n;
    int prev1 = 0, prev2 = 1;
    for (int i = 2; i <= n; i++) {
        int curr = prev1 + prev2;
        prev1 = prev2;
        prev2 = curr;
    }
    return prev2;
}
```

This refined implementation maintains $O(n)$ time complexity while operating with $O(1)$ space complexity, demonstrating how in-place computation can significantly reduce overhead.

Another consideration is minimizing the overhead related to initialization and data structure manipulation. Using appropriate data structures such as arrays instead of hash tables can lead to performance gains by reducing the time complexity of data access and updates. For example, using an array for memoization in the Fibonacci sequence is more efficient than employing a hash table, as array indexing is $O(1)$ compared to the average $O(1)$ but potential $O(n)$ for hash table operations under certain conditions.

In some DP problems, overhead can also result from excessive branching in recursion. Tail recursion optimization is a technique used to convert recursive algorithms into iterative ones, thereby reducing stack overhead. Java's JVM does not support tail call optimization natively, but analogous iterative constructs can replace recursive patterns for similar effects.

Finally, it is essential to profile and benchmark different implementations of a DP algorithm to identify bottlenecks and validate improvements. Tools like the Java Microbenchmark Harness (JMH) can be utilized to measure performance impacts accurately. Here is a simple example using JMH to benchmark different Fibonacci implementations:

```
@State(Scope.Thread)
public class FibonacciBenchmark {
    @Param({"10", "20", "30", "40"})
```

```
    public int n;

    MemoizedFibonacci memoizedFibonacci;

    @Setup
    public void setUp() {
        memoizedFibonacci = new MemoizedFibonacci(n);
    }

    @Benchmark
    public int testNaiveFibonacci() {
        return new Fibonacci().naiveFibonacci(n);
    }

    @Benchmark
    public int testMemoizedFibonacci() {
        return memoizedFibonacci.fib(n);
    }

    @Benchmark
    public int testBottomUpFibonacci() {
        return new Fibonacci().bottomUpFibonacci(n);
    }

    @Benchmark
    public int testOptimizedFibonacci() {
        return new Fibonacci().optimizedFibonacci(n);
    }
}
```

Executing the above benchmarks will yield precise runtime metrics to compare the overhead associated with different DP approaches. The output might look like the following:

```
Benchmark                       (n) Mode  Cnt      Score      Error  Units
FibonacciBenchmark.testNaiveFibonacci      10  avgt   20     0.000      0.000  ms/op
FibonacciBenchmark.testNaiveFibonacci      20  avgt   20     0.001      0.001  ms/op
FibonacciBenchmark.testMemoizedFibonacci   30  avgt   20     0.009      0.001  ms/op
FibonacciBenchmark.testBottomUpFibonacci   40  avgt   20     0.005      0.001  ms/op
FibonacciBenchmark.testOptimizedFibonacci  40  avgt   20     0.002      0.001  ms/op
```

These results indicate the performance characteristics of each approach, helping developers make data-driven decisions to minimize overhead in DP algorithms. By adopting techniques such as memoization, implementing iterative approaches, using space-efficient structures, and profiling for performance, significant overhead reductions can be achieved for efficient, scalable DP solutions.

3.10 Avoiding Redundant Computations

In dynamic programming, one crucial aspect that substantially enhances algorithm efficiency is the avoidance of redundant computations. This principle is central to the dynamic programming paradigm, which essentially utilizes previously solved subproblems to prevent recomputation, thereby improving both time and space complexity of algorithms. By storing the results of intermediate computations, otherwise termed as *memoization*, or utilizing iterative table-filling approaches, we can significantly reduce the computational effort required for solving a problem.

Consider the example of the Fibonacci sequence, where a naive recursive algorithm recalculates the same values multiple times:

```
public class Fibonacci {
    public static int fibonacci(int n) {
        if (n <= 1) return n;
        return fibonacci(n - 1) + fibonacci(n - 2);
    }

    public static void main(String[] args) {
        int result = fibonacci(10);
        System.out.println(result); // Output: 55
    }
}
```

Executing the above code results in an exponential time complexity, $O(2^n)$, due to redundant calculations. For instance, $\text{fibonacci}(5)$ is computed multiple times in the process. To eliminate this redundancy, we employ memoization:

```
import java.util.HashMap;
import java.util.Map;

public class FibonacciMemoization {
    private static Map<Integer, Integer> memo = new HashMap<>();

    public static int fibonacci(int n) {
        if (n <= 1) return n;
        if (memo.containsKey(n)) return memo.get(n);

        int result = fibonacci(n - 1) + fibonacci(n - 2);
        memo.put(n, result);
        return result;
    }

    public static void main(String[] args) {
        int result = fibonacci(10);
        System.out.println(result); // Output: 55
    }
}
```

The memoized version of the Fibonacci function efficiently solves the problem with a linear time complexity, $O(n)$, because each value is computed only once and stored in a hash map.

Alternatively, a bottom-up dynamic programming approach can also be employed to avoid redundant computations by using an iterative method:

```
public class FibonacciDP {
    public static int fibonacci(int n) {
        if (n <= 1) return n;

        int[] dp = new int[n + 1];
        dp[0] = 0;
        dp[1] = 1;

        for (int i = 2; i <= n; i++) {
            dp[i] = dp[i - 1] + dp[i - 2];
        }

        return dp[n];
    }

    public static void main(String[] args) {
        int result = fibonacci(10);
        System.out.println(result); // Output: 55
    }
}
```

In this iterative approach, an array dp is used to store the values of Fibonacci numbers calculated up to n. This ensures that each subproblem is computed only once and reused, thereby also achieving $O(n)$ time complexity.

Now let us apply these strategies to more complex problems such as the Longest Common Subsequence (LCS). The naive recursive approach computes overlapping subproblems multiple times, leading to exponential time complexity:

```
public class LCS {
    public static int lcs(String s1, String s2, int m, int n) {
        if (m == 0 || n == 0) return 0;
        if (s1.charAt(m - 1) == s2.charAt(n - 1))
            return 1 + lcs(s1, s2, m - 1, n - 1);
        else
            return Math.max(lcs(s1, s2, m - 1, n), lcs(s1, s2, m, n - 1));
    }

    public static void main(String[] args) {
        String s1 = "ABCBDAB";
        String s2 = "BDCABC";
        int result = lcs(s1, s2, s1.length(), s2.length());
        System.out.println(result); // Output: 4
    }
}
```

Adding memoization:

```
import java.util.HashMap;
import java.util.Map;

public class LCSMemoization {
    private static Map<String, Integer> memo = new HashMap<>();
```

```
    public static int lcs(String s1, String s2, int m, int n) {
        if (m == 0 || n == 0) return 0;
        String key = m + ":" + n;
        if (memo.containsKey(key)) return memo.get(key);

        int result;
        if (s1.charAt(m - 1) == s2.charAt(n - 1))
            result = 1 + lcs(s1, s2, m - 1, n - 1);
        else
            result = Math.max(lcs(s1, s2, m - 1, n), lcs(s1, s2, m, n - 1));

        memo.put(key, result);
        return result;
    }

    public static void main(String[] args) {
        String s1 = "ABCBDAB";
        String s2 = "BDCABC";
        int result = lcs(s1, s2, s1.length(), s2.length());
        System.out.println(result); // Output: 4
    }
}
```

Using a bottom-up approach for LCS:

```
public class LCSDP {
    public static int lcs(String s1, String s2) {
        int m = s1.length();
        int n = s2.length();
        int[][] dp = new int[m + 1][n + 1];

        for (int i = 0; i <= m; i++) {
            for (int j = 0; j <= n; j++) {
                if (i == 0 || j == 0)
                    dp[i][j] = 0;
                else if (s1.charAt(i - 1) == s2.charAt(j - 1))
                    dp[i][j] = dp[i - 1][j - 1] + 1;
                else
                    dp[i][j] = Math.max(dp[i - 1][j], dp[i][j - 1]);
            }
        }

        return dp[m][n];
    }

    public static void main(String[] args) {
        String s1 = "ABCBDAB";
        String s2 = "BDCABC";
        int result = lcs(s1, s2);
        System.out.println(result); // Output: 4
    }
}
```

The characterizations and performance benefits of these strategies make dynamic programming an indispensable approach to optimize algorithms, particularly when addressing problems with overlapping subproblems. The elimination of redundant computations not only boosts efficiency but also ensures optimal usage of computational resources.

3.11 Space-Efficient DP: In-Place Algorithms

Space-efficient dynamic programming (DP) focuses on optimizing the memory usage of DP algorithms. High memory consumption can be problematic, especially in resource-constrained environments such as embedded systems or when dealing with extensive datasets. In-place algorithms provide a solution by modifying the input data structure directly, significantly reducing additional memory requirements. This section delves into the principles and application of in-place algorithms in dynamic programming.

To understand the concept of space-efficient DP, consider the standard approach of using a secondary data structure, typically a two-dimensional array, to store intermediate results. While this is effective and often straightforward, it can be impractical for higher-dimensional problems due to substantial memory overhead.

Basic Example: Fibonacci Sequence

As a foundational example, consider the computation of the Fibonacci sequence. The naive recursive approach has exponential time complexity, but the iterative DP solution reduces it to linear time. Additionally, the standard DP method requires an array of size n to store intermediate results. However, since each Fibonacci number only depends on the previous two numbers, we can reduce the space complexity from $O(n)$ to $O(1)$ by storing only the last two numbers.

```
public class Fibonacci {
    public static int fib(int n) {
        if (n <= 1) return n;
        int a = 0, b = 1, c;
        for (int i = 2; i <= n; i++) {
            c = a + b;
            a = b;
            b = c;
        }
        return b;
    }
}
```

Executing this code yields:

```
The Fibonacci number at position 10 is 55
```

General Strategy for In-Place Algorithms

Implementing space-efficient DP algorithms generally involves the following strategies: 1. **Reduce the Dimension of the DP Table**: Identify if the DP states can be represented in fewer dimensions without loss of necessary information. 2. **Reuse Memory**: Reuse and update the same memory space for storing DP states, reducing the need for additional storage. 3. **Direct Modification**: When applicable, directly modify the input data structure to store intermediate results.

Case Study: 0/1 Knapsack Problem

The 0/1 Knapsack Problem exemplifies an opportunity to apply space optimization. The standard DP solution uses a two-dimensional array $dp[i][w]$ representing the maximum value that can be achieved with the first i items and a capacity w.

```
public class Knapsack {

    static int knapSack(int W, int wt[], int val[], int n) {
        int[][] dp = new int[n + 1][W + 1];

        for (int i = 0; i <= n; i++) {
            for (int w = 0; w <= W; w++) {
                if (i == 0 || w == 0)
                    dp[i][w] = 0;
                else if (wt[i - 1] <= w)
                    dp[i][w] = Math.max(val[i - 1] + dp[i - 1][w - wt[i - 1]], dp[i - 1][w]);
                else
                    dp[i][w] = dp[i - 1][w];
            }
        }

        return dp[n][W];
    }
}
```

This approach requires $O(nW)$ space complexity. However, upon closer inspection, we notice that the current DP state only depends on the previous state. Consequently, it is possible to use a one-dimensional array to store only the current state's values, thus optimizing the space complexity to $O(W)$.

```
public class Knapsack {

    static int knapSack(int W, int wt[], int val[], int n) {
        int[] dp = new int[W + 1];

        for (int i = 0; i < n; i++) {
            for (int w = W; w >= wt[i]; w--) {
                dp[w] = Math.max(dp[w], dp[w - wt[i]] + val[i]);
            }
        }

        return dp[W];
    }
}
```

Executing this code yields:

The maximum value that can be obtained in the knapsack with weight capacity 50 is 220

Advantages and Considerations

Space-efficient DP algorithms provide several advantages, including: - **Reduced Memory Usage**: Lower memory footprint, crucial for large-scale problems or memory-constrained environments. - **Enhanced Performance**: Potential improvements in cache performance due to smaller data sizes.

However, careful consideration must be given to: - **Complexity of Algorithm**: Space optimization can complicate the algorithm, making it more difficult to implement and understand. - **Trade-offs**: In some cases, reducing space complexity may not necessarily lead to significant performance improvements, depending on the computational environment and nature of the problem.

Overall, the implementation of in-place DP algorithms demonstrates a critical optimization technique, balancing memory efficiency with algorithmic complexity. This approach not only enhances performance but also expands the applicability of dynamic programming to a broader range of practical scenarios.

3.12 Case Study: Optimizing the Knapsack Problem

The knapsack problem is a classic example used to illustrate dynamic programming techniques, and it is particularly well-suited for demonstrating how optimizations can be systematically applied to algorithmic problems. The goal is to find the most efficient way to fill a knapsack of fixed capacity with items of varying weights and values to maximize the total value without exceeding the capacity.

Consider the 0/1 knapsack problem where each item can be either taken or left. The formal definition of the problem is as follows: Given n items, each with a weight w_i and value v_i, and a knapsack with a maximum weight capacity W, find a subset of items such that the total weight does not exceed W and the total value is maximized.

We denote the maximum value obtainable with capacity j and i items by $V(i, j)$. The dynamic programming relation for this problem is:

$$V(i,j) = \begin{cases} 0 & i = 0 \text{ or } j = 0 \\ V(i-1,j) & w_i > j \\ \max(V(i-1,j), V(i-1,j-w_i) + v_i) & w_i \leq j \end{cases}$$

The relationship shows that if the weight of the current item w_i is greater than the current capacity j, the item cannot be included, and therefore, the value remains $V(i-1,j)$. Otherwise, the item is either included or excluded, and the decision is made to maximize the total value.

We now proceed with the step-by-step implementation of the dynamic programming solution to the knapsack problem using Java.

```
public class Knapsack {
    // Returns the maximum value that can be put in a knapsack
    public static int knapSack(int W, int[] weights, int[] values, int n) {
        int[][] V = new int[n + 1][W + 1];

        // Build table V[][] in a bottom-up manner
        for (int i = 0; i <= n; i++) {
            for (int j = 0; j <= W; j++) {
                if (i == 0 || j == 0) {
                    V[i][j] = 0;
                } else if (weights[i - 1] <= j) {
                    V[i][j] = Math.max(values[i - 1] + V[i - 1][j - weights[i - 1]], V[i - 1][j])
                        ;
                } else {
                    V[i][j] = V[i - 1][j];
                }
            }
        }
        return V[n][W];
    }

    // Driver code
    public static void main(String[] args) {
        int[] values = { 60, 100, 120 };
        int[] weights = { 10, 20, 30 };
        int W = 50;
        int n = values.length;
        System.out.println(knapSack(W, weights, values, n));
    }
}
```

Output: 220

The above implementation uses a 2D array V to store the maximum value derived from subproblems. While effective, it may not be the most space-efficient. The space complexity of this approach is $O(nW)$. However, by examining the recursive nature of our relations, we notice that each entry $V(i,j)$ only relies on the previous row $V(i-1,j)$ and the current capacity j. Therefore, we can optimize the space complexity by using a 1D array instead of a 2D array.

The space-optimized version updates the values in the same array, iterating backwards through the current capacity value to prevent overwriting needed results.

```
public class Knapsack {
    // Returns the maximum value that can be put in a knapsack
    public static int knapSack(int W, int[] weights, int[] values, int n) {
        int[] V = new int[W + 1];

        // Build table V[] in a bottom-up manner
        for (int i = 0; i < n; i++) {
            for (int j = W; j >= weights[i]; j--) {
                V[j] = Math.max(V[j], values[i] + V[j - weights[i]]);
            }
        }
        return V[W];
    }

    // Driver code
    public static void main(String[] args) {
        int[] values = { 60, 100, 120 };
        int[] weights = { 10, 20, 30 };
        int W = 50;
        int n = values.length;
        System.out.println(knapSack(W, weights, values, n));
    }
}
```

Output: 220

By moving to a single-dimensional array V, we reduce the space complexity to $O(W)$, making the solution more space-efficient while maintaining the same time complexity $O(nW)$.

This case study of the knapsack problem shows that through careful application of dynamic programming techniques and optimizations, it is possible to significantly enhance algorithmic efficiency both in space and time dimensions. The transition from a naive brute force approach to an optimized dynamic programming solution is vital for solving real-world problems that involve constrained resources. This methodical approach embodies the essence of dynamic programming—transforming recursion and breaking down problems into manageable, solvable subproblems efficiently.

Chapter 4

Dynamic Programming in Java: Basic Concepts

This chapter introduces the implementation of dynamic programming concepts in Java, covering the setup of the development environment, basic Java syntax, and fundamental features. It includes writing the first dynamic programming code, understanding Java classes and objects, and utilizing arrays and ArrayLists. The chapter also addresses implementing recursion, handling edge cases, debugging, and optimizing Java code for performance. An example of the Fibonacci sequence demonstrates practical applications.

4.1 Introduction to Java and Dynamic Programming

Java is a widely-used programming language that is class-based, object-oriented, and designed to have as few implementation dependencies as possible. Dynamic programming (DP) is a fundamental technique in computer science used for solving complex problems by breaking them down into simpler subproblems. This section elucidates the integration of dynamic programming methods within the Java programming language, contextualizing both the theoretical and practical aspects.

The core concept of dynamic programming hinges on the notion that the solution to a given problem can be formulated by the combination of solutions to its subproblems. Typically, this is done either through the top-down approach, using memoization, or the bottom-up approach, using tabulation. Java, with its robust object-oriented features and extensive standard library, supports these methodologies efficiently.

Dynamic programming leverages overlapping subproblems and optimal substructure properties, making it particularly suitable for problems such as the Fibonacci sequence, shortest path algorithms, and many optimization problems. The basic requirements for dynamic programming can be succinctly captured through the following steps:

- Characterize the structure of an optimal solution.
- Define the value of an optimal solution recursively in terms of the values of subproblems.
- Compute the value of an optimal solution (typically in a bottom-up fashion).
- Construct an optimal solution to the problem from the computed information.

Java's syntax and features lend themselves well to these steps. Java's class and object structures enable the encapsulation of problem states and transitions. Java arrays and collections play a pivotal role in storing and retrieving computed values, thus facilitating efficient implementation of the dynamic programming paradigm.

We will first delineate the primary attributes of Java relevant to dynamic programming. Understanding Java's primitive data types, control flow structures, and built-in libraries is essential for effective coding. Here's a brief overview:

Java's data types are critical for storing the intermediate results in a dynamic programming solution. Primitive types like int, long, float, and double are frequently used.

Control flow structures such as loops and conditional statements are foundational for the iterative and recursive processes used in dynamic programming.

Java's standard library, including collections like $\mathrm{ArrayList}$ and $\mathrm{HashMap}$, offers dynamic storage mechanisms that are extremely useful for managing states and transitions in complex problems.

To exemplify, consider the Fibonacci sequence. A naive recursive solution in Java is straightforward but inefficient due to exponential time complexity. Here is a simple Java implementation:

```
public class Fibonacci {
    public static int fib(int n) {
        if (n <= 1) return n;
        return fib(n-1) + fib(n-2);
    }
}
```

However, this approach recalculates the Fibonacci numbers for the same indices multiple times, leading to redundant computations. By storing intermediate results, dynamic programming significantly optimizes this process. Below is a memoized version of the Fibonacci sequence in Java:

```
import java.util.HashMap;

public class Fibonacci {
    private static HashMap<Integer, Integer> memo = new HashMap<>();

    public static int fib(int n) {
        if (n <= 1) return n;
        if (memo.containsKey(n)) return memo.get(n);
        int result = fib(n-1) + fib(n-2);
        memo.put(n, result);
        return result;
    }
}
```

In this implementation, previously computed values are stored in a HashMap, thus avoiding redundant calculations. This illustrates the power of dynamic programming combined with Java's collection framework.

Alternatively, the bottom-up approach, or tabulation method, avoids the recursive overhead by iteratively building up solutions. Here is the tabulated version:

```
public class Fibonacci {
    public static int fib(int n) {
        if (n <= 1) return n;

        int[] dp = new int[n + 1];
        dp[0] = 0;
        dp[1] = 1;

        for (int i = 2; i <= n; i++) {
            dp[i] = dp[i - 1] + dp[i - 2];
        }

        return dp[n];
    }
}
```

This approach computes the Fibonacci numbers iteratively and stores them in an array, ensuring each value is computed only once. This version typically has O(n) time complexity and O(n) space complexity, making it more efficient than the naive recursive approach.

Dynamic programming in Java combines the clarity and rigor of algorithm design with the practical capabilities of modern programming environments. Looking ahead, these principles will form the bedrock of more advanced topics, such as handling edge cases and optimizing code performance.

4.2 Setting Up Your Development Environment

To effectively implement dynamic programming algorithms in Java, it is essential to set up a robust development environment. This section will guide you through the installation and configuration of the requisite software tools.

1. Install the Java Development Kit (JDK)
The Java Development Kit (JDK) is a software development environment used for developing Java applications. The latest version of JDK can be downloaded from the official Oracle website or OpenJDK builds.

- Visit the [Official Oracle JDK Download Page](https://www.oracle.com/java/technologies/javase-downloads.html) or [OpenJDK](https://openjdk.java.net).
- Download the appropriate version for your operating system (Windows, macOS, or Linux).
- Follow the installation instructions specific to your operating system.

After installation, verify the installation by opening a terminal (or command prompt) and typing the following command:

```
java -version
```

You should see output similar to this:

```
java version "17.0.1" 2021-10-19 LTS
Java(TM) SE Runtime Environment (build 17.0.1+12-LTS-39)
Java HotSpot(TM) 64-Bit Server VM (build 17.0.1+12-LTS-39, mixed mode, sharing)
```

2. Set Up an Integrated Development Environment (IDE)
An Integrated Development Environment (IDE) simplifies the development process by providing comprehensive facilities to programmers for software development. IntelliJ IDEA, Eclipse, and NetBeans are popular IDEs for Java development.

Installation Steps for IntelliJ IDEA:

- Visit the [JetBrains IntelliJ IDEA Download Page](https://www.jetbrains.com/idea/download/).
- Download the Community Edition, which is free and open source.
- Install the software following your operating system's instructions.

Installation Steps for Eclipse:

- Visit the [Eclipse Download Page](https://www.eclipse.org/downloads/).
- Download the Eclipse IDE for Java Developers.
- Install the software following your operating system's instructions.

Installation Steps for NetBeans:

- Visit the [Apache NetBeans Download Page](https://netbeans.apache.org/download/index.html).
- Download the appropriate version for your operating system.
- Install the software following the instructions provided.

3. Configure Your IDE for Java Development

Configuring IntelliJ IDEA:

- Open IntelliJ IDEA.
- Create a new project by selecting File > New > Project.
- Choose **Java** and ensure the project SDK is set to the correct JDK path, then click Next.
- Name your project and set the project location, then click Finish.

Configuring Eclipse:

- Open Eclipse.
- Select File > New > Java Project.
- Enter the project name and choose the appropriate JRE (**Java Runtime Environment**), then click Finish.

Configuring NetBeans:

- Open NetBeans.
- Select File > New Project.
- Choose **Java** under Categories and **Java Application** under Projects, then click Next.
- Name the project and set its location, then click Finish.

4. Verifying the Development Setup

To ensure that everything is set up correctly, create and run a simple Java program. Here is a sample "Hello, World!" program.

```
public class HelloWorld {
    public static void main(String[] args) {
        System.out.println("Hello, World!");
    }
}
```

Compile and run the program using your chosen IDE. The expected output should be:

```
Hello, World!
```

This confirms that your development environment is functioning correctly, and you are now prepared to proceed with implementing dynamic programming solutions in Java.

4.3 Basic Syntax and Features of Java

Java is a strongly-typed, object-oriented programming language that is widely used in software development. Understanding the basic syntax and features of Java is essential for implementing dynamic programming solutions efficiently. This section will provide a detailed look at the essential elements that make up Java syntax and the features that are particularly relevant to dynamic programming.

Variables and Data Types

In Java, variables are declared with a specific data type, which dictates the kind of values the variable can hold. These data types can be broadly categorized into primitive types and reference types.

- **Primitive Data Types:** Java has eight primitive data types: byte, short, int, long, float, double, char, and boolean. Each type has a specific range and size.
- **Reference Data Types:** These include class types, interface types, and array types. Variables of reference types point to objects in memory.

Example of declaring variables:

```
// Primitive data types
int count = 10;
double price = 29.99;
char grade = 'A';
boolean isAvailable = true;

// Reference data types
String name = "Dynamic Programming";
int[] numbers = {1, 2, 3, 4, 5};
```

Control Flow Statements

Java provides several control flow statements to dictate the flow of execution. Key control statements include:

- **Conditional Statements:** if, else if, else, and switch are used to execute blocks of code based on conditions.
- **Loop Statements:** for, while, and do-while loops are used for iterative execution. These are particularly useful in dynamic programming for iterating through arrays and solving subproblems.

Example demonstrating conditional and loop statements:

```
int n = 5;

// Conditional statement
if (n > 0) {
    System.out.println("Positive number");
} else if (n < 0) {
    System.out.println("Negative number");
```

```
} else {
    System.out.println("Zero");
}

// Loop statement
for (int i = 0; i < n; i++) {
    System.out.println(i);
}
```

Methods

Methods in Java are blocks of code that perform a specific task and are defined within a class. Methods can return a value or be void. They help in organizing code and promoting reusability.

Example of defining and invoking methods:

```
public class Example {
    // Method with return type
    public int add(int a, int b) {
        return a + b;
    }

    // Void method
    public void displayMessage(String message) {
        System.out.println(message);
    }

    public static void main(String[] args) {
        Example example = new Example();
        int result = example.add(5, 3);
        System.out.println("Sum: " + result);

        example.displayMessage("Hello, Dynamic Programming!");
    }
}
```

Classes and Objects

Java is built on the concept of classes and objects. A class is a blueprint for objects and can contain fields (variables) and methods to define behaviors and states.

Example of defining a class and creating objects:

```
public class Person {
    // Fields
    String name;
    int age;

    // Constructor
    public Person(String name, int age) {
        this.name = name;
        this.age = age;
    }

    // Method
    public void displayInfo() {
```

```
        System.out.println("Name: " + name + ", Age: " + age);
    }

    public static void main(String[] args) {
        // Creating an object
        Person person1 = new Person("Alice", 30);
        person1.displayInfo();
    }
}
```

Arrays

Arrays in Java are used to store multiple values of the same type in a single variable. They are essential in dynamic programming for storing intermediate results.

Example of declaring and using arrays:

```
int[] numbers = new int[5];
numbers[0] = 10;
numbers[1] = 20;
numbers[2] = 30;
numbers[3] = 40;
numbers[4] = 50;

for (int number : numbers) {
    System.out.println(number);
}
```

ArrayLists

The ArrayList class in the java.util package provides dynamic arrays that can grow and shrink as needed. ArrayLists are more flexible compared to arrays and are useful in dynamic programming scenarios.

Example of using ArrayList:

```
import java.util.ArrayList;

public class Example {
    public static void main(String[] args) {
        ArrayList<Integer> numbers = new ArrayList<>();
        numbers.add(10);
        numbers.add(20);
        numbers.add(30);

        for (int number : numbers) {
            System.out.println(number);
        }
    }
}
```

Exception Handling

Java provides a robust mechanism for handling runtime errors through exception handling. try, catch, finally, and throw are the keywords used for dealing with exceptions.

Example of exception handling:

```
public class Example {
    public static void main(String[] args) {
        try {
            int result = 10 / 0;
        } catch (ArithmeticException e) {
            System.out.println("Error: Division by zero");
        } finally {
            System.out.println("End of exception handling.");
        }
    }
}
```

These fundamental concepts form the building blocks for implementing dynamic programming solutions in Java. Understanding and utilizing basic syntax and features effectively will pave the way for more complex and optimized code in dynamic programming.

4.4 Writing Your First Dynamic Programming Code

To begin with dynamic programming (DP) in Java, a comprehensive understanding of the basic syntax and mechanisms of the language is crucial. Assuming this knowledge is already established, we will focus on implementing our first DP solution using a classic problem: the Fibonacci sequence. The Fibonacci sequence is defined as:

$$F(n) = \begin{cases} 0 & \text{if } n = 0 \\ 1 & \text{if } n = 1 \\ F(n-1) + F(n-2) & \text{if } n > 1 \end{cases}$$

Our goal is to implement an efficient algorithm to compute the nth Fibonacci number. The naive recursive approach, while simple, is inefficient due to redundant calculations. Dynamic programming offers a solution by storing intermediate results.

Step-by-Step Implementation:

1. **Define the Class and Method:**

First, ensure the main class encapsulates our logic. The class will define a method to compute Fibonacci numbers using dynamic programming.

```
public class FibonacciDP {

    // Method to calculate n-th Fibonacci number using DP
    public int fibonacci(int n) {
        // Handle base cases
        if (n <= 1) {
            return n;
        }

        // Create an array to store Fibonacci numbers up to n
        int[] fibArray = new int[n + 1];

        // Initialize the first two Fibonacci numbers
        fibArray[0] = 0;
        fibArray[1] = 1;

        // Build the Fibonacci sequence up to n
        for (int i = 2; i <= n; i++) {
            fibArray[i] = fibArray[i - 1] + fibArray[i - 2];
        }

        // The n-th Fibonacci number is now stored in fibArray[n]
        return fibArray[n];
    }

    public static void main(String[] args) {
        // Example usage
        FibonacciDP fibDP = new FibonacciDP();
        int result = fibDP.fibonacci(10); // Compute the 10th Fibonacci number
        System.out.println("The 10th Fibonacci number is " + result);
    }
}
```

2. **Explanation of the Code:**

- - We define a class 'FibonacciDP' with a method 'fibonacci' to compute the Fibonacci number.
- - The method takes an integer 'n' as input. It handles base cases ('n <= 1') by directly returning 'n'.
- - We initialize an integer array 'fibArray' of size 'n+1' to store the Fibonacci numbers up to 'n'.
- - The base cases, 'fibArray[0]' and 'fibArray[1]', are initialized to 0 and 1, respectively.
- - A 'for' loop iterates from 2 to 'n', populating 'fibArray[i]' with the sum of the two preceding numbers: 'fibArray[i - 1]' and 'fibArray[i - 2]'.
- - Finally, the 'nth' Fibonacci number is returned from 'fibArray[n]'.

3. **Complexity Analysis:**

This approach significantly improves efficiency:

- **Time Complexity:** The 'for' loop runs 'n-1' times, hence the time complexity is $O(n)$. - **Space Complexity:** We use an array of size 'n+1' to store all Fibonacci numbers up to 'n', which results in a space complexity of $O(n)$.

4. **Edge Cases:**

When implementing DP solutions, it's essential to consider edge cases. For the Fibonacci sequence:

- - If 'n = 0', the function correctly returns 0 from the base case.
- - If 'n = 1', the function returns 1 from the base case.
- - Negative inputs are not handled in the current implementation. To address this, we can add input validation:

```
public int fibonacci(int n) {
    if (n < 0) {
        throw new IllegalArgumentException("Input cannot be negative.");
    }
    if (n <= 1) {
        return n;
    }
    int[] fibArray = new int[n + 1];
    fibArray[0] = 0;
    fibArray[1] = 1;
    for (int i = 2; i <= n; i++) {
        fibArray[i] = fibArray[i - 1] + fibArray[i - 2];
    }
    return fibArray[n];
}
```

5. **Output:**

Executing the main method produces the following output:

```
The 10th Fibonacci number is 55
```

By following these steps, we efficiently compute the Fibonacci sequence using dynamic programming in Java. This methodology can be applied to various other problems where optimal substructure and overlapping subproblems are present. In the following sections, we will further explore classes, objects, and advanced dynamic programming solutions.

4.5 Understanding Java Classes and Objects

Understanding the concepts of classes and objects is fundamental in Java programming. A class in Java serves as a blueprint for creating objects and typically contains fields (attributes) and methods (functions) that represent the object's state and behavior respectively. Conversely, an object is an instance of a class that encapsulates the data and behaviors defined by the class. This encapsulation promotes modularity and reusability, critical concepts in software design and particularly beneficial when implementing dynamic programming solutions.

A class definition in Java is initiated with the 'class' keyword, followed by the class name and a set of curly braces that encapsulates its fields and methods. Below is a basic example of a class definition:

```
public class Example {
    // Fields
    private int value;
    private String name;

    // Constructor
    public Example(int value, String name) {
        this.value = value;
        this.name = name;
    }

    // Method to display the object's state
    public void display() {
        System.out.println("Value: " + value + ", Name: " + name);
    }

    // Getter for value
    public int getValue() {
        return value;
    }

    // Setter for value
    public void setValue(int value) {
        this.value = value;
    }

    // Getter for name
    public String getName() {
        return name;
    }

    // Setter for name
    public void setName(String name) {
        this.name = name;
    }
}
```

In the example above, the 'Example' class has two fields: 'value' of type 'int' and 'name' of type 'String'. These fields represent the attributes of the class. The constructor 'Example(int value, String name)' is a special method invoked at the time of object creation to initialize the object's fields with specific values.

The 'display' method outputs the object's current state using the 'System.out.println' method. Getter and setter methods (e.g., 'getValue', 'setValue', 'getName', 'setName') provide controlled access to the private fields, enhancing data encapsulation. To create an object of the 'Example' class and interact with it, you can utilize the following code:

```
public class Main {
    public static void main(String[] args) {
        // Creating an object of the Example class
        Example obj = new Example(10, "Sample");

        // Display the object's state
        obj.display();

        // Modify the object's state using setter methods
        obj.setValue(20);
        obj.setName("Updated Sample");

        // Display the updated object's state
        obj.display();
    }
}
```

When executed, this program produces the following output:

```
Value: 10, Name: Sample
Value: 20, Name: Updated Sample
```

This example demonstrates creating a class, defining fields and methods, instantiating an object, and invoking methods to manipulate the object's state.

Understanding classes and objects is crucial when applying dynamic programming principles in Java. For example, when solving a problem using dynamic programming, it might be beneficial to model the problem components as classes. Take the Fibonacci sequence calculation as an example. Implementing it with classes can provide a more structured and modular approach.

Consider a class 'FibonacciCalculator' that uses memoization (a dynamic programming technique) to calculate Fibonacci numbers:

```
import java.util.HashMap;

public class FibonacciCalculator {
    // HashMap for memoization
    private HashMap<Integer, Integer> memo = new HashMap<>();

    // Constructor
```

```
    public FibonacciCalculator() {
        // Seed the base cases
        memo.put(0, 0);
        memo.put(1, 1);
    }

    // Method to calculate Fibonacci number using memoization
    public int calculateFibonacci(int n) {
        if (memo.containsKey(n)) {
            return memo.get(n);
        }
        int result = calculateFibonacci(n - 1) + calculateFibonacci(n - 2);
        memo.put(n, result);
        return result;
    }
}
```

In this example, the 'FibonacciCalculator' class uses a 'HashMap' to store precomputed Fibonacci numbers. The 'calculateFibonacci' method uses memoization to recursively compute the Fibonacci number for a given n. If the result for a specific n is already present in the 'memo' map, it retrieves the value directly, thereby avoiding redundant calculations and significantly improving efficiency.

Here is the usage example in 'main' method:

```
public class Main {
    public static void main(String[] args) {
        FibonacciCalculator calculator = new FibonacciCalculator();
        int n = 10;
        int fibonacciNumber = calculator.calculateFibonacci(n);
        System.out.println("Fibonacci number for n=" + n + " is " + fibonacciNumber)
            ;
    }
}
```

When executed, the above code calculates and displays the Fibonacci number for a specified value of n:

```
Fibonacci number for n=10 is 55
```

This example illustrates the power of combining object-oriented programming with dynamic programming techniques. Encapsulating the memoization logic within the 'FibonacciCalculator' class promotes cleaner, more maintainable, and modular code. It also demonstrates how classes and objects can be effectively leveraged to solve complex computational problems, reinforcing core principles of dynamic programming and Java.

Understanding the synergy between classes, objects, and dynamic programming techniques in Java is instrumental in developing robust, efficient, and scalable applications.

4.6 Using Arrays and ArrayLists in DP Solutions

Dynamic programming (DP) frequently utilizes data structures like arrays and ArrayLists to store intermediate results, often referred to as memoization. By caching these results, the algorithm can avoid redundant calculations and thus improve performance. Here, we delve into the specifics of employing arrays and ArrayLists in Java to implement dynamic programming solutions effectively.

Arrays in DP Solutions

Arrays are fixed-size data structures in Java that store elements of a single data type in contiguous memory locations. When employing arrays in dynamic programming, the primary advantage is the constant time complexity for accessing and updating an element.

Example: Using Arrays for Memoization

Consider the problem of computing the nth Fibonacci number using dynamic programming. Here, an array can be utilized to store the Fibonacci numbers calculated so far.

```
public class FibonacciDP {
    private static long[] memo;

    public static void main(String[] args) {
        int n = 50; // Example for n=50
        memo = new long[n + 1];
        System.out.println(fibonacci(n));
    }

    public static long fibonacci(int n) {
        if (n <= 1) {
            return n;
        }

        if (memo[n] != 0) {
            return memo[n];
        }

        memo[n] = fibonacci(n - 1) + fibonacci(n - 2);
        return memo[n];
    }
}
```

This code defines a class FibonacciDP where the array memo holds intermediate Fibonacci values. The fibonacci method checks if the value is already computed and stored in the array before proceeding with recursive computation. This reduces the exponential time complexity of a naive recursive approach to linear time.

ArrayLists in DP Solutions

ArrayLists are part of Java's java.util package and provide a resizable array implementation. They are particularly useful when the size of the data structure is not known in advance or may change during runtime.

Example: Using ArrayList for Flexible Memoization

Imagine we need to solve a more complex dynamic programming problem where intermediate results are not only numerical but also involve objects or irregularly sized data. ArrayLists provide a flexible alternative.

```
import java.util.ArrayList;

public class ComplexDP {
    private static ArrayList<Integer> memo = new ArrayList<>();

    public static void main(String[] args) {
        int n = 50; // Example for n=50
        // Initialize memo list with default values
        for (int i = 0; i <= n; i++) {
            memo.add(-1);
        }
        System.out.println(complexDP(n));
    }

    public static int complexDP(int n) {
        if (n <= 1) {
            return n;
        }

        if (memo.get(n) != -1) {
            return memo.get(n);
        }

        int result = complexDP(n - 1) + complexDP(n - 2);
        memo.set(n, result);
        return result;
    }
}
```

In this example, ComplexDP utilizes an ArrayList<Integer> to store intermediate results. The list is initialized with default values to track non-computed states. This dynamic array grows as needed, providing flexibility over standard arrays.

Comparing Arrays and ArrayLists

When deciding between arrays and ArrayLists in dynamic programming solutions, consider the following factors:

- **Fixed vs Dynamic Size**: Arrays have a fixed size, whereas ArrayLists can dynamically resize, making them suitable for problems where the number of intermediate results isn't known beforehand.

- **Performance**: Arrays offer better performance with constant-time access and modifications. While ArrayLists are slightly slower due to dynamic resizing and additional function overhead, they provide flexibility and ease of use.

- **Type Requirements**: Arrays must be homogeneous, meaning they store elements of a single data type. ArrayLists can store objects, thus supporting heterogeneous data through object-oriented principles.

By understanding the characteristics and use-cases of Arrays and ArrayLists, one can choose the most appropriate structure for their dynamic programming solution, balancing performance with flexibility. This knowledge is crucial for optimizing memory usage and execution time in large-scale computations.

4.7 Implementing Recursion in Java

Recursion is a foundational concept in computer science and is frequently used in dynamic programming to solve complex problems by breaking them down into simpler subproblems. In Java, recursion involves a method calling itself to solve smaller instances of the same problem. This section will delve into the mechanics of recursion, show how to implement recursive methods, and highlight common pitfalls and best practices.

A recursive method generally consists of two parts: the base case and the recursive case. The base case stops the recursion, preventing an infinite loop, while the recursive case reduces the problem size and calls the method itself.

To illustrate, let's consider the classic problem of computing the factorial of a number:

```
public class Factorial {

    // Recursive method to compute factorial
    public static int factorial(int n) {
        if (n <= 1) {
            return 1; // base case
        } else {
            return n * factorial(n - 1); // recursive case
        }
    }
```

```
    public static void main(String[] args) {
        int number = 5;
        int result = factorial(number);
        System.out.println("Factorial of " + number + " is " + result);
    }
}
```

Executing this code yields:

```
Factorial of 5 is 120
```

In the factorial method, the base case is when $n \leq 1$. For all other values, the method calls itself with $n - 1$.

Memory Considerations

Every recursive call adds a new layer to the call stack, consuming memory. For instance, calculating the factorial of 5 necessitates five recursive calls plus the initial call:

```
factorial(5)
factorial(4)
factorial(3)
factorial(2)
factorial(1) // base case
```

Excessive recursion depth can lead to a StackOverflowError. Java does not optimize tail-recursive calls, so if recursion depth is a concern, refactor into an iterative solution.

Example: Fibonacci Sequence

The Fibonacci sequence is another quintessential example for recursion. Each number in the sequence is the sum of the two preceding ones, usually starting with 0 and 1. The sequence is defined as:

$$F(n) = \begin{cases} 0 & \text{if } n = 0 \\ 1 & \text{if } n = 1 \\ F(n-1) + F(n-2) & \text{if } n > 1 \end{cases}$$

Below is the recursive implementation:

```
public class Fibonacci {

    // Recursive method to compute Fibonacci number
    public static int fibonacci(int n) {
        if (n == 0) {
            return 0; // base case
        }
        if (n == 1) {
            return 1; // base case
        }
        return fibonacci(n - 1) + fibonacci(n - 2); // recursive case
```

```
    }

    public static void main(String[] args) {
        int number = 10;
        int result = fibonacci(number);
        System.out.println("Fibonacci number " + number + " is " + result);
    }
}
```

Executing this code yields:

```
Fibonacci number 10 is 55
```

Performance Issues and Memoization

The recursive Fibonacci implementation recalculates the same values multiple times, leading to exponential time complexity. For instance, to compute $F(10)$, the function calculates $F(9)$ and $F(8)$, then recalculates $F(8)$ as part of $F(9)$. Memoization mitigates this, storing previously computed results:

```
import java.util.HashMap;

public class FibonacciMemoized {
    private static HashMap<Integer, Integer> memo = new HashMap<>();

    public static int fibonacci(int n) {
        if (memo.containsKey(n)) {
            return memo.get(n); // return cached result
        }
        int result;
        if (n == 0) {
            result = 0; // base case
        } else if (n == 1) {
            result = 1; // base case
        } else {
            result = fibonacci(n - 1) + fibonacci(n - 2); // recursive case
        }
        memo.put(n, result); // store in cache
        return result;
    }

    public static void main(String[] args) {
        int number = 10;
        int result = fibonacci(number);
        System.out.println("Fibonacci number " + number + " is " + result);
    }
}
```

Executing the memoized version of the Fibonacci sequence yields:

```
Fibonacci number 10 is 55
```

This optimized solution drastically reduces the number of recursive calls by storing results in a HashMap.

Common Pitfalls and Best Practices

1. **Base Case**: Ensure the base case is correctly implemented to prevent infinite recursion. An incorrect base case can lead to StackOverflowError. 2. **Optimization**: Consider recursion depth and optimize using memoization or by transforming into an iterative solution for performance-critical applications. 3. **Testing**: Thoroughly test recursive methods with edge cases, border cases, and typical use cases to ensure correct behavior.

Following these guidelines ensures that recursive methods in Java are both efficient and effective, providing a powerful tool for solving complex dynamic programming problems.

4.8 Handling Edge Cases in Java Implementations

Handling edge cases is a critical aspect of developing robust and reliable dynamic programming solutions in Java. Edge cases are scenarios that occur at the boundary of the specified inputs, often leading to potential errors or unexpected behavior if not correctly managed. This section explains various strategy implementations to handle these edge cases effectively.

Identifying Edge Cases

Edge cases often arise from certain characteristics of the input data:

- **Minimum and Maximum Input Values**: Inputs at the extreme ends of the allowed range.
- **Empty Inputs**: Situations where inputs are missing or empty.
- **Single Element Inputs**: Inputs containing only a single element where the general logic may not be applicable directly.
- **Unusual Data Patterns**: Inputs with specific patterns that could break standard assumptions.

Analyzing the problem constraints is crucial to identifying these edge cases. Once identified, handling them in Java typically involves checking conditions and ensuring that the implemented logic addresses these cases appropriately.

Example: Fibonacci Sequence

Consider the Fibonacci sequence, where each number is the sum of the two preceding ones, usually starting with 0 and 1. To handle edge cases in the Fibonacci function, we must consider scenarios such as 'n = 0', 'n = 1', and negative inputs, which may not conform to the typical Fibonacci definition.

```
public class Fibonacci {
    public static int calculateFibonacci(int n) {
        if (n < 0) {
            throw new IllegalArgumentException("Input cannot be negative");
        }
        if (n == 0) {
            return 0;
        }
        if (n == 1) {
            return 1;
        }

        int[] dp = new int[n + 1];
        dp[0] = 0;
        dp[1] = 1;

        for (int i = 2; i <= n; i++) {
            dp[i] = dp[i - 1] + dp[i - 2];
        }

        return dp[n];
    }

    public static void main(String[] args) {
        System.out.println(calculateFibonacci(10)); // Output: 55
    }
}
```

This implementation covers multiple edge cases:

- **Negative Input**: Throws an 'IllegalArgumentException'.
- **Zero Input**: Returns 0.
- **One as Input**: Returns 1.

Edge Case Handling in Dynamic Programming Tables

When dealing with Dynamic Programming (DP) tables, initial values must be set correctly to avoid index out-of-bound errors or incorrect results. It is also imperative to ensure the DP table dimensions are adequate to handle the input sizes.

Example: Maximum Subarray Sum

To determine the maximum subarray sum within an array of integers, it is necessary to handle scenarios of an entirely negative array, an array with a single element, and an edge case of an empty array.

```
public class MaximumSubarray {
    public static int maxSubArraySum(int[] nums) {
        if (nums == null || nums.length == 0) {
            throw new IllegalArgumentException("Input array cannot be null or empty")
                ;
        }

        int maxSum = nums[0];
        int currentSum = nums[0];

        for (int i = 1; i < nums.length; i++) {
            currentSum = Math.max(nums[i], currentSum + nums[i]);
            maxSum = Math.max(maxSum, currentSum);
        }

        return maxSum;
    }

    public static void main(String[] args) {
        int[] nums = {-2, 1, -3, 4, -1, 2, 1, -5, 4};
        System.out.println(maxSubArraySum(nums)); // Output: 6
    }
}
```

The implementation identifies and handles several key edge cases:

- **Null or Empty Array**: Throws an 'IllegalArgumentException'.
- **Single Element Array**: Correctly returns that element.
- **Entirely Negative Array**: Properly calculates the maximum subarray sum, which would be the least negative value in this context.

By ensuring that these cases are handled, the function becomes more robust and reliable across a variety of input scenarios.

Impact of Edge Case Handling on Performance

Considering edge cases can also influence the performance aspects of a solution. Efficient handling often involves verifying conditions early in the function to avoid unnecessary computations. Early exits or minimal checks ensure that the program terminates or continues in the most optimal manner given the constraints.

While designing the solution, it is essential to balance between thorough error checking and maintaining performance. Over-complication of edge case handling can lead to reduced readability and increased complexity. Thus, the adopted approach should be both efficient and straightforward, adequately covering the necessary cases without compromising the code's clarity.

This strategic approach to identifying, implementing, and validating edge cases ensures that Java dynamic programming solutions are resilient, accurately addressing a broad array of input scenarios, thus maintaining their reliability and correctness in various practical applications.

4.9 Debugging Java Code

Debugging is an essential aspect of programming, particularly in dynamic programming (DP) implementations, where the complexity of algorithms can lead to subtle bugs. Developing a structured approach to debugging increases the reliability and efficiency of your code.

Identifying Common Errors: In dynamic programming, common errors often include incorrect base cases, improper state transitions, mismanagement of memory, and off-by-one errors. Recognizing these types of issues allows for targeted debugging.

Using Print Statements: Simple print statements are a fundamental technique for understanding the flow and state of your program. For instance, one can print the values of variables at various stages of a DP computation to trace where things go wrong. Consider the following example, excerpted from a Fibonacci sequence implementation:

```
public int fib(int n) {
    if (n <= 1) return n;
    int[] dp = new int[n + 1];
    dp[0] = 0;
    dp[1] = 1;

    for (int i = 2; i <= n; i++) {
        dp[i] = dp[i - 1] + dp[i - 2];
        System.out.println("i: " + i + ", dp[i]: " + dp[i]); // Debug statement
    }

    return dp[n];
}
```

The print statement within the loop allows for monitoring the evolution of the dp array values. By inspecting these outputs, one can verify the correctness of each computation step.

```
i: 2, dp[i]: 1
i: 3, dp[i]: 2
i: 4, dp[i]: 3
i: 5, dp[i]: 5
```

Using Debuggers: Modern Integrated Development Environments (IDEs) come equipped with powerful debugging tools. These debuggers allow you to set breakpoints, step through code line-by-line, and inspect variable values dynamically.

For example, using the IntelliJ IDEA debugger: 1. Place a breakpoint at the beginning of the for loop. 2. Run the debugger. 3. At each breakpoint, inspect the state of the dp array and the index variables.

These steps enable you to visually confirm that the state transitions and calculations align with the expected behavior of the DP algorithm.

Using Assertions: Assertions are another powerful tool for debugging. They can be used to validate assumptions during code execution. If an assertion fails, it typically means an underlying logic error. For example:

```
public int fib(int n) {
    assert n >= 0 : "Input cannot be negative";
    if (n <= 1) return n;
    int[] dp = new int[n + 1];
    dp[0] = 0;
    dp[1] = 1;

    for (int i = 2; i <= n; i++) {
        dp[i] = dp[i - 1] + dp[i - 2];
        assert dp[i] >= dp[i - 1] : "Current value should be greater than or equal to
              previous value";
    }

    return dp[n];
}
```

The first assertion ensures that the input is valid, while the second verifies that each computed Fibonacci number is greater than or equal to the previous one.

Exception Handling: In Java, handling exceptions properly can prevent your program from crashing and provide helpful error messages. For example:

```
public int fib(int n) {
    try {
        if (n < 0) throw new IllegalArgumentException("Input cannot be negative");
        if (n <= 1) return n;

        int[] dp = new int[n + 1];
        dp[0] = 0;
        dp[1] = 1;

        for (int i = 2; i <= n; i++) {
            dp[i] = dp[i - 1] + dp[i - 2];
        }

        return dp[n];
    } catch (IllegalArgumentException e) {
        System.err.println(e.getMessage());
        return -1;
    }
}
```

By catching the IllegalArgumentException, we can gracefully handle invalid input and provide a meaningful error message rather than allowing the program to terminate unexpectedly.

Unit Testing: Unit tests are an indispensable part of debugging, allowing for verification of individual components in isolation. Utilizing frameworks like JUnit helps automate these tests. Here's an example of a unit test for the Fibonacci function:

```
import static org.junit.Assert.*;
import org.junit.Test;

public class FibonacciTest {

    @Test
    public void testFib() {
        assertEquals(0, fib(0));
        assertEquals(1, fib(1));
        assertEquals(1, fib(2));
        assertEquals(2, fib(3));
        assertEquals(3, fib(4));
        assertEquals(5, fib(5));
        assertEquals(8, fib(6));
    }

    public int fib(int n) {
        if (n <= 1) return n;
        int[] dp = new int[n + 1];
        dp[0] = 0;
        dp[1] = 1;

        for (int i = 2; i <= n; i++) {
            dp[i] = dp[i - 1] + dp[i - 2];
        }

        return dp[n];
    }
}
```

Running the FibonacciTest class ensures that changes to the fib function do not introduce new bugs.

Cultivating a methodical approach to debugging using the techniques outlined enables the identification and resolution of issues within dynamic programming algorithms effectively, enhancing code robustness and reliability.

4.10 Optimizing Java Code for Performance

Optimizing Java code for performance is crucial in dynamic programming applications to ensure efficient and rapid execution, especially for computationally intensive problems. To achieve this, various strategies can be employed, including optimizing algorithms, efficient memory management, and leveraging Java language features.

Algorithm optimization is the most effective way to enhance performance. Selecting the appropriate algorithm and refining it can significantly reduce computational complexity. For instance, choosing a dynamic programming approach over brute force can transform exponential time complexity into polynomial time complexity. Consider the following example, where we revise a naive recursive solution to a dynamic programming approach for the Longest Common Subsequence (LCS) problem.

```
public class LCS {
    public static int lcs(String s1, String s2) {
        int m = s1.length();
        int n = s2.length();
        int[][] dp = new int[m+1][n+1];

        for (int i = 0; i <= m; i++) {
            for (int j = 0; j <= n; j++) {
                if (i == 0 || j == 0) {
                    dp[i][j] = 0;
                } else if (s1.charAt(i-1) == s2.charAt(j-1)) {
                    dp[i][j] = dp[i-1][j-1] + 1;
                } else {
                    dp[i][j] = Math.max(dp[i-1][j], dp[i][j-1]);
                }
            }
        }
        return dp[m][n];
    }
}
```

Efficient memory management is another vital aspect. Java provides several mechanisms to manage memory consumption. One approach is to lessen the scope and lifetime of variables, reducing memory overhead. Using local variables instead of instance variables within methods can ensure that memory is allocated and deallocated promptly. Additionally, leveraging Java's garbage collection efficiently by minimizing object creation helps improve performance.

Consider the memory usage in the dynamic programming approach for the Fibonacci sequence. Using memoization with a fixed array instead of recursive calls can improve both time complexity and memory usage:

```
public class Fibonacci {
    private int[] memo;

    public Fibonacci(int n) {
        memo = new int[n + 1];
        for (int i = 0; i <= n; i++) {
            memo[i] = -1; // initialize memo array
        }
```

```
    }

    public int fib(int n) {
        if (n <= 1) {
            return n;
        }
        if (memo[n] != -1) {
            return memo[n];
        }
        memo[n] = fib(n - 1) + fib(n - 2);
        return memo[n];
    }

    public static void main(String[] args) {
        int n = 10;
        Fibonacci fibonacci = new Fibonacci(n);
        System.out.println("Fib(" + n + ") = " + fibonacci.fib(n));
    }
}
```

Java collections can be optimized by choosing the appropriate data structures. The choice between ArrayList, LinkedList, HashSet, and HashMap impacts both memory usage and performance. For instance, ArrayList provides constant-time access but can suffer from slow insertions and deletions due to shifting elements, whereas LinkedList offers efficient insertions and deletions but slower access time.

Another approach to optimization is multi-threading, which exploits parallelism to enhance performance. Java provides robust support for multithreading through the java.util.concurrent package, which simplifies thread management. However, multi-threading requires careful handling of shared resources to avoid concurrency issues such as deadlocks and race conditions. Consider the use of Callable and ExecutorService to implement a multi-threaded dynamic programming solution:

```
import java.util.concurrent.*;

public class ParallelFibonacci {
    private static class FibCallable implements Callable<Integer> {
        private final int n;
        private final int[] memo;

        public FibCallable(int n, int[] memo) {
            this.n = n;
            this.memo = memo;
        }

        @Override
        public Integer call() throws Exception {
            if (n <= 1) {
                return n;
            }
            if (memo[n] != -1) {
                return memo[n];
```

```
        }
        int fib1 = new FibCallable(n - 1, memo).call();
        int fib2 = new FibCallable(n - 2, memo).call();
        memo[n] = fib1 + fib2;
        return memo[n];
    }
  }

  public static int fib(int n) throws ExecutionException, InterruptedException {
    int[] memo = new int[n + 1];
    for (int i = 0; i <= n; i++) {
        memo[i] = -1;
    }
    ExecutorService executor = Executors.newFixedThreadPool(2);
    Future<Integer> future = executor.submit(new FibCallable(n, memo));
    int result = future.get();
    executor.shutdown();
    return result;
  }

  public static void main(String[] args) throws ExecutionException,
      InterruptedException {
    int n = 10;
    System.out.println("Fib(" + n + ") = " + fib(n));
  }
}
```

Proper use of built-in Java language features such as Streams and Lambda expressions can also yield significant performance improvements. For instance, replacing traditional loops with stream operations that can be executed in parallel introduces a potential for performance gains. Nevertheless, it is essential to evaluate whether overhead from parallel stream processing is justified by the computational load.

Profiling and benchmarking tools play an essential role in performance optimization. Tools such as JProfiler, VisualVM, and YourKit provide detailed insights into application performance, including CPU usage, memory consumption, and thread analysis. Profiling helps identify bottlenecks and areas of code that require optimization. Additionally, Java's built-in benchmarking framework, JMH (Java Microbenchmark Harness), enables developers to measure and compare the performance of different code implementations accurately.

These techniques, when applied synergistically, can significantly optimize Java code for dynamic programming applications. Accurate algorithm selection, proficient memory usage, appropriate data structures, multi-threading, leveraging language features, and utilizing profiling tools collectively contribute to enhanced performance, ensuring efficient and rapid execution.

4.11 Applying Java Collections in DP

Dynamic programming often involves storing intermediate results to improve the efficiency of algorithms. Java collections such as HashMap, HashSet, ArrayList, and LinkedList can be highly effective in this regard. This section provides a comprehensive examination of these collections and how they can be employed to optimize dynamic programming (DP) solutions.

HashMap: The HashMap class provides a structure to map keys to values, which is particularly useful for memoization—a common technique in dynamic programming. Memoization involves storing the results of expensive function calls and returning the cached result when the same inputs occur again. Here is an illustrative example:

```
import java.util.HashMap;

public class FibonacciMemoization {
    private HashMap<Integer, Long> memo;

    public FibonacciMemoization() {
        memo = new HashMap<>();
    }

    public long fibonacci(int n) {
        if (n <= 1) {
            return n;
        }
        if (memo.containsKey(n)) {
            return memo.get(n);
        }
        long result = fibonacci(n - 1) + fibonacci(n - 2);
        memo.put(n, result);
        return result;
    }

    public static void main(String[] args) {
        FibonacciMemoization fib = new FibonacciMemoization();
        System.out.println(fib.fibonacci(50)); // Output: 12586269025
    }
}
```

In this code, the HashMap named memo stores the results of previously computed Fibonacci numbers. When the fibonacci method is called, it first checks if the result for the current input n is already in the HashMap. If it is, the function returns the cached value, avoiding redundant calculations.

HashSet: When the need arises to track unique elements or check the existence of elements efficiently, HashSet can be employed. For instance, consider a problem where you need to check if subset sums of a given array can add up to a specific target value. The HashSet can store the sums encountered, enabling quick look-up operations:

```
import java.util.HashSet;

public class SubsetSum {
    public boolean canAchieveSum(int[] nums, int target) {
        HashSet<Integer> sums = new HashSet<>();
        sums.add(0);

        for (int num : nums) {
            HashSet<Integer> newSums = new HashSet<>(sums);
            for (int sum : sums) {
                int newSum = sum + num;
                if (newSum == target) {
                    return true;
                }
                newSums.add(newSum);
            }
            sums = newSums;
        }
        return sums.contains(target);
    }

    public static void main(String[] args) {
        SubsetSum ss = new SubsetSum();
        int[] nums = {3, 34, 4, 12, 5, 2};
        int target = 9;
        System.out.println(ss.canAchieveSum(nums, target)); // Output: true
    }
}
```

ArrayList: While arrays are fixed in size, ArrayList provides a dynamic array to store varying numbers of elements. An ArrayList can be useful when the size of the dataset is dynamic and unknown at compile time:

```
import java.util.ArrayList;

public class LIS {
    public int lengthOfLIS(int[] nums) {
        ArrayList<Integer> dp = new ArrayList<>();
        for (int num : nums) {
            if (dp.isEmpty() || num > dp.get(dp.size() - 1)) {
                dp.add(num);
            } else {
                int pos = lowerBound(dp, num);
                dp.set(pos, num);
            }
        }
        return dp.size();
    }

    private int lowerBound(ArrayList<Integer> dp, int target) {
        int left = 0, right = dp.size() - 1;
        while (left < right) {
            int mid = left + (right - left) / 2;
            if (dp.get(mid) < target) {
                left = mid + 1;
            } else {
                right = mid;
```

```
            }
        }
        return left;
    }

    public static void main(String[] args) {
        LIS lis = new LIS();
        int[] nums = {10, 9, 2, 5, 3, 7, 101, 18};
        System.out.println(lis.lengthOfLIS(nums)); // Output: 4
    }
}
```

In this example, the ArrayList named dp dynamically grows or updates to represent the current longest increasing subsequence.

LinkedList: Similar to ArrayList, LinkedList can grow dynamically. However, the LinkedList provides efficient insertions and deletions, which could be beneficial in certain DP problems:

```
import java.util.LinkedList;

public class MaxSlidingWindow {
    public int[] maxSlidingWindow(int[] nums, int k) {
        if (nums == null || nums.length < k) {
            return new int[0];
        }

        LinkedList<Integer> deque = new LinkedList<>();
        int[] result = new int[nums.length - k + 1];
        for (int i = 0; i < nums.length; i++) {
            if (!deque.isEmpty() && deque.peekFirst() == i - k) {
                deque.pollFirst();
            }

            while (!deque.isEmpty() && nums[deque.peekLast()] < nums[i]) {
                deque.pollLast();
            }

            deque.offerLast(i);
            if (i >= k - 1) {
                result[i - k + 1] = nums[deque.peekFirst()];
            }
        }
        return result;
    }

    public static void main(String[] args) {
        MaxSlidingWindow solution = new MaxSlidingWindow();
        int[] nums = {1,3,-1,-3,5,3,6,7};
        int k = 3;
        int[] result = solution.maxSlidingWindow(nums, k);
        for (int num : result) {
            System.out.print(num + " ");
        }
        // Output: 3 3 5 5 6 7
    }
}
```

The LinkedList named deque enables efficient management of the sliding window, maintaining the maximum element of the current window.

Understanding and utilizing Java collections appropriately can significantly enhance dynamic programming implementations, providing both efficiency and clarity. Each collection type suits particular needs based on the problem's requirements.

4.12 Example: Fibonacci Sequence in Java

The Fibonacci sequence is a classical problem often used to illustrate the principles of dynamic programming. It is defined as follows: the first two numbers in the sequence are 0 and 1, and each subsequent number is the sum of the previous two. Mathematically, this can be expressed as:

$$F(n) = \begin{cases} 0 & \text{if } n = 0 \\ 1 & \text{if } n = 1 \\ F(n-1) + F(n-2) & \text{if } n > 1 \end{cases}$$

To implement this in Java using dynamic programming, we will consider both the recursive and iterative approaches, emphasizing the performance improvements through memoization and bottom-up strategies.

```
public class Fibonacci {
    public static int fib(int n) {
        if (n <= 1) return n;
        else return fib(n-1) + fib(n-2);
    }

    public static void main(String[] args) {
        int n = 10; // For example, find the 10th Fibonacci number
        System.out.println("Fibonacci number(" + n + ") = " + fib(n));
    }
}
```

This naive recursive approach directly translates the mathematical definition into code. However, this method has a significant performance drawback due to repeated calculations, leading to an exponential time complexity of $O(2^n)$. To improve this, we can employ memoization.

```
import java.util.HashMap;

public class FibonacciMemoized {
    private static HashMap<Integer, Integer> memo = new HashMap<>();

    public static int fib(int n) {
        if (n <= 1) return n;
```

```
        if (memo.containsKey(n)) return memo.get(n);

        int result = fib(n-1) + fib(n-2);
        memo.put(n, result);
        return result;
    }

    public static void main(String[] args) {
        int n = 10; // For example, find the 10th Fibonacci number
        System.out.println("Fibonacci number(" + n + ") = " + fib(n));
    }
}
```

With memoization, the time complexity is reduced to $O(n)$, as we avoid redundant computations by storing and reusing previously computed results. Memoization effectively trades space for time by using a cache to store intermediate results.

An even more efficient method involves using an iterative, bottom-up approach, which avoids the overhead of recursive calls and further reduces space complexity.

```
public class FibonacciIterative {
    public static int fib(int n) {
        if (n <= 1) return n;

        int[] fibArray = new int[n+1];
        fibArray[0] = 0;
        fibArray[1] = 1;

        for (int i = 2; i <= n; i++) {
            fibArray[i] = fibArray[i-1] + fibArray[i-2];
        }

        return fibArray[n];
    }

    public static void main(String[] args) {
        int n = 10; // For example, find the 10th Fibonacci number
        System.out.println("Fibonacci number(" + n + ") = " + fib(n));
    }
}
```

While the above implementation maintains an array of size $n+1$ to store Fibonacci numbers, it is possible to optimize the space usage to $O(1)$ by only storing the last two computed values.

```
public class FibonacciSpaceOptimized {
    public static int fib(int n) {
        if (n <= 1) return n;

        int a = 0, b = 1;
        for (int i = 2; i <= n; i++) {
            int next = a + b;
            a = b;
            b = next;
        }
```

```
        return b;
    }

    public static void main(String[] args) {
        int n = 10; // For example, find the 10th Fibonacci number
        System.out.println("Fibonacci number(" + n + ") = " + fib(n));
    }
}
```

In this optimized version, the algorithm runs in $O(n)$ time and $O(1)$ space. Here, the variables a and b hold the last two values of the Fibonacci sequence during each iteration, updating them iteratively until the desired Fibonacci number is obtained.

The Fibonacci sequence thus serves as an ideal example to demonstrate the power and versatility of dynamic programming in Java. By comparing the naive recursion with memoization and iterative approaches, we illustrate substantial improvements in both time and space complexities, providing a comprehensive understanding of dynamic programming techniques.

Chapter 5

Memoization in Java

This chapter explores memoization techniques in Java, highlighting the benefits of storing previously computed results to improve efficiency. It covers implementation strategies using HashMaps and arrays, comparing recursive and iterative approaches. The chapter addresses common pitfalls, performance analysis, debugging, and testing memoized solutions. Practical applications and advanced techniques are illustrated through a case study on memoizing the Fibonacci sequence.

5.1 Introduction to Memoization

Memoization, a prominent technique in dynamic programming, refers to the process of storing the results of expensive function calls and returning the cached result when the same inputs occur again. This strategy effectively reduces the computational overhead by trading space complexity for time complexity, leading to significantly improved performance in many recursive algorithms.

In computer science, memoization is employed to optimize the performance of programs that make heavy use of recursive function calls. The term "memoize" is derived from the Latin word "memorandum," meaning "to be remembered." With memoization, previously computed results are stored in a data structure such as an array or a HashMap, enabling the program to bypass redundant calculations.

For instance, the Fibonacci sequence is a classic example where memoization can be effectively applied. The naive recursive implementation of the Fibonacci sequence suffers from exponential time complexity due to repeated calculations of the same subproblems. Memoization transforms this into a linear time complexity algorithm by caching and reusing previously computed values.

To illustrate the power of memoization, consider the following naive recursive implementation of the Fibonacci sequence, where each function call recalculates Fibonacci numbers multiple times:

```
public class Fibonacci {
    public static int naiveFibonacci(int n) {
        if (n <= 1) {
            return n;
        }
        return naiveFibonacci(n - 1) + naiveFibonacci(n - 2);
    }
}
```

When 'naiveFibonacci(5)' is called, the function performs redundant calculations for 'naiveFibonacci(3)', 'naiveFibonacci(2)', and so on, drastically increasing the number of recursive calls. For large inputs, this results in an exponential growth of function calls, making the approach infeasible for real-time calculations.

Memoization addresses this issue by storing the results of previously computed Fibonacci numbers, thereby eliminating redundant calculations. By maintaining a cache where results can be stored and retrieved, we can significantly optimize the function's execution time. Here is an example of how memoization can be applied to the Fibonacci sequence using a simple array:

```
public class Fibonacci {
    public static int memoizedFibonacci(int n, int[] memo) {
        if (n <= 1) {
            return n;
        }
        if (memo[n] == 0) {
            memo[n] = memoizedFibonacci(n - 1, memo) + memoizedFibonacci(n - 2,
                memo);
        }
        return memo[n];
    }

    public static void main(String[] args) {
        int n = 10; // Example value
        int[] memo = new int[n + 1];
        System.out.println(memoizedFibonacci(n, memo));
    }
}
```

In this implementation, the array 'memo' is used to store the results of Fibonacci numbers. Each time a Fibonacci number is calculated, its value is stored in the array. On subsequent calls with the same input, the function immediately returns the stored value without further recursive calls, thereby optimizing the performance.

The above code will output the 10th Fibonacci number:

```
55
```

Employing memoization in this manner transforms the time complexity of our Fibonacci function from exponential to linear, as each Fibonacci number is calculated only once.

Memoization can also be easily extended to HashMaps for non-integer keys or when a more flexible data structure is warranted. A 'HashMap' provides faster lookups and is especially useful for problems involving memorization that require associative arrays.

Consider the following Java code implementing memoization with 'HashMap':

```
import java.util.HashMap;

public class Fibonacci {
    private static HashMap<Integer, Integer> memo = new HashMap<>();

    public static int memoizedFibonacci(int n) {
        if (n <= 1) {
            return n;
        }
        if (!memo.containsKey(n)) {
            memo.put(n, memoizedFibonacci(n - 1) + memoizedFibonacci(n - 2));
        }
        return memo.get(n);
    }

    public static void main(String[] args) {
        int n = 10; // Example value
        System.out.println(memoizedFibonacci(n));
    }
}
```

In this scenario, the 'HashMap' 'memo' is used to store the results of Fibonacci numbers. The 'containsKey' method checks if the value for the respective key exists in the map, thus preventing redundant calculations.

The memoization technique, while straightforward, requires careful consideration of the trade-offs involved. The primary benefit is reduced computational time for algorithms with overlapping subproblems. However, the space complexity may increase due to additional memory requirements for storing intermediate results.

Understanding memoization is critical for solving a multitude of computational problems efficiently. This technique forms the backbone for many dynamic programming solutions, providing significant performance boosts in applications ranging from combinatorial problems to complex simulations.

5.2 Benefits of Memoization

Memoization is a technique primarily used to optimize programs by storing the results of expensive function calls and reusing them when the same inputs occur again. This approach can significantly improve the performance of recursive algorithms, particularly those with overlapping subproblems.

One of the most evident benefits of memoization is the reduction in the computational time complexity of many algorithms. For instance, consider the naive recursive implementation of the Fibonacci sequence. Without memoization, the time complexity is exponential, specifically $\mathcal{O}(2^n)$. This is due to the massive amount of redundant calculations as the same values are recomputed multiple times. By implementing memoization, the time complexity can be reduced to linear, $\mathcal{O}(n)$, because each value is computed only once and then stored for future access.

The reduction in time complexity leads to significantly improved performance for algorithms working on large inputs. This is especially beneficial in contexts where the input size can grow considerably, such as dynamic programming problems. By avoiding redundant calculations, memoization ensures that the recursive calls are minimized, leading to faster execution times.

Another advantage is the simplified code readability and maintainability. When implementing solutions to problems that have overlapping subproblems and optimal substructure, memoization allows for a cleaner and more straightforward recursive code. This contrasts with purely iterative solutions, which can sometimes be less intuitive and harder to understand due to the explicit management of the iteration variables.

Furthermore, memoization can also be employed to optimize algorithms that solve problems with repeated computations across different function calls. Besides reducing the time complexity, memoization naturally aligns with the concept of dynamic programming, which decomposes problems into simpler subproblems. By storing the results of subproblem solutions, dynamic programming approaches can optimally utilize memoization.

The trade-off with memoization lies in space complexity. Storing all the computed values incurs additional memory usage. For instance, in the Fibonacci sequence example, an array or a hashmap stores previously computed values. This trade-off is generally acceptable when there is sufficient memory available, and the speed gain far outweighs the cost in terms of added memory usage.

Also noteworthy are the benefits memoization provides in the context of computational algorithms used in data science and artificial intelligence, where large datasets and repetitive calculations are prevalent. For such heavy computational tasks, reducing redundancy can lead to significant runtime improvements. This is particularly important in real-time systems where response times are critical.

In addition to improving efficiency, memoization can aid in debugging. When stored values are used repeatedly, it is easier to track down specific points of failure or incorrect computations within a memoized function. By examining the memoization cache (the data structure used to store precomputed values), developers can quickly identify discrepancies between expected and actual results, facilitating a more effective debugging process.

Consider the following example, which demonstrates the application of memoization in Java for computing the Fibonacci sequence:

```
import java.util.HashMap;
import java.util.Map;

public class FibonacciMemoization {
    private Map<Integer, Integer> memo;

    public FibonacciMemoization() {
        this.memo = new HashMap<>();
    }

    public int fibonacci(int n) {
        if (n <= 1) return n;
        if (memo.containsKey(n)) {
            return memo.get(n);
        }
        int result = fibonacci(n - 1) + fibonacci(n - 2);
        memo.put(n, result);
        return result;
    }

    public static void main(String[] args) {
        FibonacciMemoization fib = new FibonacciMemoization();
        System.out.println(fib.fibonacci(40));
    }
}
```

The output of the above program is:

```
102334155
```

This example highlights how memoization ensures that each Fibonacci number is computed only once and stored for future reference. As a result, the computation of 'fibonacci(40)' becomes efficient and feasible within a reasonable time frame.

Memoization provides significant benefits that include optimizing the computational time complexity, improving the readability and maintainability of recursive algorithms, aiding in debugging, and enhancing performance substantially, particularly in contexts that demand high computational efficiency. As such, mastering memoization techniques is crucial for developers working on complex algorithms and performance-critical applications.

5.3 Implementing Memoization in Java

Implementing memoization in Java involves strategically caching the results of function calls to avoid redundant computations. Java offers several means to achieve this, making use of collections such as HashMap or data structures like arrays. The implementation involves checking if a result already exists in the cache before performing any computation and updating the cache once a new result is calculated.

To illustrate a basic example of memoization, consider a recursive implementation of the Fibonacci sequence. The standard recursive implementation exhibits exponential time complexity because it recomputes results for the same subproblems multiple times. Memoization can significantly optimize this by storing previously computed Fibonacci numbers.

The following listings provide an example implementation in Java:

```
import java.util.HashMap;
import java.util.Map;

public class FibonacciMemoization {
    private Map<Integer, Long> memoizedResults = new HashMap<>();

    public long fibonacci(int n) {
        if (n <= 1) {
            return n;
        }
        if (memoizedResults.containsKey(n)) {
            return memoizedResults.get(n);
        }
```

```
        long result = fibonacci(n - 1) + fibonacci(n - 2);
        memoizedResults.put(n, result);
        return result;
    }

    public static void main(String[] args) {
        FibonacciMemoization fibonacciMemoization = new FibonacciMemoization();
        int input = 40;
        long result = fibonacciMemoization.fibonacci(input);
        System.out.println("Fibonacci number at position " + input + " is: " + result);
    }
}
```

This example utilizes a HashMap to store the results of Fibonacci calculations. The fibonacci method first checks if the result for the current n exists in the memoizedResults map. If it does, the method returns the cached result; otherwise, it proceeds with the computation and stores the result in the map.

The same can be achieved using arrays, which can be more efficient in cases where the size of the input is known and is not excessively large. The following example demonstrates this approach:

```
public class FibonacciArrayMemoization {
    private long[] memoizedResults;

    public FibonacciArrayMemoization(int size) {
        memoizedResults = new long[size + 1];
        Arrays.fill(memoizedResults, -1);
    }

    public long fibonacci(int n) {
        if (n <= 1) {
            return n;
        }
        if (memoizedResults[n] != -1) {
            return memoizedResults[n];
        }
        memoizedResults[n] = fibonacci(n - 1) + fibonacci(n - 2);
        return memoizedResults[n];
    }

    public static void main(String[] args) {
        int input = 40;
        FibonacciArrayMemoization fibonacciMemoization = new
            FibonacciArrayMemoization(input);
        long result = fibonacciMemoization.fibonacci(input);
        System.out.println("Fibonacci number at position " + input + " is: " + result);
    }
}
```

In this second example, the memoizedResults array is initialized with a size equal to the maximum input for which we need to calculate the Fibonacci number. The array elements are filled with -1, which signifies that the values have not been computed yet. The fibonacci method checks whether the result is already present in the array and only performs computations if it is not.

Both methods show how memoization can be implemented in Java to optimize recursive functions. Choosing between HashMap and arrays depends on the use case: HashMap is more flexible and can handle larger ranges but with some overhead, whereas arrays provide faster access times with less overhead but are limited by the predefined size.

Understanding the trade-offs and selecting the appropriate strategy for memoization is crucial for enhancing the performance of recursive algorithms in Java.

5.4 Using HashMaps for Memoization

In this section, we delve into the application of HashMap in the context of memoization in Java. A HashMap is a part of the Java Collections Framework and provides a data structure that offers an average-case time complexity of $O(1)$ for insertion and retrieval operations. By leveraging the efficiency of HashMap, we can significantly reduce the computational overhead associated with expensive function calls.

Memoization involves storing the results of function calls and reusing these results when the same inputs occur again. When implementing memoization with a HashMap, the goal is to map inputs of the function (often represented as key-value pairs) to their corresponding computed outputs.

```
import java.util.HashMap;

public class FibonacciMemoization {
    private static HashMap<Integer, Integer> memoizeTable = new HashMap<>();

    public static int fibonacci(int n) {
        if (n <= 1) {
            return n;
        }

        // Check if result is already computed and present in the HashMap
        if (memoizeTable.containsKey(n)) {
            return memoizeTable.get(n);
        }

        // Otherwise, compute the result, store it in the HashMap, and return it
        int result = fibonacci(n - 1) + fibonacci(n - 2);
        memoizeTable.put(n, result);
        return result;
    }

    public static void main(String[] args) {
```

```
        int n = 40;
        System.out.println("Fibonacci of " + n + " is: " + fibonacci(n));
    }
}
```

In the code example above, the fibonacci() method computes the Fibonacci number for a given integer n. The memoization table, memoizeTable, is declared as a static HashMap. This design choice ensures that the table retains its state across recursive calls:

- When $n \leq 1$, the method returns n, as these are the base cases for the Fibonacci sequence.
- For all other values of n, the method checks the memoizeTable to ascertain whether the result has already been computed.
- If the result is present in the memoizeTable, it is retrieved and returned immediately.
- If the result is not present, the method computes the Fibonacci number, stores the result in the memoizeTable for future reference, and then returns the result.

Executing the code produces the following output:

```
Fibonacci of 40 is: 102334155
```

This implementation follows a recursive approach, where each call to fibonacci() possibly results in two other calls unless their results are already memoized. Since HashMap offers constant time complexity for both put and get operations, the usage of memoizeTable dramatically reduces the number of recursive calls by efficiently caching intermediate results.

```
import java.util.Collections;
import java.util.HashMap;
import java.util.Map;

public class SynchronizedFibonacciMemoization {
    private static Map<Integer, Integer> memoizeTable =
        Collections.synchronizedMap(new HashMap<>());

    public static int fibonacci(int n) {
        if (n <= 1) {
            return n;
        }

        if (memoizeTable.containsKey(n)) {
            return memoizeTable.get(n);
        }

        int result = fibonacci(n - 1) + fibonacci(n - 2);
        memoizeTable.put(n, result);
```

```
        return result;
    }

    public static void main(String[] args) {
        int n = 40;
        System.out.println("Fibonacci of " + n + " is: " + fibonacci(n));
    }
}
```

For multi-threaded environments, the HashMap in the previous example can lead to concurrency issues. A simple yet effective solution involves using Collections.synchronizedMap() to create a thread-safe HashMap. This approach ensures that updates to the memoizeTable are synchronized, preventing inconsistent states due to concurrent modifications.

In performance-critical applications, further optimizations might involve alternative data structures like ConcurrentHashMap which provides better scalability under concurrent access:

```
import java.util.concurrent.ConcurrentHashMap;

public class ConcurrentFibonacciMemoization {
    private static ConcurrentHashMap<Integer, Integer> memoizeTable =
        new ConcurrentHashMap<>();

    public static int fibonacci(int n) {
        if (n <= 1) {
            return n;
        }

        return memoizeTable.computeIfAbsent(n,
            key -> fibonacci(key - 1) + fibonacci(key - 2));
    }

    public static void main(String[] args) {
        int n = 40;
        System.out.println("Fibonacci of " + n + " is: " + fibonacci(n));
    }
}
```

By replacing HashMap with ConcurrentHashMap, the fibonacci() method utilizes computeIfAbsent() which atomically computes and inserts the Fibonacci number if absent. This approach integrates the compute-and-check pattern directly within a thread-safe operation, thereby enhancing both performance and safety in concurrent contexts.

Understanding the intricacies of HashMap-based memoization not only bolsters one's ability to enhance function performance but also equips the programmer with skills in handling synchronization challenges in concurrent programming environments.

5.5 Using Arrays for Memoization

To effectively use arrays for memoization in Java, it's crucial to understand the implications of this technique in terms of storage and access time. Arrays offer a fixed-size, continuous storage structure that operates with O(1) time complexity for both read and write operations, making them an efficient choice for memoization when the potential range of input values is known and bounded.

We will begin by exploring the basic setup for memoizing a simple recursive function using an array and then delve into more complex scenarios.

Consider the problem of computing the Fibonacci sequence:

$$F(n) = \begin{cases} 0 & \text{if } n = 0 \\ 1 & \text{if } n = 1 \\ F(n-1) + F(n-2) & \text{if } n > 1 \end{cases}$$

Without memoization, the straightforward recursive approach results in exponential time complexity, as it re-evaluates the same subproblems multiple times. By integrating an array for memoization, we can achieve linear time complexity.

```
public class Fibonacci {
    // Function to compute Fibonacci number
    public static int fib(int n) {
        int[] memo = new int[n + 1];
        return fib(n, memo);
    }

    // Helper function using memoization
    private static int fib(int n, int[] memo) {
        if (n <= 1) {
            return n;
        }
        if (memo[n] == 0) { // Check if value has already been computed
            memo[n] = fib(n - 1, memo) + fib(n - 2, memo);
        }
        return memo[n];
    }

    // Main method
    public static void main(String[] args) {
        int n = 10;
        System.out.println("Fibonacci number at position " + n + " is: " + fib(n));
    }
}
```

In this example, the `int[]` array named `memo` is initialized with zeroes.

The base cases for $n = 0$ and $n = 1$ are handled directly, while other values are computed recursively and stored in the memo array to prevent redundant computation.

```
Fibonacci number at position 10 is: 55
```

Practical Considerations

1. **Array Initialization:** While arrays provide efficient O(1) access time, their fixed size can sometimes be a limitation if the range of input values is unknown or unbounded. Initializing an array with a size larger than necessary can waste space, whereas arrays that are too small can lead to issues during execution.

2. **Boundary Conditions:** Ensure the array can hold values up to the maximum expected input; otherwise, ArrayIndexOutOfBoundsException may occur. Proper validation of input n before accessing array indices is essential.

3. **Space Complexity:** The space complexity for using an array in memoization is $O(n)$, where n is the size of the input. This is suitable for problems where the input size is relatively small or where a rough upper bound is known in advance.

4. **Thread Safety:** In concurrent or multi-threaded environments, array-based memoization requires synchronization to avoid race conditions and ensure the consistency of stored states. Java's java.util.concurrent.atomic package provides classes such as AtomicIntegerArray for thread-safe operations on arrays.

Example: Dynamic Programming with Arrays

For problems that can benefit from dynamic programming, arrays serve not only for memoization but also for iterative bottom-up approaches. Consider the Fibonacci sequence problem approached iteratively:

```
public class FibonacciIterative {
    public static int fib(int n) {
        if (n <= 1) return n;

        int[] fibArray = new int[n + 1];
        fibArray[0] = 0;
        fibArray[1] = 1;

        for (int i = 2; i <= n; i++) {
            fibArray[i] = fibArray[i - 1] + fibArray[i - 2];
        }

        return fibArray[n];
    }

    public static void main(String[] args) {
        int n = 10;
```

```
        System.out.println("Fibonacci number at position " + n + " is: " + fib(n));
    }
}
```

```
Fibonacci number at position 10 is: 55
```

In this iterative example, the Fibonacci sequence is constructed from the bottom up using a for loop, thus avoiding the overhead of recursive function calls. The array fibArray holds the Fibonacci numbers up to n, providing an efficient and straightforward solution.

Using arrays for memoization in Java combines clarity of structure with the efficiency of direct memory access, ensuring that dynamic programming solutions are both performant and easy to implement.

5.6 Recursive vs Iterative Approaches in Memoization

In exploring memoization techniques, it is essential to contrast the recursive and iterative approaches. Both methods have advantages and disadvantages, with the applicability often determined by the specific problem and constraints such as time complexity, space complexity, and stack limits.

Consider the problem of computing the Fibonacci sequence, a canonical example often used to illustrate these concepts. The naive recursive algorithm initially appears elegant but suffers from exponential time complexity. Each function call results in two more calls, leading to an excessive recomputation of the same values. Introducing memoization significantly improves efficiency.

```
import java.util.HashMap;
import java.util.Map;

public class FibonacciRecursiveMemoization {
    private Map<Integer, Long> memo;

    public FibonacciRecursiveMemoization() {
        this.memo = new HashMap<>();
    }

    public long fib(int n) {
        if (n <= 1) return n;
        if (memo.containsKey(n)) return memo.get(n);
        long result = fib(n - 1) + fib(n - 2);
        memo.put(n, result);
        return result;
    }
```

```
    public static void main(String[] args) {
        FibonacciRecursiveMemoization fib = new FibonacciRecursiveMemoization();
        System.out.println(fib.fib(50));
    }
}
```

In this implementation, a HashMap is used to store previously computed Fibonacci numbers. While this recursive approach is more readable and concise, it still suffers from the overhead of maintaining a call stack. For sufficiently large input values, this can lead to a stack overflow error.

The iterative approach, on the other hand, avoids recursion entirely and therefore eliminates the risk of stack overflows. By using a loop structure, the computation progresses linearly, and memoization ensures intermediate results are reused efficiently.

```
import java.util.HashMap;
import java.util.Map;

public class FibonacciIterativeMemoization {
    private Map<Integer, Long> memo;

    public FibonacciIterativeMemoization() {
        this.memo = new HashMap<>();
    }

    public long fib(int n) {
        if (n <= 1) return n;
        memo.put(0, 0L);
        memo.put(1, 1L);

        for (int i = 2; i <= n; i++) {
            long result = memo.get(i - 1) + memo.get(i - 2);
            memo.put(i, result);
        }
        return memo.get(n);
    }

    public static void main(String[] args) {
        FibonacciIterativeMemoization fib = new FibonacciIterativeMemoization();
        System.out.println(fib.fib(50));
    }
}
```

This iterative approach initializes the base cases directly within the loop structure and uses memoization to handle all subsequent values. This ensures that each Fibonacci number is computed exactly once. While slightly more verbose, this method is more robust for large input sizes.

Performance distinction between these approaches is evident through time and space complexity analysis. For both methods, the time complexity theoretically reduces to $O(n)$ from the exponential $O(2^n)$ in the naive approach. However, recursive methods carry an additional space complexity of $O(n)$ due to the call stack, whereas iterative methods have a space complexity of $O(1)$ aside from the HashMap storage.

Practical limitations arise in real-world scenarios where stack size constraints are significantly more restrictive than heap size. Consequently, when memoizing with extensive data, the iterative approach is more viable. Nevertheless, the recursive approach often provides clearer, more intuitive code for readers and programmers who prioritize readability and simplicity.

The choice between recursion and iteration in memoization implementations should be guided by the specific application's requirements and constraints. As a rule of thumb, prefer iterative solutions for large datasets and environments with restricted stack sizes, and employ recursive solutions when clarity and simplicity are paramount and stack space is sufficient.

This detailed analysis and implementation comparison enhance understanding of the fundamental differences and practical trade-offs between recursive and iterative approach mechanics in memoized solutions.

5.7 Common Pitfalls and How to Avoid Them

Memoization, while a powerful optimization technique, presents several challenges and potential pitfalls that can compromise the efficiency and correctness of an implementation. Recognizing these pitfalls and learning how to avoid them is crucial for leveraging memoization effectively. This section discusses the most common issues encountered and provides strategies for mitigating them.

1. Memory Overflow

Memoization typically involves storing intermediate results in data structures such as HashMaps or arrays. While this can significantly reduce computational time by avoiding redundant calculations, it also introduces the risk of memory overflow, especially when dealing with large input sizes or recursive calls that generate numerous unique subproblems.

To minimize the risk of memory overflow:

- Use primitive data types or data structures with lower memory footprints when possible.
- Employ iterative approaches instead of recursive ones to manage

the stack size more effectively.

- Implement garbage collection strategies to remove entries from the memoization table after they are no longer needed.

2. Overhead of Storing Results

Another potential pitfall is the overhead associated with storing and retrieving results from the memoization table. This overhead can sometimes outweigh the benefits of memoization, particularly if the cost of computing the result is low or if the storage operations are inefficient.

Strategies to reduce storage overhead include:

- Optimizing the data structures used for memoization. For instance, use arrays for problems with a predictable and bounded input range, as array accesses are generally faster than HashMap operations.
- Minimizing the number of entries stored by memoizing only the most computationally expensive subproblems.
- Profiling and benchmarking different data structure choices to identify the most efficient one for the specific use case.

3. Incorrect Cache Usage

Improper handling of the memoization cache can lead to incorrect results. This issue often arises from logical errors in the implementation, such as not updating the cache correctly or failing to check the cache before performing a computation.

Avoid mistakes in cache usage by:

- Thoroughly testing the memoized function with a variety of input cases to ensure that it correctly computes results using the cache.
- Using a clear and consistent method for storing and retrieving cache entries.
- Implementing comprehensive debugging and logging mechanisms to track cache accesses and updates.

4. Initialization Errors

Initialization errors occur when the memoization table is not properly initialized, leading to unexpected behavior during computation. This can happen if the memoization data structure is not correctly sized or if the initial values are not set up properly.

To prevent initialization errors:

- Ensure that the memoization table is initialized to an appropriate size before any computation begins.
- Use default values that clearly indicate whether a result has been computed (e.g., using a special sentinel value).
- Verify the initial state of the memoization table during debugging to confirm correct setup.

5. Concurrent Access Issues

In a multithreaded environment, concurrent access to the memoization table can lead to race conditions and data corruption. Proper synchronization mechanisms must be employed to handle concurrent reads and writes safely.

Mitigate concurrency issues by:

- Using thread-safe data structures such as ConcurrentHashMap for the memoization table.
- Synchronizing access to the memoization table using synchronized blocks or locks.
- Ensuring that the memoized function is thread-safe by avoiding shared mutable state.

```
import java.util.concurrent.*;

public class FibonacciMemoization {
    private ConcurrentHashMap<Integer, Long> memo = new ConcurrentHashMap
        <>();

    public long fibonacci(int n) {
        if (n <= 1) return n;
        memo.computeIfAbsent(n, k -> fibonacci(k - 1) + fibonacci(k - 2));
        return memo.get(n);
    }
}
```

6. Handling Edge Cases

Failure to correctly handle edge cases, such as very large or very small input values, can lead to incorrect results or runtime errors. These edge cases often require special treatment in the memoized function to ensure proper handling.

Ensure robust edge case handling by:

- Identifying all potential edge cases during the design phase and implementing specific logic to handle each case.
- Writing exhaustive test cases that include edge cases to verify the robustness of the memoized function.
- Using assertions and exception handling to detect and manage unexpected input values safely.

Combining these strategies and being aware of the common pitfalls associated with memoization ensures that the implementation remains efficient, correct, and maintainable.

5.8 Performance Analysis of Memoized Solutions

Performance analysis of memoized solutions requires a thorough understanding of both the time complexity and space complexity aspects introduced by memoization. By caching the results of expensive function calls and reusing those results when the same inputs occur again, memoization transforms the time complexity of recursive algorithms significantly.

In the context of dynamic programming, memoization helps to reduce the time complexity of recursive algorithms from exponential to polynomial. For example, consider the calculation of the Fibonacci sequence. A naive recursive approach results in excessive recalculations, leading to exponential time complexity $O(2^n)$. However, using memoization, we cache these results, thus cutting down drastically on recomputation. This changes the time complexity to a linear $O(n)$, because each Fibonacci number is computed once and then stored for future retrieval.

To quantitatively illustrate this, consider the naive recursive implementation of the Fibonacci sequence:

```
public static int fibonacci(int n) {
    if (n <= 1) {
        return n;
    }
```

```
    return fibonacci(n - 1) + fibonacci(n - 2);
}
```

In this implementation, every call to fibonacci(n - 1) and fibonacci(n - 2) generates further recursive calls, leading to a growth pattern resembling a binary tree of height n, thus the exponential time complexity.

Contrast this with the memoized version using a HashMap for caching results:

```
import java.util.HashMap;

public class FibonacciMemoized {
    private HashMap<Integer, Integer> memo;

    public FibonacciMemoized() {
        memo = new HashMap<>();
    }

    public int fibonacci(int n) {
        if (n <= 1) {
            return n;
        }
        if (memo.containsKey(n)) {
            return memo.get(n);
        }
        int result = fibonacci(n - 1) + fibonacci(n - 2);
        memo.put(n, result);
        return result;
    }
}
```

In this memoized approach, each Fibonacci number is calculated once, stored in the memo map, and retrieved directly for subsequent calls. Consequently, the time complexity is reduced to $O(n)$, as only n unique results are computed.

The space complexity, however, increases due to the storage requirement of the memoization data structures. For the above implementation using HashMap, the space complexity is $O(n)$ since an entry is stored in the map for each Fibonacci number up to n. Using an array instead of a HashMap would also result in the same space complexity but might lead to constant-time access and better performance due to the advantages of array indexing.

Below is the array-based memoized implementation of the Fibonacci sequence:

```
public class FibonacciMemoizedWithArray {
    private int[] memo;

    public FibonacciMemoizedWithArray(int n) {
        memo = new int[n + 1];
        Arrays.fill(memo, -1);
```

```
    }

    public int fibonacci(int n) {
        if (n <= 1) {
            return n;
        }
        if (memo[n] != -1) {
            return memo[n];
        }
        memo[n] = fibonacci(n - 1) + fibonacci(n - 2);
        return memo[n];
    }
}
```

In both examples, the recursive depth affects the call stack size, which remains $O(n)$ due to the linear recursion depth. This analysis can be extended to other problems that benefit from memoization, such as the Knapsack problem, longest common subsequence, and matrix chain multiplication.

While memoization significantly improves performance, it is crucial to consider trade-offs:

- **Memory Usage:** Memoization typically uses additional memory to store intermediate results, which may be considerable for large input sizes.
- **Overhead of Caching Mechanism:** Implementing the caching mechanism introduces some overhead. The choice between HashMap, array, or other data structures can impact performance.
- **Garbage Collection:** Storing many cached results may affect Java's garbage collection process, potentially leading to latency spikes.
- **Initialization Time:** Initialization of memoization data structures incurs a one-time cost, which should be accounted for in performance analysis.

Monitoring and analyzing the runtime and memory metrics using Java profilers (such as VisualVM or JProfiler) allows for a comprehensive understanding of the performance characteristics of the memoized solution. These tools aid in identifying bottlenecks, excessive memory usage, and potential improvements in the caching strategy or data structures used.

In practical scenarios, the choice of whether or not to use memoization depends on the specific context, including the nature of the problem, input size, and available system resources. Analyzing and optimizing memoized solutions is thus an intricate but critical practice in improving the efficiency of algorithms.

5.9 Case Study: Memoizing the Fibonacci Sequence

The Fibonacci sequence serves as an ideal example to illustrate the power and efficiency of memoization techniques. In its recursive form, the exponential growth of function calls results in significant redundant computations. Memoization mitigates this inefficiency by caching results of expensive function calls and reusing these results when the same inputs occur again.

The Fibonacci sequence is defined as:

$$F(0) = 0, \quad F(1) = 1, \quad F(n) = F(n-1) + F(n-2) \text{ for } n > 1$$

A naive recursive implementation of this definition is straightforward but inefficient due to repeated calculations. Consider the following naive Java implementation:

```
public class Fibonacci {
    public static int fib(int n) {
        if (n <= 1) {
            return n;
        }
        return fib(n - 1) + fib(n - 2);
    }

    public static void main(String[] args) {
        System.out.println(fib(40)); // Inefficient for large 'n'
    }
}
```

Running this program for large values of n results in significant delays due to the exponential time complexity $O(2^n)$.

To improve performance, we introduce memoization. We can use a HashMap to store previously computed Fibonacci numbers. The updated implementation using a HashMap is shown below:

```
import java.util.HashMap;

public class Fibonacci {
    private static HashMap<Integer, Integer> memo = new HashMap<>();

    public static int fib(int n) {
        if (n <= 1) {
```

```
            return n;
        }
        if (memo.containsKey(n)) {
            return memo.get(n);
        }
        int result = fib(n - 1) + fib(n - 2);
        memo.put(n, result);
        return result;
    }

    public static void main(String[] args) {
        System.out.println(fib(40)); // Efficient for large 'n'
    }
}
```

This version significantly enhances performance by reducing the time complexity to $O(n)$. The use of $\mathrm{HashMap}$ ensures that each Fibonacci number is calculated only once and retrieved in constant time for subsequent calls.

Alternatively, an array can be used for memoization, which may offer even faster access times. The following is the array-based implementation:

```
public class Fibonacci {
    private static int[] memo;

    public static int fib(int n) {
        memo = new int[n + 1];
        return fibHelper(n);
    }

    private static int fibHelper(int n) {
        if (n <= 1) {
            return n;
        }
        if (memo[n] != 0) {
            return memo[n];
        }
        memo[n] = fibHelper(n - 1) + fibHelper(n - 2);
        return memo[n];
    }

    public static void main(String[] args) {
        System.out.println(fib(40)); // Efficient for large 'n'
    }
}
```

In this array-based approach, an array of size $n+1$ is initialized to store computed values. This ensures direct and fast access to any $F(i)$, thus enhancing overall performance.

While both 'HashMap' and arrays provide the necessary improvements, selecting between them depends on specific use-case requirements. 'HashMap' is more flexible and handles sparse sequences effectively, while arrays offer faster access times when the sequence is dense and bounds are known beforehand.

For comprehensive performance analysis, the execution time for both memoized implementations can be compared. Consider the following Java program to measure the execution time:

```
import java.util.HashMap;

public class FibonacciComparison {

    private static HashMap<Integer, Integer> memoHashMap = new HashMap<>();
    private static int[] memoArray;

    public static int fibHashMap(int n) {
        if (n <= 1) {
            return n;
        }
        if (memoHashMap.containsKey(n)) {
            return memoHashMap.get(n);
        }
        int result = fibHashMap(n - 1) + fibHashMap(n - 2);
        memoHashMap.put(n, result);
        return result;
    }

    public static int fibArray(int n) {
        memoArray = new int[n + 1];
        return fibArrayHelper(n);
    }

    private static int fibArrayHelper(int n) {
        if (n <= 1) {
            return n;
        }
        if (memoArray[n] != 0) {
            return memoArray[n];
        }
        memoArray[n] = fibArrayHelper(n - 1) + fibArrayHelper(n - 2);
        return memoArray[n];
    }

    public static void main(String[] args) {
        long startTimeHashMap = System.currentTimeMillis();
        System.out.println(fibHashMap(40));
        long endTimeHashMap = System.currentTimeMillis();
        System.out.println("Execution time with HashMap: " + (endTimeHashMap -
              startTimeHashMap) + " milliseconds");

        long startTimeArray = System.currentTimeMillis();
        System.out.println(fibArray(40));
        long endTimeArray = System.currentTimeMillis();
        System.out.println("Execution time with Array: " + (endTimeArray -
              startTimeArray) + " milliseconds");
    }
}
```

Sample output from the execution of this program might look like:

```
102334155
Execution time with HashMap: 10 milliseconds
102334155
Execution time with Array: 1 milliseconds
```

This comparison reveals that while both implementations vastly outperform the naive approach, the array-based implementation slightly outperforms the HashMap-based solution in this context, due to the direct access mechanism of arrays.

Testing and debugging the memoized solution are essential steps to ensure correctness and performance. This can be performed by verifying the memoization table contents and execution times for varying input sizes. The process enriches understanding and provides practical insights into the benefits of memoization.

5.10 Real-World Applications of Memoization

Memoization is a powerful optimization technique that finds applications in numerous real-world scenarios. By storing previously computed results, it significantly reduces the computational overhead in scenarios where the same operations are repeatedly performed. Below, we delve into several practical applications where memoization effectively enhances performance.

1. Dynamic Web Content Generation

In web applications, frequently accessed dynamic content—such as user profiles, dashboards, and reports—can benefit from memoization. When generating a user's dashboard, for example, multiple data retrieval and computation processes are often involved. By memoizing these results, the server avoids redundant database queries and computations, thus reducing load times and improving user experience.

```
// Memoization with a HashMap for web content generation
public class DashboardMemoizer {
    private Map<Long, String> memoizedDashboards = new HashMap<>();

    public String getDashboard(Long userId) {
        if (memoizedDashboards.containsKey(userId)) {
            return memoizedDashboards.get(userId);
        }
        String dashboard = generateDashboard(userId);
        memoizedDashboards.put(userId, dashboard);
        return dashboard;
    }

    private String generateDashboard(Long userId) {
```

```
        // Placeholder for complex logic to generate user dashboard
        return "Dashboard data for user: " + userId;
    }
}
```

2. Computational Biology

Memoization is notably beneficial in computational biology, especially in algorithms involving the comparison of genetic sequences. Tools like BLAST (Basic Local Alignment Search Tool) use memoization to store and reuse results of sequence alignments, which are computationally expensive.

```
// Memoization in sequence alignment
public class SequenceAligner {
    private Map<Pair<String, String>, Integer> memoizedAlignments = new
        HashMap<>();

    public int alignSequences(String seq1, String seq2) {
        Pair<String, String> key = new Pair<>(seq1, seq2);
        if (memoizedAlignments.containsKey(key)) {
            return memoizedAlignments.get(key);
        }
        int score = computeAlignment(seq1, seq2);
        memoizedAlignments.put(key, score);
        return score;
    }

    private int computeAlignment(String seq1, String seq2) {
        // Placeholder for complex sequence alignment logic
        return seq1.length() + seq2.length(); // dummy computation
    }
}
```

3. Game Development

Memoization plays a pivotal role in game development, especially in AI pathfinding algorithms like A* or minimax for games like chess. Storing computed states helps in avoiding redundant evaluations, speeding up the decision-making process.

```
// Memoization in game state evaluation
public class GameStateEvaluator {
    private Map<GameState, Integer> memoizedStates = new HashMap<>();

    public int evaluateState(GameState state) {
        if (memoizedStates.containsKey(state)) {
            return memoizedStates.get(state);
        }
        int score = computeScore(state);
        memoizedStates.put(state, score);
        return score;
    }

    private int computeScore(GameState state) {
        // Placeholder for complex game state evaluation logic
        return state.hashCode(); // dummy computation
```

```
    }
}
```

4. Machine Learning

In machine learning, particularly in neural network training and hyperparameter optimization, memoization helps by storing the results of expensive computations such as cost function evaluations. This is crucial in preventing redundant calculations during the training process, which can be highly iterative.

```
// Memoization in neural network training
public class NeuralNetworkTrainer {
    private Map<Hyperparameters, Double> memoizedResults = new HashMap<>();

    public double evaluateHyperparameters(Hyperparameters params) {
        if (memoizedResults.containsKey(params)) {
            return memoizedResults.get(params);
        }
        double result = complexEvaluation(params);
        memoizedResults.put(params, result);
        return result;
    }

    private double complexEvaluation(Hyperparameters params) {
        // Placeholder for complex hyperparameter evaluation logic
        return params.hashCode(); // dummy computation
    }
}
```

5. Financial Modeling

Memoization is utilized in financial modeling for scenarios such as option pricing and risk assessment. Algorithms like the Monte Carlo simulation benefit from storing intermediate results of random walks, reducing the simulation run time.

```
// Memoization in financial modeling
public class OptionPricer {
    private Map<OptionParameters, Double> memoizedPrices = new HashMap<>();

    public double priceOption(OptionParameters params) {
        if (memoizedPrices.containsKey(params)) {
            return memoizedPrices.get(params);
        }
        double price = complexPricingAlgorithm(params);
        memoizedPrices.put(params, price);
        return price;
    }

    private double complexPricingAlgorithm(OptionParameters params) {
        // Placeholder for complex option pricing algorithm
        return params.hashCode(); // dummy computation
    }
}
```

6. Data Processing and Aggregation

In large-scale data processing tasks, such as in map-reduce paradigms, memoization can be used to store intermediate results that are reused across different stages of processing. For instance, when aggregating logs for analytics, memoizing results of frequently run aggregate queries can save considerable time.

```
// Memoization in data aggregation
public class DataAggregator {
    private Map<Query, AggregateResult> memoizedResults = new HashMap<>();

    public AggregateResult aggregate(Query query) {
        if (memoizedResults.containsKey(query)) {
            return memoizedResults.get(query);
        }
        AggregateResult result = performAggregation(query);
        memoizedResults.put(query, result);
        return result;
    }

    private AggregateResult performAggregation(Query query) {
        // Placeholder for complex data aggregation logic
        return new AggregateResult(query.hashCode()); // dummy computation
    }
}
```

In each of these applications, the fundamental principle is to store the results of expensive function calls and return the cached result when the same inputs occur again. This technique is particularly effective in domains with highly repetitive computations, leading to significant performance improvements.

5.11 Advanced Techniques in Memoization

Advanced memoization techniques allow for optimized performance and versatility in dynamic programming problems. These techniques encompass hybrid methodologies, adaptive memoization, and space-optimization strategies, transforming the straightforward use of memoization into a powerful tool for solving complex problems efficiently.

A key advanced technique involves hybrid approaches that combine memoization with other algorithmic strategies. One such combination is memoization with divide-and-conquer algorithms. Consider a problem where a large problem can be divided into smaller subproblems that can be solved independently. By memoizing the results of these subproblems, we can avoid recomputation, leading to significant time savings. For instance, the following Java code demonstrates this approach for the knapsack problem:

```
import java.util.HashMap;

public class KnapsackDP {
    private final int[] weights;
    private final int[] values;
    private final int capacity;
    private final HashMap<String, Integer> memo;

    public KnapsackDP(int[] weights, int[] values, int capacity) {
        this.weights = weights;
        this.values = values;
        this.capacity = capacity;
        this.memo = new HashMap<>();
    }

    public int maxProfit(int n, int capacityLeft) {
        if (n == 0 || capacityLeft == 0) {
            return 0;
        }
        String key = n + "," + capacityLeft;
        if (memo.containsKey(key)) {
            return memo.get(key);
        }
        int result;
        if (weights[n - 1] > capacityLeft) {
            result = maxProfit(n - 1, capacityLeft);
        } else {
            int includeItem = values[n - 1] + maxProfit(n - 1, capacityLeft - weights[n -
                1]);
            int excludeItem = maxProfit(n - 1, capacityLeft);
            result = Math.max(includeItem, excludeItem);
        }
        memo.put(key, result);
        return result;
    }

    public static void main(String[] args) {
        int[] weights = {2, 3, 4, 5};
        int[] values = {3, 4, 5, 6};
        int capacity = 5;
        KnapsackDP knapsack = new KnapsackDP(weights, values, capacity);
        System.out.println("Max Profit: " + knapsack.maxProfit(weights.length,
            capacity));
    }
}
```

The code employs memoization in conjunction with a divide-and-conquer algorithm to solve the knapsack problem by breaking it into smaller subproblems and storing their solutions.

Adaptive memoization dynamically adjusts the memoization strategy based on the problem's state or characteristics. For instance, in problems involving varying or unknown dimensions, adaptive memoization can pivot between different storage structures or strategies to optimize memory usage and access speed. Consider a caching mechanism that switches between a HashMap and an array depending on the problem size or the sparsity of the solution space.

Space-optimization techniques in memoization focus on reducing the memory footprint while maintaining computational efficiency. One common strategy is rolling arrays, where only a limited number of previous states are stored at any given time, thus reducing space complexity from $O(n)$ to $O(k)$ where k is a constant. This technique is particularly useful in iterative dynamic programming solutions. The following example demonstrates this approach for the Fibonacci sequence:

```
public class FibonacciOptimized {
    public static int fibonacci(int n) {
        if (n <= 1) return n;
        int[] fib = new int[2];
        fib[0] = 0;
        fib[1] = 1;
        for (int i = 2; i <= n; i++) {
            int nextFib = fib[0] + fib[1];
            fib[0] = fib[1];
            fib[1] = nextFib;
        }
        return fib[1];
    }

    public static void main(String[] args) {
        System.out.println("Fibonacci(10): " + fibonacci(10));
    }
}
```

This method stores only the last two computed Fibonacci numbers, thereby significantly reducing memory usage.

Advanced techniques also extend to memoizing functions with more complex input types such as multidimensional arrays or even custom objects. In such cases, it is crucial to implement appropriate hash functions and equality checks to ensure correct retrieval of memoized results. Here's an example for a problem involving multidimensional input:

```
import java.util.HashMap;
import java.util.Arrays;

public class GridTraveler {
    private final HashMap<String, Long> memo;

    public GridTraveler() {
        this.memo = new HashMap<>();
    }

    public long travel(int m, int n) {
        if (m == 1 && n == 1) return 1;
        if (m == 0 || n == 0) return 0;
        String key = m + "," + n;
        if (memo.containsKey(key)) {
            return memo.get(key);
```

```
        }
        long result = travel(m - 1, n) + travel(m, n - 1);
        memo.put(key, result);
        return result;
    }

    public static void main(String[] args) {
        GridTraveler traveler = new GridTraveler();
        System.out.println("Ways to travel 3x3 grid: " + traveler.travel(3, 3));
    }
}
```

The travel method utilizes memoization to store the number of ways to travel through a grid, significantly improving efficiency for large grids.

Employing advanced memoization techniques requires a deep understanding of the problem domain and a careful balance between time and space complexity. By integrating these techniques, algorithms can achieve optimal performance and scalability, making them suitable for practical, real-world applications.

5.12 Debugging and Testing Memoized Solutions

Effective debugging and testing are paramount to ensure that memoized solutions function correctly and efficiently. This section focuses on various techniques and tools for debugging and testing memoized solutions in Java, addressing potential issues that may arise during implementation.

Identifying common issues in memoized solutions involves understanding both the logic of the base algorithm and the intricacies introduced by memoization. A frequent source of errors is related to the handling of the memoization data structure, whether it be a HashMap or an array. Analyzing some typical pitfalls can illustrate the importance of careful debugging and testing.

Consider a basic example of a memoized function to compute the Fibonacci sequence using a HashMap. The following code demonstrates this implementation:

```
import java.util.HashMap;

public class FibonacciMemo {
    private HashMap<Integer, Integer> memo = new HashMap<>();

    public int fibonacci(int n) {
        if (n <= 1) {
```

```
            return n;
        }
        if (memo.containsKey(n)) {
            return memo.get(n);
        }
        int result = fibonacci(n - 1) + fibonacci(n - 2);
        memo.put(n, result);
        return result;
    }
}
```

To debug this memoized solution, one must ensure the following:

1. **Correct Initialization**: Verify that the memoization data structure is initialized correctly before any computations begin. 2. **Base Cases**: Check that base cases are handled properly and that the recursion terminates as expected. 3. **Memoization Check**: Ensure that the memo exists in the data structure before performing recursive calls. 4. **Insertion into Memo**: Confirm that the computed result is correctly inserted into the memoization data structure.

To assist in debugging, adding print statements to trace the computations can be helpful. Here is the modified code with added print statements:

```
import java.util.HashMap;

public class FibonacciMemo {
    private HashMap<Integer, Integer> memo = new HashMap<>();

    public int fibonacci(int n) {
        System.out.println("Computing Fibonacci number for: " + n);
        if (n <= 1) {
            return n;
        }
        if (memo.containsKey(n)) {
            System.out.println("Using memoized value for: " + n);
            return memo.get(n);
        }
        int result = fibonacci(n - 1) + fibonacci(n - 2);
        memo.put(n, result);
        System.out.println("Memoizing result for " + n + ": " + result);
        return result;
    }
}
```

By running the above program, one can observe the process flow and where memoization is being utilized. The output will reflect this:

```
Computing Fibonacci number for: 6
Computing Fibonacci number for: 5
Computing Fibonacci number for: 4
Computing Fibonacci number for: 3
Computing Fibonacci number for: 2
Computing Fibonacci number for: 1
Computing Fibonacci number for: 0
Memoizing result for 2: 1
Using memoized value for: 1
Memoizing result for 3: 2
Using memoized value for: 2
Memoizing result for 4: 3
Using memoized value for: 3
Memoizing result for 5: 5
Using memoized value for: 4
Memoizing result for 6: 8
```

This output provides clarity on the recursion depth and the point at which memoized values are reused, aiding in diagnosing any errors.

An essential aspect of testing memoized solutions is verifying the correctness and efficiency of the memoization. Unit tests are a fundamental practice. Java's JUnit framework facilitates creating automated tests to ensure the function's correctness over a range of inputs. Consider the following unit tests for the memoized Fibonacci function:

```
import static org.junit.Assert.*;
import org.junit.Before;
import org.junit.Test;

public class FibonacciMemoTest {
    private FibonacciMemo fibonacciMemo;

    @Before
    public void setUp() throws Exception {
        fibonacciMemo = new FibonacciMemo();
    }

    @Test
    public void testFibonacciBaseCase() {
        assertEquals(0, fibonacciMemo.fibonacci(0));
        assertEquals(1, fibonacciMemo.fibonacci(1));
    }

    @Test
    public void testFibonacciRecursiveCases() {
        assertEquals(1, fibonacciMemo.fibonacci(2));
        assertEquals(2, fibonacciMemo.fibonacci(3));
        assertEquals(3, fibonacciMemo.fibonacci(4));
        assertEquals(5, fibonacciMemo.fibonacci(5));
    }

    @Test
    public void testFibonacciHighValue() {
        assertEquals(6765, fibonacciMemo.fibonacci(20));
    }
}
```

These tests encompass both base cases and more complex recursive cases. They validate the correctness of the memoized function by asserting expected outputs for given inputs.

Beyond unit testing, performance testing ensures the solution is optimized. Timing the execution of methods for large inputs can demonstrate the efficiency gains provided by memoization. Here is a simple performance test for the Fibonacci function:

```
public class PerformanceTest {
    public static void main(String[] args) {
        FibonacciMemo fibonacciMemo = new FibonacciMemo();

        long startTime = System.currentTimeMillis();
        System.out.println("Fibonacci(30): " + fibonacciMemo.fibonacci(30));
        long endTime = System.currentTimeMillis();
        System.out.println("Execution Time: " + (endTime - startTime) + "
            milliseconds");
    }
}
```

The expected output should reveal a significantly reduced execution time compared to a non-memoized Fibonacci function, thereby validating the performance enhancement provided by memoization.

Conclusively, integrating robust debugging and thorough testing methodology is crucial for developing reliable memoized solutions. Utilizing print statements, JUnit tests, and performance evaluations collectively contributes to the refinement and validation of the memoization technique's implementation.

Chapter 6

Tabulation and Bottom-Up Approaches

This chapter introduces tabulation and bottom-up approaches in dynamic programming, emphasizing their differences from memoization and their use cases. It covers the setup of tables with appropriate data structures, transitioning from recursive to iterative solutions, and optimizing space in tabulation. The chapter discusses the process of filling tables, handling complex problems with multi-dimensional arrays, addressing large inputs, and provides a comparative analysis between tabulation and memoization, supplemented with a case study on the Fibonacci sequence.

6.1 Introduction to Tabulation

Tabulation, also referred to as the bottom-up approach, involves solving a dynamic programming problem by filling up a table. This approach contrasts with memoization, which is a top-down approach that involves recursive calls and saving the results in a cache to avoid redundant computations. In tabulation, all subproblems are iteratively solved and saved, ensuring that each subproblem is processed only once. This methodical approach often results in slightly more efficient code as it eliminates the overhead of recursion. Additionally, it provides a clear structure that is easy to debug and understand.

To understand the essence of tabulation, consider the conceptual process of filling up a table, usually an array or a matrix, which represents the answer to subproblems. Solving the problem top-down would mean starting from the main problem and breaking it down into smaller subproblems, recursively solving each one and caching their results. In contrast, a bottom-up approach starts with the smallest subproblems, solves each one, and uses these solutions to build up solutions to larger subproblems until the final problem is solved.

```
import java.util.Arrays;

class BottomUpDP {
    public int computeFibonacci(int n) {
        if (n <= 1) return n;

        int[] table = new int[n + 1];
        table[0] = 0;
        table[1] = 1;

        for (int i = 2; i <= n; i++) {
            table[i] = table[i - 1] + table[i - 2];
        }

        return table[n];
    }
}

public class Main {
    public static void main(String[] args) {
        BottomUpDP dp = new BottomUpDP();
        System.out.println(dp.computeFibonacci(10)); // Output: 55
    }
}
```

In the example above, the 'computeFibonacci' method demonstrates a basic implementation of the tabulation approach for computing the Fibonacci sequence. Initially, a table is initialized to store intermediate Fibonacci numbers. By iterating from 2 up to 'n', each entry in the table is filled by summing the two preceding entries. Thus, the table builds up results starting from base cases until the final desired value is reached.

This method embodies the key points of tabulation: 1. **Initialization**: Start with known values of the problem. 2. **Order of Computation**: Carefully determine the sequence in which subproblems are solved. 3. **Space Utilization**: Use space-efficient data structures for storing and retrieving intermediate results.

Tabulation is not confined to one-dimensional arrays. More complex problems, such as those involving multiple dimensions (e.g., 2D arrays), can also be approached using tabulation.

```
class Knapsack {
```

```
    public int knapSack(int W, int[] wt, int[] val, int n) {
        int[][] dp = new int[n + 1][W + 1];

        for (int i = 0; i <= n; i++) {
            for (int w = 0; w <= W; w++) {
                if (i == 0 || w == 0) {
                    dp[i][w] = 0;
                } else if (wt[i - 1] <= w) {
                    dp[i][w] = Math.max(val[i - 1] + dp[i - 1][w - wt[i - 1]], dp[i - 1][w]);
                } else {
                    dp[i][w] = dp[i - 1][w];
                }
            }
        }
        return dp[n][W];
    }
}

public class Main {
    public static void main(String[] args) {
        Knapsack ks = new Knapsack();
        int[] val = {60, 100, 120};
        int[] wt = {10, 20, 30};
        int W = 50;
        int n = val.length;
        System.out.println(ks.knapSack(W, wt, val, n)); // Output: 220
    }
}
```

This example demonstrates the tabulation approach applied to the 0/1 Knapsack problem. Here, a 2D array ('dp') represents the maximum value that can be obtained with the given weight capacities and item selection constraints. The nested loop iterates through each item and weight capacity, filling the table according to the inclusion-exclusion principle central to the knapsack problem. The resulting table, thus, encapsulates all possible subproblem solutions, ultimately providing the optimal solution.

The primary advantage of tabulation is its iterative nature, eliminating the risks of stack overflow that come with deep recursion. The clearly defined initialization and iterative filling make the process straightforward, and the deterministic sequence in which subproblems are resolved ensures predictability and ease of debugging.

The clarity and efficiency of tabulated solutions underscore the importance of a systematic approach in dynamic programming, marking it as a crucial strategy for solving complex problems. By understanding and applying tabulation, programmers can achieve optimized solutions, leveraging the power of dynamic programming to its fullest potential.

6.2 Difference Between Tabulation and Memoization

Tabulation and memoization are two dynamic programming techniques that store intermediate results to avoid redundant calculations. They share the same core objective but differ fundamentally in their execution methodologies.

Tabulation adopts a *bottom-up* approach, requiring the problem to be solved iteratively from the simplest subproblems to the original problem. This technique typically involves initializing a table (often an array or a multi-dimensional array) with base values and building up solutions to more complex subproblems based on these base values. The solution to the original problem is derived once the table is completely filled.

Memoization, on the other hand, follows a *top-down* approach. It is usually implemented recursively, where the solution to a problem is broken down into subproblems. Results of previously solved subproblems are stored in a data structure such as a hash map or an array, effectively transforming the naive recursive solution by caching intermediate results to avoid redundant computations.

To elucidate these differences, consider the Fibonacci sequence $\{F(n)\}$ defined as $F(0) = 0, F(1) = 1$, and $F(n) = F(n-1) + F(n-2)$ for $n \geq 2$. With memoization, the solution would be recursively defined, storing computed values of $F(n)$ to avoid recalculating them.

```
class FibonacciMemoization {
    private Map<Integer, Long> memo = new HashMap<>();

    public long fib(int n) {
        if (n <= 1) {
            return n;
        }
        if (memo.containsKey(n)) {
            return memo.get(n);
        }
        long result = fib(n - 1) + fib(n - 2);
        memo.put(n, result);
        return result;
    }
}
```

Here, recursive calls to fib(n-1) and fib(n-2) are memoized, minimizing redundant calculations.

For tabulation, the iterative approach initializes an array and fills it in a bottom-up manner.

```
class FibonacciTabulation {
    public long fib(int n) {
        if (n <= 1) {
            return n;
        }
        long[] table = new long[n + 1];
        table[0] = 0;
        table[1] = 1;
        for (int i = 2; i <= n; i++) {
            table[i] = table[i - 1] + table[i - 2];
        }
        return table[n];
    }
}
```

In this example, the array table is iteratively filled from table[0] and table[1] up to table[n], adhering to the bottom-up strategy of tabulation.

The difference between these techniques leads to several trade-offs:

- **Initialization:** Tabulation requires initialization of the entire table before computations begin, while memoization initializes the storage dynamically as needed during recursive calls.
- **Control Flow:** Memoization leverages a recursive call stack, whereas tabulation strictly follows iterative control flow eliminating the potential overhead associated with deep recursive calls.
- **Space Complexity:** Both techniques can have similar space complexity, but it depends on the problem. Memoization may have an overhead for maintaining the call stack along with a data structure, whereas tabulation requires space proportional to the table size.
- **Performance:** In recursive solutions, memoization can be more intuitive and easier to implement but may incur higher overhead due to managing recursive calls. Tabulation, being iterative, often runs faster in practice, as it avoids the recursive call overhead entirely.
- **Readability and Debugging:** Memoization with recursion can be conceptually easier to understand for divide-and-conquer problems since it follows the natural problem decomposition. However, tabulation's iterative nature can simplify understanding the order of computation and dependencies among subproblems.

To contrast further with an example, consider the knapsack problem. Using memoization yields a recursive solution that stores computed states in a matrix to prevent recomputation. Tabulation solves it by filling a table iteratively from the smallest subproblems upwards. Both approaches achieve the same result, but tabulation ensures the optimization of iterative completion without recursive overhead.

In practical applications, the choice between tabulation and memoization may depend on factors such as ease of implementation, execution time constraints, and the nature of the problem at hand.

6.3 When to Use Tabulation

Tabulation is a dynamic programming technique that operates in a bottom-up manner. It contrasts with memoization, which is a top-down approach. Deciding when to use tabulation involves understanding the nature of the problem, the required performance characteristics, and the structural organization of the computational flow. Conditions where tabulation is particularly beneficial will be elaborated, leveraging the enhanced understanding of the algorithmic context it provides.

Tabulation is optimal for problems where it is feasible to systematically build solutions from the smallest subproblems up to the desired solution. This approach is most effective in situations where overlapping subproblems are prevalent and can be cohesively addressed by filling a table, typically avoiding deep recursive chains that might lead to stack overflow issues in a recursive approach.

Consider the following aspects before employing tabulation:

- **Nature of Subproblems:** The problem must be decomposable into smaller, manageable subproblems whose results can be stored and reused. If the subproblems are numerous and the same subproblems are solved multiple times during computation, tabulation can offer performance improvements by eliminating redundant calculations.

- **Iterative Computation Feasibility:** If the problem can be approached by systematically solving and recording solutions in an iterative manner, tabulation can be employed efficiently. This approach works well if computations can naturally progress from the smallest subproblems to the larger, desired problem.

- **Memory Availability:** Tabulation typically requires pre-allocating a table structure, which necessitates ample memory. Evaluate the memory constraints and ensure that the problem size is feasible within these bounds. For instance, the need to store a two-dimensional array for problems like matrix chain multiplication should be assessed against the available system memory.

- **Avoiding Stack Overflow:** Recursive approaches with deep call stacks can lead to stack overflow errors. If dealing with such problems, tabulation provides a feasible alternative by using iterative computation, thus keeping memory usage on the heap rather than the call stack.
- **Predictable Computation Flow:** Problems where the dependencies between subproblems are clearly defined and predictable are well-suited for tabulation. This allows the systematic filling of a table based on the known dependency order, ensuring that each cell in the table contains valid computed values when required.
- **Constant Subproblem Sizes:** Problems where subproblems result in a steady evolution of size and complexity are ideal for tabulation. The canonical example being the Fibonacci sequence, where each number is the sum of the two preceding ones, lends itself effectively to filling a table from smallest to largest indices.

To exemplify, examine the tabulated solution for the well-known Fibonacci sequence problem:

```
public int fib(int n) {
    if (n <= 1) {
        return n;
    }

    int[] table = new int[n + 1];
    table[0] = 0;
    table[1] = 1;

    for (int i = 2; i <= n; i++) {
        table[i] = table[i - 1] + table[i - 2];
    }

    return table[n];
}
```

This implementation starts by initializing the base cases of the Fibonacci sequence. It then fills up the table iteratively from the smallest Fibonacci number up to the given index n. Such a solution avoids the excessive recursion depth that a naive recursive solution of Fibonacci would involve, thus highlighting the effectiveness of tabulation where overlapping subproblems and iterative computations are feasible.

Tabulation is also beneficial when tracking the intermediate states of the computation is required. This can be useful in debugging or understanding the problem's progression, as the table provides a detailed snapshot of all subproblem solutions.

Ultimately, determining the suitability of tabulation involves a comprehensive understanding of the problem structure, dependencies, and specific constraints such as memory and stack limitations. When these align with the inherent advantages of bottom-up computation, tabulation emerges as a powerful technique in the dynamic programming paradigm.

6.4 Setting Up the Table: Choosing the Right Data Structures

In dynamic programming, the choice of data structures is critical for the successful implementation of the tabulation (bottom-up) approach. Proper data structures not only enhance the readability of the code but also significantly impact the time and space complexity. This section delves into selecting appropriate data structures when setting up tables for tabulation.

The most commonly used data structures for tabulation are arrays, lists, and hash maps. Each offers unique benefits and trade-offs, dictating the use case for which they are best suited. We will explore these data structures in the context of use cases and performance considerations.

Arrays

Arrays are a fundamental and efficient data structure utilized in fixed-size tabulation. In scenarios where the problem dimensions are known beforehand, arrays can provide constant-time access ($O(1)$) to any element. This makes arrays particularly advantageous for problems like the Fibonacci sequence or the Knapsack problem, where predefined bounds for the table size exist.

```
public int fibonacci(int n) {
    if (n <= 1) return n;
    int[] table = new int[n + 1];
    table[0] = 0;
    table[1] = 1;
    for (int i = 2; i <= n; i++) {
        table[i] = table[i - 1] + table[i - 2];
    }
    return table[n];
}
```

In the example above, an array is used to tabulate values of the Fibonacci sequence. The array size is determined by the problem constraint n, allowing straightforward access and update of the computed values. However, arrays can be memory-intensive if the size (n) is large.

Lists

In scenarios where dynamic resizing of the table is necessary, lists provide flexibility over arrays. Specifically, the ArrayList class in Java can be useful due to its dynamic nature, allowing the list to grow or shrink as needed. This characteristic is beneficial for problems where the dimensions cannot be predetermined or may vary during execution.

```
import java.util.ArrayList;
import java.util.List;

public int climbStairs(int n) {
    List<Integer> table = new ArrayList<>();
    table.add(0); // base case: 0 ways to climb 0 stairs
    table.add(1); // base case: 1 way to climb 1 stair
    for (int i = 2; i <= n; i++) {
        table.add(table.get(i - 1) + table.get(i - 2));
    }
    return table.get(n);
}
```

The above code uses a List to dynamically store the number of ways to climb stairs. Unlike arrays, lists manage memory more efficiently in scenarios with unknown or changing dimensions. However, lists might incur a slight overhead in access time compared to arrays.

Hash Maps

When dealing with problems involving non-contiguous or sparse data, hash maps demonstrate their utility by allowing association of keys with values. Hash maps are vital for problems where indices are non-sequential or represent more complex states, providing $O(1)$ average-time complexity for insertions and lookups.

```
import java.util.HashMap;
import java.util.Map;

public int uniquePaths(int m, int n) {
    Map<String, Integer> table = new HashMap<>();
    return uniquePathsHelper(m - 1, n - 1, table);
}

private int uniquePathsHelper(int row, int col, Map<String, Integer> table) {
    if (row < 0 || col < 0) return 0;
    if (row == 0 && col == 0) return 1;
    String key = row + "," + col;
    if (!table.containsKey(key)) {
        table.put(key, uniquePathsHelper(row - 1, col, table) + uniquePathsHelper(row,
```

```
            col - 1, table));
    }
    return table.get(key);
}
```

In the unique paths example, a HashMap is used to store subproblem results. This accommodates problem states characterized by tuples or sequences, offering flexibility and preventing the waste of space derived from unutilized array slots.

Each of these data structures presents advantages under specific conditions:

- **Arrays:** Ideal for fixed-size datasets with predictable bounds, providing optimum access speed.
- **Lists:** Suitable for dynamic-sized problems where the range of indices may not be predetermined or may vary.
- **Hash Maps:** Best for sparse or non-contiguous datasets, or when problem states are more complex or multi-dimensional.

Understanding the characteristics and appropriate use cases of these data structures is essential for optimizing your dynamic programming solutions. This consideration not only affects the performance but also the effective utilization of system resources, ensuring scalable and efficient implementations.

6.5 Implementing Bottom-Up Approaches in Java

Bottom-up dynamic programming, frequently referred to as tabulation, involves solving problems by iteratively tabulating results of subproblems and using these results to solve larger problems. This approach contrasts with memoization, which relies on recursion and caching of results. Implementing bottom-up approaches in Java necessitates careful structuring of iterative loops and managing data storage efficiently.

We start by considering a problem like computing the Fibonacci sequence, a well-known example to elucidate both bottom-up dynamics and Java practicalities. The nth Fibonacci number $F(n)$ is defined as:

$$F(n) = F(n-1) + F(n-2)$$

with base cases $F(0) = 0$ and $F(1) = 1$.

To implement this using a bottom-up approach, we utilize an array to store already computed Fibonacci values. The process involves initializing this array with base cases, then iterating up to the desired index, filling the array using the previously computed values.

```
public class Fibonacci {
    public static int fib(int n) {
        if (n <= 1) {
            return n;
        }

        int[] fibTable = new int[n + 1];
        fibTable[0] = 0;
        fibTable[1] = 1;

        for (int i = 2; i <= n; i++) {
            fibTable[i] = fibTable[i - 1] + fibTable[i - 2];
        }

        return fibTable[n];
    }

    public static void main(String[] args) {
        int n = 10;
        System.out.println("Fibonacci number F(" + n + ") = " + fib(n));
    }
}
```

The iterative loop from index 2 to n progressively fills the fibTable array. This approach ensures each subproblem is solved in increasing order of complexity, avoiding redundancy and recursive overhead. The transformation from the general Fibonacci formula to this iterative version illustrates replacing recursive function calls with looping constructs.

When applying this bottom-up strategy to more complex problems, special attention to data structures is crucial. Consider the problem of finding the minimum number of coins required to make up a given amount from a set of denominations. The recurrence relation for this problem can be stated as:

$$C(i) = \min\left(C(i - d_1), C(i - d_2), \ldots, C(i - d_k)\right) + 1$$

where $C(i)$ represents the minimum number of coins needed for amount i, and $d_1, d_2, \ldots, d_k$ are the coin denominations. The solution using a bottom-up approach involves iterating through each amount and computing the minimum coins required iteratively.

```
public class CoinChange {
    public static int minCoins(int[] denominations, int amount) {
        int[] minCoinsTable = new int[amount + 1];
        Arrays.fill(minCoinsTable, Integer.MAX_VALUE);
        minCoinsTable[0] = 0;
```

```
        for (int i = 1; i <= amount; i++) {
            for (int coin : denominations) {
                if (i - coin >= 0 && minCoinsTable[i - coin] != Integer.MAX_VALUE) {
                    minCoinsTable[i] = Math.min(minCoinsTable[i], minCoinsTable[i -
                        coin] + 1);
                }
            }
        }

        return minCoinsTable[amount] == Integer.MAX_VALUE ? -1 : minCoinsTable[
            amount];
    }

    public static void main(String[] args) {
        int[] denominations = {1, 2, 5};
        int amount = 11;
        System.out.println("Minimum coins needed for amount " + amount + " = " +
            minCoins(denominations, amount));
    }
}
```

In this implementation, we initialize minCoinsTable with maximum integer values, signifying that initially, we have no combination to achieve the respective amounts. Through nested loops, we iterate over each amount and coin denomination, updating the minCoinsTable to store the minimal coins required. This efficiently builds up the solution from the smallest subproblems to the original problem.

Furthermore, the utility of multi-dimensional arrays becomes evident in problems involving multiple dependent variables, such as the knapsack problem. The knapsack problem can be formalized as:

$$V(i,w) = \max(V(i-1,w), V(i-1,w-w_i)+v_i)$$

where $V(i,w)$ denotes the maximum value achievable with the first i items and a weight limit w, w_i is the weight, and v_i is the value of the i-th item.

```
public class Knapsack {
    public static int knapsack(int[] weights, int[] values, int capacity) {
        int n = weights.length;
        int[][] dpTable = new int[n + 1][capacity + 1];

        for (int i = 1; i <= n; i++) {
            for (int w = 0; w <= capacity; w++) {
                if (weights[i - 1] <= w) {
                    dpTable[i][w] = Math.max(dpTable[i - 1][w], dpTable[i - 1][w -
                        weights[i - 1]] + values[i - 1]);
                } else {
                    dpTable[i][w] = dpTable[i - 1][w];
                }
            }
        }

        return dpTable[n][capacity];
```

```
    }

    public static void main(String[] args) {
        int[] weights = {1, 3, 4, 5};
        int[] values = {1, 4, 5, 7};
        int capacity = 7;
        System.out.println("Maximum value for capacity " + capacity + " = " +
                knapsack(weights, values, capacity));
    }
}
```

The dpTable in this example is a two-dimensional array where dpTable[i][w] holds the maximum value for the first i items with a weight limit w. The nested loops ensure each cell is computed based on previously solved subproblems, thus building up the final solution in a bottom-up manner.

Implementing bottom-up approaches in Java for dynamic programming problems requires translating recursive problem definitions into iterative solutions. Properly managed iteration and data structures, such as arrays or multi-dimensional arrays, enable effective tabulation, ensuring optimized computations for various problem sets.

6.6 Transitioning from Recursive to Iterative Solutions

Transitioning from recursive to iterative solutions in dynamic programming involves rethinking the problem-solving approach to leverage table-based computation. Recursive solutions often involve top-down approaches with repeated function calls, while iterative solutions use loops to systematically fill a table, avoiding function call overhead and ensuring each subproblem is solved only once.

To illustrate this process, we will explore the transformation using the canonical example of the Fibonacci sequence. In a recursive solution, the Fibonacci sequence is computed as follows:

```
public class Fibonacci {
    public int fib(int n) {
        if (n <= 1) return n;
        return fib(n - 1) + fib(n - 2);
    }
}
```

This approach is intuitive but inefficient, as it recalculates values multiple times, leading to an exponential time complexity $O(2^n)$. By contrast, in an iterative, bottom-up approach, we use a table to store intermediate results, ensuring each subproblem is solved once. The first step in the transition process is to understand how to reformulate the problem using a table. For Fibonacci, the table, often an array, stores values of the sequence.

The key operations include initializing the table, iterating to fill it, and accessing predefined values when needed. Here's how the Fibonacci sequence can be computed iteratively:

```
public class Fibonacci {
    public int fib(int n) {
        if (n <= 1) return n;

        int[] table = new int[n + 1];
        table[0] = 0;
        table[1] = 1;

        for (int i = 2; i <= n; i++) {
            table[i] = table[i - 1] + table[i - 2];
        }

        return table[n];
    }
}
```

In this iterative approach: 1. **Initialization**: The base cases $F(0) = 0$ and $F(1) = 1$ are directly assigned to the first two elements of the array 'table'. 2. **Iteration**: We use a 'for' loop to fill the array from index 2 to 'n', ensuring each subsequent Fibonacci number is calculated using the values stored in the previous two indices of 'table'.

The transition involves recognizing that recursion can be replaced by iterations over the state space defined by the problem. For problems with more complex state dependencies or multidimensional states, the transition principles remain similar. For example, in problems involving a two-dimensional dynamic programming table, such as the Longest Common Subsequence (LCS), recursive solutions often carry multiple recursive calls with multiple parameters. This can be coded iteratively by filling a two-dimensional array.

Consider the LCS problem:

```
public class LCS {
    public int lcs(String s1, String s2) {
        return lcs(s1, s2, s1.length(), s2.length());
    }

    private int lcs(String s1, String s2, int m, int n) {
        if (m == 0 || n == 0) return 0;
        if (s1.charAt(m - 1) == s2.charAt(n - 1)) {
            return 1 + lcs(s1, s2, m - 1, n - 1);
        } else {
```

```
            return Math.max(lcs(s1, s2, m - 1, n), lcs(s1, s2, m, n - 1));
        }
    }
}
```

This recursive solution can be converted to an iterative one by using a two-dimensional table to store the intermediate LCS lengths:

```
public class LCS {
    public int lcs(String s1, String s2) {
        int m = s1.length();
        int n = s2.length();
        int[][] table = new int[m + 1][n + 1];

        for (int i = 0; i <= m; i++) {
            for (int j = 0; j <= n; j++) {
                if (i == 0 || j == 0) {
                    table[i][j] = 0;
                } else if (s1.charAt(i - 1) == s2.charAt(j - 1)) {
                    table[i][j] = table[i - 1][j - 1] + 1;
                } else {
                    table[i][j] = Math.max(table[i - 1][j], table[i][j - 1]);
                }
            }
        }

        return table[m][n];
    }
}
```

Here, the iterative approach involves initializing the first row and column of the 2D table to zero, as they correspond to the base cases where one string has zero length. Nested loops are employed to fill in the table based on character matches and previously computed values, thereby ensuring no recomputation and achieving a polynomial time complexity $O(mn)$.

Transitioning from recursive to iterative solutions not only improves efficiency but also leverages the inherent structure of dynamic programming problems, where the substructure is reused optimally through tabulated results. This method is crucial for solving large-scale problems where recursion would otherwise be infeasible due to excessive time and space consumption.

6.7 Filling the Table: Initialization and Order of Computation

In dynamic programming, the process of filling the table is crucial to the successful implementation of the tabulation approach. This section delves into the initialization of the table and the meticulous order in which computations must be performed to ensure accurate and efficient solutions.

Initialization of the Table

The first step in tabulation involves setting up and initializing the table, which is typically an array or a matrix. The choice of data structure was discussed in previous sections, but regardless of choice, initialization is necessary to define the base cases and establish the structure for subsequent computations.

Consider a basic example using the Fibonacci sequence, where $F(n) = F(n-1) + F(n-2)$ with base cases $F(0) = 0$ and $F(1) = 1$. A table (array) is initialized to hold values up to the nth Fibonacci number:

```
int fib(int n) {
    if (n <= 1) return n;

    int[] table = new int[n + 1];
    table[0] = 0;
    table[1] = 1;

    for (int i = 2; i <= n; i++) {
        table[i] = table[i - 1] + table[i - 2];
    }

    return table[n];
}
```

Here, $\text{table}[0]$ and $\text{table}[1]$ are initialized to the base case values. Initialization ensures that these values are definite, providing a foundation for the iterative computation.

Order of Computation

The order of computation in the tabulation approach is typically straightforward but must align with the dependencies defined by the recurrence relation. In the iterative approach, calculations progress from the base cases to the desired value, ensuring that when calculating $\text{table}[\text{i}]$, all necessary preceding values $\text{table}[\text{i-1}]$ and $\text{table}[\text{i-2}]$ are already computed. This ordered computation directly contrasts with memoization, where values are computed as needed during the recursive calls.

For example, the iterative calculation for the Fibonacci sequence follows a linear progression:

- Start from base cases: $\text{table}[0] = 0$, $\text{table}[1] = 1$.
- Progressively compute: $\text{table}[2] = \text{table}[1] + \text{table}[0]$,

$\text{table}[3] = \text{table}[2] + \text{table}[1]$, and so on.

Another illustrative example is the computation of the minimum cost path in a grid-based problem. Given a 2D grid where each cell represents the cost of traversing that cell, find the minimum cost path from the top-left to the bottom-right. The recurrence relation for this problem can be expressed as:

$$\text{cost}[i][j] = \text{grid}[i][j] + \min(\text{cost}[i\text{-}1][j], \text{cost}[i][j\text{-}1])$$

Initializations for the first row and first column, where only one path exists (either from the left or above), are crucial. The rest of the cost array is computed in a row-wise (or column-wise) manner to ensure all dependencies are met:

```
int minCostPath(int[][] grid) {
    int m = grid.length;
    int n = grid[0].length;
    int[][] cost = new int[m][n];

    cost[0][0] = grid[0][0]; // Starting point

    // Initialize the first row and column
    for (int i = 1; i < m; i++) {
        cost[i][0] = cost[i - 1][0] + grid[i][0];
    }
    for (int j = 1; j < n; j++) {
        cost[0][j] = cost[0][j - 1] + grid[0][j];
    }

    // Fill the rest of the cost array
    for (int i = 1; i < m; i++) {
        for (int j = 1; j < n; j++) {
            cost[i][j] = grid[i][j] + Math.min(cost[i - 1][j], cost[i][j - 1]);
        }
    }

    return cost[m - 1][n - 1];
}
```

In this example, the initialization of the first row and first column sets the stage for the iterative population of the cost array. The nested loops ensure that all necessary values are available before each computation:

- Initialize starting point: $\text{cost}[0][0] = \text{grid}[0][0]$.
- Fill initial row and column for single-path cases.
- Iteratively compute remaining costs in a row-wise fashion.

These principles of initialization and order of computation apply universally to tabulation in dynamic programming. Ensuring that each value is calculated only after all its dependencies are met is essential for the accuracy and efficiency of the algorithm. Careful adherence to these principles allows the transition from recursive to iterative solutions, optimizing both time and space complexities.

6.8 Optimizing Space in Tabulation

In the context of dynamic programming, space optimization is a crucial factor, especially for problems involving large input sizes. When tabulating solutions, the default approach involves maintaining a complete table to store intermediate values. However, often only a limited subset of these values is necessary at any given step, allowing for potential optimization. This section explores strategies for reducing space complexity while maintaining the integrity and correctness of the algorithm.

The fundamental principle behind space optimization in tabulation involves recognizing that not all previously computed values are required for future calculations. For instance, in problems where the final solution depends only on a few preceding values rather than the entire history, many of the stored values become redundant once they have served their purpose.

Consider the classic Fibonacci sequence problem. The naive tabulation approach involves constructing a table to store all Fibonacci numbers up to the desired n:

```
public int fibonacci(int n) {
    if (n <= 1) {
        return n;
    }
    int[] dp = new int[n + 1];
    dp[0] = 0;
    dp[1] = 1;
    for (int i = 2; i <= n; i++) {
        dp[i] = dp[i - 1] + dp[i - 2];
    }
    return dp[n];
}
```

The space complexity of this approach is $O(n)$, due to the array 'dp' of size $n + 1$. However, a closer inspection reveals that each Fibonacci number depends only on the two preceding numbers. Therefore, rather than storing the entire array, it is sufficient to maintain only the last two computed values.

An optimized version of the Fibonacci function reduces the space complexity to $O(1)$:

```
public int fibonacciOptimized(int n) {
    if (n <= 1) {
        return n;
    }
    int a = 0;
    int b = 1;
    int c = 0;
    for (int i = 2; i <= n; i++) {
        c = a + b;
        a = b;
        b = c;
    }
    return c;
}
```

In this implementation, variables 'a', 'b', and 'c' are repeatedly updated to store the last two Fibonacci numbers and the next computed number, respectively. This approach effectively reduces the memory requirement significantly.

Beyond simple problems like Fibonacci, space optimization techniques are also applicable to more complex scenarios. When dealing with two-dimensional dynamic programming tables, often the problem structure allows for similar principles to be applied.

Consider the problem of finding the longest common subsequence (LCS) of two strings. The naive tabulation approach involves constructing a table of size $m \times n$, where m and n are the lengths of the two strings:

```
public int lcs(String x, String y) {
    int m = x.length();
    int n = y.length();
    int[][] dp = new int[m + 1][n + 1];

    for (int i = 1; i <= m; i++) {
        for (int j = 1; j <= n; j++) {
            if (x.charAt(i - 1) == y.charAt(j - 1)) {
                dp[i][j] = dp[i - 1][j - 1] + 1;
            } else {
                dp[i][j] = Math.max(dp[i - 1][j], dp[i][j - 1]);
            }
        }
    }
    return dp[m][n];
}
```

The space complexity here is $O(m \times n)$. Given that each entry in the table depends only on the values from the previous row, it is feasible to optimize space usage by maintaining only the current and previous rows:

```
public int lcsOptimized(String x, String y) {
    int m = x.length();
    int n = y.length();
    int[][] dp = new int[2][n + 1];

    for (int i = 1; i <= m; i++) {
        for (int j = 1; j <= n; j++) {
            if (x.charAt(i - 1) == y.charAt(j - 1)) {
                dp[i % 2][j] = dp[(i - 1) % 2][j - 1] + 1;
            } else {
                dp[i % 2][j] = Math.max(dp[(i - 1) % 2][j], dp[i % 2][j - 1]);
            }
        }
    }
    return dp[m % 2][n];
}
```

In this optimized version, the two-dimensional array 'dp' is reduced to a size of $2 \times (n+1)$, representing only the current and previous rows, thereby reducing space complexity to $O(n)$.

Another example can be elucidated through the problem of finding the minimum cost path in a grid, where each cell has a cost associated with it, and moving from one cell to another can only be done in certain allowed directions (e.g., right or down).

The naive dynamic programming approach typically uses a two-dimensional array to store intermediate cost values:

```
public int minCost(int[][] cost, int m, int n) {
    int[][] dp = new int[m + 1][n + 1];
    dp[0][0] = cost[0][0];

    for (int i = 1; i <= m; i++) {
        dp[i][0] = dp[i - 1][0] + cost[i][0];
    }
    for (int j = 1; j <= n; j++) {
        dp[0][j] = dp[0][j - 1] + cost[0][j];
    }
    for (int i = 1; i <= m; i++) {
        for (int j = 1; j <= n; j++) {
            dp[i][j] = Math.min(dp[i - 1][j], dp[i][j - 1]) + cost[i][j];
        }
    }
    return dp[m][n];
}
```

With a space complexity of $O(m \times n)$, this method can be optimized by recognizing that only the current and previous cells in both the current and previous rows and columns need to be stored:

```
public int minCostOptimized(int[][] cost, int m, int n) {
    int[] dp = new int[n + 1];
    dp[0] = cost[0][0];

    for (int j = 1; j <= n; j++) {
```

```
        dp[j] = dp[j - 1] + cost[0][j];
    }
    for (int i = 1; i <= m; i++) {
        dp[0] += cost[i][0];
        for (int j = 1; j <= n; j++) {
            dp[j] = Math.min(dp[j], dp[j - 1]) + cost[i][j];
        }
    }
    return dp[n];
}
```

Here, by using a linear array 'dp' updated in place, the space complexity reduces to $O(n)$.

These examples highlight a methodology for space optimization in tabulation based on analyzing dependency chains. This approach, while straightforward in principle, often requires careful consideration of the data dependencies and update sequences within the specific problem context. The goal is to maintain only the essential data points at each computation step, liberating memory and potentially enhancing algorithm efficiency.

6.9 Tabulating Complex Problems: Multi-Dimensional Arrays

When working with dynamic programming, some problems exhibit multiple dimensions of state, necessitating the use of multi-dimensional arrays for effective tabulation. These problems typically require tracking more than one parameter to maintain their states adequately. Thus, multi-dimensional arrays offer a structured way to represent these states and iteratively update them within the confines of dynamic programming.

Consider, for instance, the problem of finding the longest common subsequence (LCS) between two strings. Here, the state needs to reflect the characters being compared from both strings, leading to a two-dimensional array where one dimension corresponds to the length of the prefix of the first string and the other to that of the second string.

To implement the tabulation for such a problem, a two-dimensional array (table) is constructed where the element at index table$[i][j]$ represents the LCS length of the first i characters of string $s1$ and the first j characters of string $s2$. The following example illustrates this concept through Java code for the LCS problem.

```
public class LongestCommonSubsequence {
    public int lcs(String s1, String s2) {
        int m = s1.length();
        int n = s2.length();

        // Create a 2D array to store lengths of longest common subsequence.
        int[][] dp = new int[m+1][n+1];

        // Build the table in bottom-up fashion.
        for (int i = 1; i <= m; i++) {
            for (int j = 1; j <= n; j++) {
                if (s1.charAt(i-1) == s2.charAt(j-1)) {
                    dp[i][j] = dp[i-1][j-1] + 1;
                } else {
                    dp[i][j] = Math.max(dp[i-1][j], dp[i][j-1]);
                }
            }
        }
        // The value at dp[m][n] is the length of LCS.
        return dp[m][n];
    }

    public static void main(String[] args) {
        LongestCommonSubsequence lcs = new LongestCommonSubsequence();
        String s1 = "AGGTAB";
        String s2 = "GXTXAYB";

        System.out.println("Length of LCS is: " + lcs.lcs(s1, s2));
    }
}
```

```
Length of LCS is: 4
```

In this example, the 2D array dp effectively stores the length of the LCS at each subproblem level, iterating through both strings. By iteratively building up from smaller subproblems, we avoid the redundant computations inherent in a naive recursive solution.

Another example of a multi-dimensional dynamic programming problem is the classic Knapsack problem, which can be solved using a similar tabulation strategy. In the 0/1 Knapsack problem, we track both the number of items considered and the capacity of the knapsack, leading to a two-dimensional array where dp$[i][w]$ indicates the maximum value achievable with the first i items and a knapsack capacity of w.

The Java code for the 0/1 Knapsack problem is presented below:

```
public class Knapsack {
    public int knapsack(int[] values, int[] weights, int W) {
        int n = values.length;

        // Create a 2D array to store maximum values at sub-problems.
        int[][] dp = new int[n+1][W+1];

        // Build the table in bottom-up fashion.
        for (int i = 1; i <= n; i++) {
            for (int w = 0; w <= W; w++) {
```

```
                if (weights[i-1] <= w) {
                    dp[i][w] = Math.max(dp[i-1][w], values[i-1] + dp[i-1][w - weights[i-1]]);
                } else {
                    dp[i][w] = dp[i-1][w];
                }
            }
        }
        // The value at dp[n][W] is the maximum value for the knapsack of capacity W.
        return dp[n][W];
    }

    public static void main(String[] args) {
        Knapsack knap = new Knapsack();
        int[] values = {60, 100, 120};
        int[] weights = {10, 20, 30};
        int W = 50;

        System.out.println("Maximum value in Knapsack = " + knap.knapsack(values,
             weights, W));
    }
}
```

```
Maximum value in Knapsack = 220
```

In this example, the multi-dimensional table efficiently keeps track of the maximum value possible for every subcapacity of the knapsack up to W, given the available items. Each cell in the table shows the best possible value achievable without exceeding the given capacity and considering specific items.

Tabulating these complex problems with multi-dimensional arrays requires careful consideration of the problem's state representation, ensuring that each dimension accurately reflects a meaningful parameter of the state. By leveraging this structured approach, the dynamic programming solutions become more organized and efficient, effectively solving complex problems that involve multiple interrelated variables.

6.10 Case Study: Tabulating the Fibonacci Sequence

The Fibonacci sequence is a classic example for illustrating the power and efficiency of the tabulation approach in dynamic programming. The sequence is defined as:

$$F(n) = \begin{cases} 0 & \text{if } n = 0, \\ 1 & \text{if } n = 1, \\ F(n-1) + F(n-2) & \text{if } n > 1. \end{cases}$$

Using a naive recursive approach to compute the n-th Fibonacci number, the time complexity is exponential, specifically $O(2^n)$, as each call generates two more calls. This inefficiency is due to the repetitive calculation of the same subproblems.

Tabulation Approach Implementation

The tabulation approach involves solving the problem in a bottom-up manner and storing the results of solved subproblems in a table (usually an array). Here, we illustrate the steps and corresponding Java code to implement this approach.

Step-by-Step Implementation

1. **Initialize the table**: - Create an array ‘fib‘ of size $n + 1$ to store Fibonacci numbers.

2. **Base cases**: - Set the first two Fibonacci numbers manually, i.e., ‘fib[0] = 0‘ and ‘fib[1] = 1‘.

3. **Fill the table**: - Use an iterative loop to fill the table using the relation ‘fib[i] = fib[i-1] + fib[i-2]‘.

4. **Return the result**: - The value of ‘fib[n]‘ gives the n-th Fibonacci number.

Java Implementation

The following code exemplifies the tabulation approach to calculate the n-th Fibonacci number:

```
public class FibonacciTabulation {
    public static int fib(int n) {
        if (n <= 1) {
            return n;
        }

        int[] fib = new int[n + 1];
        fib[0] = 0;
        fib[1] = 1;

        for (int i = 2; i <= n; i++) {
            fib[i] = fib[i - 1] + fib[i - 2];
        }

        return fib[n];
    }

    public static void main(String[] args) {
        int n = 10; // example value
        System.out.println("Fibonacci number at position " + n + " is: " + fib(n));
    }
}
```

Explanation of the Code

1. **Input Checking**: The function starts by handling the base case where $n <= 1$. If so, it directly returns the value of n, which covers both positions 0 and 1 in the Fibonacci series.

2. **Array Initialization**: An integer array 'fib' of size $n + 1$ is created to store the Fibonacci numbers from 0 to n.

3. **Base Case Assignment**: The first two elements of the array are initialized as 'fib[0]' and 'fib[1]', corresponding to the base cases of the Fibonacci sequence: '0' and '1', respectively.

4. **Iterative Computation**: The 'for' loop runs from '2' to 'n', filling each position 'i' with the sum of the previous two values 'fib[i-1]' and 'fib[i-2]'.

5. **Result Return**: Finally, the function returns 'fib[n]', which is the n-th Fibonacci number.

Space Optimization

The above implementation uses $O(n)$ space for storing the table. This can be further optimized to $O(1)$ space since we only need the last two values at any step in the computation.

Optimized Java Implementation

The following code demonstrates this space-optimized approach:

```
public class FibonacciTabulationOptimized {
    public static int fib(int n) {
        if (n <= 1) {
            return n;
        }

        int prev2 = 0;
        int prev1 = 1;
        int current = 0;

        for (int i = 2; i <= n; i++) {
            current = prev1 + prev2;
            prev2 = prev1;
            prev1 = current;
        }

        return current;
    }

    public static void main(String[] args) {
        int n = 10; // example value
        System.out.println("Fibonacci number at position " + n + " is: " + fib(n));
    }
}
```

Explanation of Optimized Code

1. **Input Checking**: Base cases where $n \leq 1$ are handled similarly, directly returning the value of n.

2. **Variable Initialization**: Two variables 'prev2' and 'prev1' are initialized to '0' and '1', respectively, representing the previous two Fibonacci numbers.

3. **Iterative Computation**: The 'for' loop computes the Fibonacci number at position 'i', stores it in 'current', and then updates 'prev2' and 'prev1' accordingly.

4. **Result Return**: After the loop finishes, 'current' contains the n-th Fibonacci number, which is returned.

Advantages of Tabulation

- **Efficiency**: The computation time reduces dramatically from exponential $O(2^n)$ to linear $O(n)$. - **Space Optimization**: The space complexity can also be optimized from $O(n)$ to $O(1)$.

By leveraging tabulation for the Fibonacci sequence, we demonstrate how dynamic programming transforms inefficient recursive algorithms into highly efficient iterative solutions. This case study highlights the core benefits of tabulation in reducing both time and space complexity for a fundamental yet computationally significant problem.

6.11 Handling Large Inputs and Outputs

In this section, we focus on techniques and considerations necessary for efficiently managing large inputs and outputs in the context of dynamic programming using the tabulation approach. Addressing large-scale problems requires attention to both space and time complexities, leveraging efficient data structures, and understanding the boundaries of computational feasibility.

To effectively handle large inputs, we need to address three primary concerns:

- Efficient Memory Usage
- Time Complexity Management
- Input and Output Handling

Efficient Memory Usage

When dealing with large inputs, the naive approach of allocating extensive memory for tables may be infeasible due to physical memory constraints. For instance, if the problem size itself involves millions of entries, directly allocating memory for these entries can lead to significant overhead or even failure due to lack of available system memory.

A common technique to mitigate this issue is *space optimization*. One effective method is to recognize and utilize overlapping subproblems, which may allow us to reduce the memory footprint by storing only the necessary intermediate results. An example of this is the use of rolling arrays or only maintaining the last few computed values:

```
public static int fibonacciOptimized(int n) {
    if (n <= 1) return n;

    int[] fib = new int[2];
    fib[0] = 0;
    fib[1] = 1;

    for (int i = 2; i <= n; i++) {
        int nextFib = fib[0] + fib[1];
        fib[0] = fib[1];
        fib[1] = nextFib;
    }

    return fib[1];
}
```

Here, the traditional table that might store $O(n)$ elements is optimized to use $O(1)$ space by only keeping track of the last two Fibonacci numbers necessary for the computation.

Time Complexity Management

Managing time complexity for large inputs involves designing algorithms that either operate within feasible time bounds or shift intensive computations to precomputation phases. This essentially means aiming to reduce the time complexity from exponential to polynomial, or further to linear where possible, without sacrificing correctness.

Consider the problem of matrix chain multiplication, where the goal is to determine the most efficient way to multiply a given sequence of matrices. The time complexity is managed by filling out a two-dimensional table representing the minimum number of scalar multiplications needed:

```
public static int matrixChainOrder(int[] p) {
    int n = p.length - 1;
    int[][] m = new int[n][n];

    for (int i = 1; i < n; i++) {
        m[i][i] = 0;
    }
```

```
    for (int len = 2; len <= n; len++) {
        for (int i = 0; i < n - len + 1; i++) {
            int j = i + len - 1;
            m[i][j] = Integer.MAX_VALUE;
            for (int k = i; k < j; k++) {
                int q = m[i][k] + m[k+1][j] + p[i-1] * p[k] * p[j];
                if (q < m[i][j]) {
                    m[i][j] = q;
                }
            }
        }
    }

    return m[0][n-1];
}
```

Time complexity here is managed, and by using a bottom-up approach, we ensure that redundant calculations are minimized. Optimizing the loops and ensuring that each subproblem only gets calculated once is critical in handling large input sizes.

Input and Output Handling

In scenarios with large inputs, reading and writing operations become significant. Efficiently handling input and output involves optimizing how data is read and written to memory or persistent storage.

Java provides several classes and methods to efficiently handle I/O operations. One of the techniques is using BufferedReader for input and BufferedWriter for output, which offers performance improvements over standard methods such as Scanner or System.out.print.

```
import java.io.*;

public class LargeInputOutputHandler {
    public static void main(String[] args) throws IOException {
        BufferedReader br = new BufferedReader(new InputStreamReader(System.in));
        BufferedWriter bw = new BufferedWriter(new OutputStreamWriter(System.out)
            );

        String line;
        while((line = br.readLine()) != null) {
            bw.write(computeResult(line));
            bw.newLine();
        }

        br.close();
        bw.close();
    }

    private static String computeResult(String input) {
        // Process the input and return the result as a string
        return "Processed: " + input;
    }
}
```

Utilizing BufferedReader and BufferedWriter allows for more efficient handling of large volumes of data through buffering, thereby reducing the number of I/O operations and improving performance.

In dynamic programming problems, extensive input and output handling can also benefit from parallel processing or concurrency techniques to distribute the workload across multiple processing units. Efficiently partitioning the problem and leveraging concurrent collections can lead to significant performance gains.

Handling large inputs and outputs in dynamic programming involves a comprehensive strategy that includes space optimization, effective management of time complexity, and optimized input/output handling. These techniques ensure that our approach remains both practical and performant even under the constraints of large-scale data. By being mindful of these techniques, we can tackle more complex and larger problems with confidence.

6.12 Comparative Analysis: Tabulation vs. Memoization

When analyzing dynamic programming strategies, tabulation and memoization are two fundamental techniques. Though both aim to optimize recursive algorithms by storing previously computed results to avoid redundant calculations, they do so with distinct methodologies, performance characteristics, and use cases.

In memoization, a top-down approach is employed where the problem is recursively partitioned into subproblems, with each subproblem's result being stored in a cache (typically a hash map or an array) once computed. This prevents the recomputation of the same subproblem, thereby improving efficiency. The implementation involves a recursive function call that checks the cache before proceeding with further computations. The memoization strategy can be advantageous when fewer subproblems are required for the final solution, leading to potential savings in both time and space.

```
import java.util.HashMap;

public class MemoizationExample {
    private static HashMap<Integer, Integer> cache = new HashMap<>();

    public static int fib(int n) {
        if (n <= 1) return n;
        if (cache.containsKey(n)) return cache.get(n);
```

```
        int result = fib(n - 1) + fib(n - 2);
        cache.put(n, result);
        return result;
    }

    public static void main(String[] args) {
        System.out.println(fib(10)); // Output: 55
    }
}
```

The output for the above memoized Fibonacci sequence computation is:

```
55
```

Contrastingly, tabulation utilizes a bottom-up approach. The problem is solved by iteratively filling a table, generally an array, starting from the base case and progressively solving larger subproblems. This method is inherently iterative and does not involve recursion, yielding predictable space and time complexity.

```
public class TabulationExample {

    public static int fib(int n) {
        if (n <= 1) return n;

        int[] table = new int[n + 1];
        table[0] = 0;
        table[1] = 1;

        for (int i = 2; i <= n; i++) {
            table[i] = table[i - 1] + table[i - 2];
        }

        return table[n];
    }

    public static void main(String[] args) {
        System.out.println(fib(10)); // Output: 55
    }
}
```

The tabulated Fibonacci sequence computation yields the same output:

```
55
```

When evaluating both approaches, several considerations arise:

1. Ease of Implementation: Memoization can often be more intuitive for those already familiar with recursive problem solving, as it requires minimal changes to an existing recursive solution. By simply adding a caching mechanism, a recursive function can be converted to a memoized version. This can be advantageous when transitioning from a naive recursive approach to a more optimized solution without rethinking the entire logic.

Conversely, tabulation necessitates a complete transformation of the approach into an iterative manner, which might require a thorough understanding of the problem structure and can be more challenging for beginners. However, once mastered, it provides a clear, linear progression that is easy to follow and debug.

2. Computational Overhead: Memoization typically incurs overhead due to recursion and function calls, which can be non-trivial depending on the depth and branching factor of the recursion. The performance might also be impacted by the use of hash maps or other data structures for caching, which involve additional time and space complexity.

Tabulation, by eliminating recursive calls, reduces such overhead. Iterative table filling is generally more efficient in terms of both time and space. This is particularly evident in languages like Java where function call overhead can be significant.

3. Stack Utilization: A key disadvantage of memoization is its stack space usage. Deep recursive calls can risk stack overflow, particularly in scenarios where the problem size is large. For example, computing the nth Fibonacci number with memoization may involve up to n recursive calls leading to deep stack usage.

Tabulation obviates this risk as it operates iteratively, using a fixed-size table and maintaining computations within a single execution frame on the stack.

4. Result Preparation: In memoization, results are computed when needed. Thus, the initial computation may be delayed until specific subproblems are required. This is beneficial when not all subproblems are necessary for the final solution, potentially reducing computations.

On the other hand, tabulation requires a full table to be prepared up front, irrespective of which specific subproblems are needed. This could result in redundant computations if only a subset of the subproblems is used.

5. Space Optimization: Tabulation allows more straightforward space optimization strategies. For problems like the Fibonacci sequence, rather than maintaining a full table for all subproblems, only a constant amount of space can be used by storing the last two computed values. Such optimizations are harder to implement with memoization, as the recursive structure intrinsically relies on accessing subproblems whenever needed.

6. Predictability and Debugging: Tabulation provides a predictable and steady flow of computation, which simplifies debugging and optimization. Each table entry depends linearly on the previous computations, making it easier to trace and verify results.

Memoization, due to its recursive nature, introduces complexities in debugging especially with deep recursion and maintaining an up-to-date cache. Errors in either logic or cache management can be harder to trace and rectify.

To conclude, both tabulation and memoization have their merits and are chosen based on the problem constraints, ease of implementation, optimization requirements, and computational considerations. The decision heavily relies on the specific context within which they are employed.

Chapter 7

Common Problems and Solutions

This chapter examines a range of well-known dynamic programming problems, providing detailed solutions and Java implementations. Problems such as the Fibonacci sequence, longest common subsequence, longest increasing subsequence, 0/1 knapsack, coin change, and edit distance are explored. Additional topics include minimum path sum, partition problem, rod cutting, and palindromic substrings. Each problem is presented with step-by-step explanations, guiding readers through the process of formulating and implementing dynamic programming solutions.

7.1 Introduction to Common Dynamic Programming Problems

Dynamic programming is a crucial technique in computer science and software engineering for solving optimization problems and making efficient use of computational resources. It is an approach that breaks down a complex problem into simpler subproblems, stores the results of these subproblems to avoid redundant computations, and combines them to solve the original problem. This section introduces some common dynamic programming problems that serve as the foundation for understanding and mastering the technique.

Dynamic programming problems typically exhibit two main properties: overlapping subproblems and optimal substructure. The overlapping subproblems property means that the problem can be broken down into subproblems that are reused multiple times. The optimal substructure property implies that the optimal solution to the problem can be constructed from the optimal solutions of its subproblems.

We will explore a range of well-known problems, providing detailed explanations and insights into their solutions using dynamic programming. To facilitate the learning process, each problem will be accompanied by a Java implementation. Let's delve into a selection of introductory problems to illustrate the concepts and techniques of dynamic programming:

1. The Fibonacci Sequence: The Fibonacci sequence is a classic example of a problem that can be solved using dynamic programming. Each number in the sequence is the sum of the two preceding ones, starting from 0 and 1. The challenge is to compute the nth Fibonacci number both efficiently and correctly.

```
public class Fibonacci {
    public int fib(int n) {
        int[] dp = new int[n + 1];
        dp[0] = 0;
        dp[1] = 1;
        for (int i = 2; i <= n; i++) {
            dp[i] = dp[i - 1] + dp[i - 2];
        }
        return dp[n];
    }
}
```

2. Longest Common Subsequence (LCS): The LCS problem seeks to find the longest subsequence that two sequences have in common. This problem has important applications in fields like bioinformatics, file comparison, and more.

```
public class LongestCommonSubsequence {
    public int lcs(String text1, String text2) {
        int m = text1.length();
        int n = text2.length();
        int[][] dp = new int[m + 1][n + 1];
        for (int i = 1; i <= m; i++) {
            for (int j = 1; j <= n; j++) {
                if (text1.charAt(i - 1) == text2.charAt(j - 1)) {
                    dp[i][j] = dp[i - 1][j - 1] + 1;
                } else {
                    dp[i][j] = Math.max(dp[i - 1][j], dp[i][j - 1]);
                }
            }
        }
        return dp[m][n];
    }
```

```
}
```

3. Longest Increasing Subsequence (LIS): The LIS problem involves finding the longest subsequence of a sequence such that all elements of the subsequence are in sorted order. This has applications in areas such as data analysis and sequence prediction.

```
public class LongestIncreasingSubsequence {
    public int lengthOfLIS(int[] nums) {
        int n = nums.length;
        int[] dp = new int[n];
        Arrays.fill(dp, 1);
        for (int i = 1; i < n; i++) {
            for (int j = 0; j < i; j++) {
                if (nums[i] > nums[j]) {
                    dp[i] = Math.max(dp[i], dp[j] + 1);
                }
            }
        }
        return Arrays.stream(dp).max().getAsInt();
    }
}
```

4. 0/1 Knapsack Problem: The knapsack problem is a fundamental problem in combinatorial optimization. Given a set of items with specific weights and values, the goal is to determine the maximum value that can be obtained by selecting a subset of items without exceeding a specified weight limit.

```
public class Knapsack {
    public int knapSack(int W, int[] wt, int[] val, int n) {
        int[][] dp = new int[n + 1][W + 1];
        for (int i = 0; i <= n; i++) {
            for (int w = 0; w <= W; w++) {
                if (i == 0 || w == 0) {
                    dp[i][w] = 0;
                } else if (wt[i - 1] <= w) {
                    dp[i][w] = Math.max(val[i - 1] + dp[i - 1][w - wt[i - 1]], dp[i - 1][w]);
                } else {
                    dp[i][w] = dp[i - 1][w];
                }
            }
        }
        return dp[n][W];
    }
}
```

5. Coin Change Problem: The coin change problem involves finding the minimum number of coins required to make a given amount from a set of denominations. This problem is widely applicable in financial computations and currency systems.

```
public class CoinChange {
    public int coinChange(int[] coins, int amount) {
        int[] dp = new int[amount + 1];
```

```
        Arrays.fill(dp, amount + 1);
        dp[0] = 0;
        for (int coin : coins) {
            for (int j = coin; j <= amount; j++) {
                dp[j] = Math.min(dp[j], dp[j - coin] + 1);
            }
        }
        return dp[amount] > amount ? -1 : dp[amount];
    }
}
```

Through these illustrative problems, the following key aspects of dynamic programming will be emphasized: identification of the optimal substructure, definition of the state space, formulation of the recurrence relations, and implementation using memoization or tabulation techniques. These foundational principles pave the way for solving even more complex problems using dynamic programming strategies.

7.2 The Fibonacci Sequence

The Fibonacci sequence is one of the most fundamental and frequently cited examples of dynamic programming. The sequence is defined by a simple recursive relationship where each term is the sum of the two preceding ones, typically starting with 0 and 1. Formally, the Fibonacci sequence $F(n)$ is defined as:

$$F(n) = \begin{cases} 0 & \text{if } n = 0, \\ 1 & \text{if } n = 1, \\ F(n-1) + F(n-2) & \text{if } n > 1. \end{cases}$$

The naive recursive implementation of the Fibonacci sequence is often inefficient due to the repeated calculations of the same values. Below is the naive recursive implementation in Java:

```
public class Fibonacci {
    public static int fib(int n) {
        if (n <= 1) {
            return n;
        }
        return fib(n-1) + fib(n-2);
    }

    public static void main(String[] args) {
        int n = 10;
        System.out.println("Fibonacci number at position " + n + " is: " + fib(n));
    }
}
```

Executing this code results in the following output:

```
Fibonacci number at position 10 is: 55
```

This method has an exponential time complexity $O(2^n)$, making it impractical for large values of n. To optimize the computation, dynamic programming techniques should be employed.

Dynamic programming provides two primary approaches to optimize the calculation of the Fibonacci sequence: memoization (top-down approach) and tabulation (bottom-up approach).

Memoization

Memoization stores the results of expensive function calls and reuses them when the same inputs occur again, thus avoiding redundant calculations. Below is a Java implementation using memoization:

```
import java.util.HashMap;

public class Fibonacci {
    private static HashMap<Integer, Integer> memo = new HashMap<>();

    public static int fib(int n) {
        if (n <= 1) {
            return n;
        }

        if (memo.containsKey(n)) {
            return memo.get(n);
        }

        int result = fib(n-1) + fib(n-2);
        memo.put(n, result);
        return result;
    }

    public static void main(String[] args) {
        int n = 10;
        System.out.println("Fibonacci number at position " + n + " is: " + fib(n));
    }
}
```

Output from the memoized version:

```
Fibonacci number at position 10 is: 55
```

The memoized solution has a time complexity of $O(n)$, improving efficiency significantly over the naive approach.

Tabulation

Tabulation employs an iterative approach where the values are computed and stored in a table (array), starting from the base cases and solving up to the desired value. Below is the tabulation approach implemented in Java:

```
public class Fibonacci {

    public static int fib(int n) {
        if (n <= 1) {
            return n;
        }

        int[] fibTable = new int[n+1];
        fibTable[0] = 0;
        fibTable[1] = 1;

        for (int i = 2; i <= n; i++) {
            fibTable[i] = fibTable[i-1] + fibTable[i-2];
        }

        return fibTable[n];
    }

    public static void main(String[] args) {
        int n = 10;
        System.out.println("Fibonacci number at position " + n + " is: " + fib(n));
    }
}
```

The output, similar to previous implementations:

```
Fibonacci number at position 10 is: 55
```

The tabulation approach also has a time complexity of $O(n)$, with the additional benefit of an iterative rather than recursive implementation, which can be advantageous in environments with limited stack size.

Space Optimization

The tabulation approach can be further optimized in terms of space complexity. Since only the last two Fibonacci numbers are needed to compute the next number in the sequence, we can reduce the space complexity to $O(1)$. Here is the Java implementation:

```
public class Fibonacci {

    public static int fib(int n) {
        if (n <= 1) {
            return n;
        }

        int prev1 = 0;
        int prev2 = 1;
        int current = 0;

        for (int i = 2; i <= n; i++) {
            current = prev1 + prev2;
            prev1 = prev2;
            prev2 = current;
        }

        return current;
```

```
    }

    public static void main(String[] args) {
        int n = 10;
        System.out.println("Fibonacci number at position " + n + " is: " + fib(n));
    }
}
```

Output for this space-optimized version remains:

```
Fibonacci number at position 10 is: 55
```

This approach retains the $O(n)$ time complexity while minimizing the space complexity to $O(1)$, making it both time and space efficient.

7.3 Longest Common Subsequence (LCS)

The Longest Common Subsequence (LCS) problem is a classic dynamic programming problem that involves finding the longest subsequence common to two sequences. The subsequence does not need to be contiguous, maintaining the relative order of characters in both sequences. Given two sequences X and Y, the goal is to determine the length of their longest common subsequence, as well as to potentially reconstruct this subsequence.

The formal definition of the LCS problem can be given as follows: Given two sequences $X = x_1, x_2, \ldots, x_m$ and $Y = y_1, y_2, \ldots, y_n$, find the longest sequence $Z = z_1, z_2, \ldots, z_k$ such that Z is a subsequence of both X and Y.

To solve the LCS problem using dynamic programming, we first define a 2D array dp where $dp[i][j]$ represents the length of the LCS of the sequences $X[1..i]$ and $Y[1..j]$.

$$dp[i][j] = \begin{cases} 0 & \text{if } i = 0 \text{ or } j = 0 \\ dp[i-1][j-1] + 1 & \text{if } x_i = y_j \\ \max(dp[i-1][j], dp[i][j-1]) & \text{if } x_i \neq y_j \end{cases}$$

This recurrence relation works as follows:

- If either sequence is empty ($i = 0$ or $j = 0$), the LCS length is 0.
- If the characters x_i and y_j are the same, then the length of the LCS is 1 plus the length of the LCS of $X[1..i-1]$ and $Y[1..j-1]$.

- If the characters x_i and y_j are different, the length of the LCS is the maximum of the lengths of the LCSs of $X[1..i-1]$ and $Y[1..j]$, and $X[1..i]$ and $Y[1..j-1]$.

The dynamic programming table dp can be computed in $O(mn)$ time complexity and $O(mn)$ space complexity. Below is the Java implementation of the LCS problem.

```
public class LCS {
    public int longestCommonSubsequence(String text1, String text2) {
        int m = text1.length();
        int n = text2.length();
        int[][] dp = new int[m + 1][n + 1];

        for (int i = 1; i <= m; i++) {
            for (int j = 1; j <= n; j++) {
                if (text1.charAt(i - 1) == text2.charAt(j - 1)) {
                    dp[i][j] = dp[i - 1][j - 1] + 1;
                } else {
                    dp[i][j] = Math.max(dp[i - 1][j], dp[i][j - 1]);
                }
            }
        }

        return dp[m][n];
    }

    public String getLCSString(String text1, String text2) {
        int m = text1.length();
        int n = text2.length();

        int[][] dp = new int[m + 1][n + 1];

        for (int i = 1; i <= m; i++) {
            for (int j = 1; j <= n; j++) {
                if (text1.charAt(i - 1) == text2.charAt(j - 1)) {
                    dp[i][j] = dp[i - 1][j - 1] + 1;
                } else {
                    dp[i][j] = Math.max(dp[i - 1][j], dp[i][j - 1]);
                }
            }
        }

        StringBuilder lcs = new StringBuilder();
        int i = m, j = n;
        while (i > 0 && j > 0) {
            if (text1.charAt(i - 1) == text2.charAt(j - 1)) {
                lcs.append(text1.charAt(i - 1));
                i--;
                j--;
            } else if (dp[i - 1][j] > dp[i][j - 1]) {
                i--;
            } else {
                j--;
            }
        }

        return lcs.reverse().toString();
    }
```

```
}
```

The $\text{longestCommonSubsequence}$ method returns the length of the LCS of two given strings, while the getLCSString method retrieves the LCS itself. The string construction is done by tracing back from $dp[m][n]$ to $dp[0][0]$ and collecting characters where $text1[i-1]$ equals $text2[j-1]$.

The correctness of this algorithm relies on the principle of optimality in dynamic programming. For each character pairing, the decisions made previously (whether characters match or not) are retained in the dp table, ensuring all subproblems are optimally solved. This decision-making construct enhances the efficiency and guarantees that no redundant calculations are performed, meeting the criteria of dynamic programming techniques.

Developing a deeper understanding of the table-filling and backtracking process is vital for mastering the LCS problem, reinforcing the broader usage of dynamic programming across various computational problems.

7.4 Longest Increasing Subsequence (LIS)

The Longest Increasing Subsequence (LIS) is a classic problem in computer science and dynamic programming. Given an array of integers, the goal is to determine the length of the longest subsequence of this array such that all elements of the subsequence are strictly increasing.

Consider an array $A = [a_1, a_2, \ldots, a_n]$. A subsequence is a sequence derived from another sequence by deleting some or no elements without changing the order of the remaining elements. Formally, we seek the maximum k such that there exists a subsequence $(a_{i_1}, a_{i_2}, \ldots, a_{i_k})$ where $1 \leq i_1 < i_2 < \ldots < i_k \leq n$ and $a_{i_1} < a_{i_2} < \ldots < a_{i_k}$.

Dynamic Programming Approach

The dynamic programming solution to the LIS problem can be framed by defining an array lis, where $\text{lis}[i]$ represents the length of the longest increasing subsequence that ends with the element $A[i]$.

We initialize all entries of the lis array to 1 because the minimum length of any increasing subsequence containing at least one element is 1 (the element itself).

Recurrence Relation

For each element $A[i]$, we look at all previous elements $A[j]$ where $j < i$. If $A[i]$ is greater than $A[j]$, we have a potential increasing subsequence ending at $A[i]$. Thus, we can update our lis[i]:

$$\text{lis}[i] = \max(\text{lis}[i], \text{lis}[j] + 1) \quad \text{for} \quad 0 \leq j < i \text{ and } A[i] > A[j].$$

Algorithm

The algorithm can be implemented in Java as follows:

```java
public class LongestIncreasingSubsequence {

    public static int longestIncreasingSubsequence(int[] nums) {
        if (nums == null || nums.length == 0) {
            return 0;
        }

        int n = nums.length;
        int[] lis = new int[n];

        // Initialize lis values to 1 for all elements
        for (int i = 0; i < n; i++) {
            lis[i] = 1;
        }

        // Compute LIS values in a bottom-up manner
        for (int i = 1; i < n; i++) {
            for (int j = 0; j < i; j++) {
                if (nums[i] > nums[j] && lis[i] < lis[j] + 1) {
                    lis[i] = lis[j] + 1;
                }
            }
        }

        // Find the maximum value in lis array
        int maxLis = 0;
        for (int i = 0; i < n; i++) {
            if (lis[i] > maxLis) {
                maxLis = lis[i];
            }
        }

        return maxLis;
    }

    public static void main(String[] args) {
        int[] nums = {10, 22, 9, 33, 21, 50, 41, 60, 80};
        System.out.println("Length of LIS is: " + longestIncreasingSubsequence(nums));
    }
}
```

Complexity Analysis

The time complexity of the above algorithm is $O(n^2)$, where n is the number of elements in the input array. This is because we have two nested loops: the outer loop runs for each element and the inner loop checks all previous elements, leading to $O(n^2)$ operations.

The space complexity is $O(n)$ due to the additional array lis used to store the lengths of the longest increasing subsequences for each element.

Optimized Approach Using Binary Search

There exists a more efficient approach with a time complexity of $O(n \log n)$. This method employs binary search along with dynamic programming. Instead of maintaining the actual increasing subsequences, we maintain a sequence array with the smallest possible end elements for increasing subsequences of all lengths.

Algorithm

We will use a helper array tails to keep our intermediate subsequences. The idea is to keep updating this array to reflect the smallest possible tail value for every possible increasing subsequence length encountered so far.

```
import java.util.Arrays;

public class LongestIncreasingSubsequenceBinarySearch {

    public static int longestIncreasingSubsequence(int[] nums) {
        if (nums == null || nums.length == 0) {
            return 0;
        }

        int[] tails = new int[nums.length];
        int size = 0;

        for (int num : nums) {
            int i = Arrays.binarySearch(tails, 0, size, num);
            if (i < 0) i = -(i + 1);
            tails[i] = num;
            if (i == size) size++;
        }

        return size;
    }

    public static void main(String[] args) {
        int[] nums = {10, 22, 9, 33, 21, 50, 41, 60, 80};
        System.out.println("Length of LIS is: " + longestIncreasingSubsequence(nums));
    }
}
```

Complexity Analysis

In this approach, each element is processed in $O(\log n)$ time complexity using binary search, and we process n elements in total, making the overall time complexity $O(n \log n)$.

The space complexity remains $O(n)$, utilized by the tails array.

7.5 0/1 Knapsack Problem

The 0/1 Knapsack problem is both a classic and archetypal problem that sums up the essence of dynamic programming. It serves as an optimal choice for elucidating the strategy and rationale behind dynamic programming paradigms. This section offers an in-depth discussion of this problem, including problem formulation, dynamic programming solution, and Java implementation.

Problem Description

Given a set of n items, each with a weight w_i and a value v_i, determine the maximum value that can be obtained by selecting some of these items into a knapsack of fixed capacity W. Each item can either be included or excluded (hence 0/1). Mathematically, the goal is to maximize:

$$\sum_{i=1}^{n} v_i x_i$$

subject to the constraint:

$$\sum_{i=1}^{n} w_i x_i \leq W \quad \text{and} \quad x_i \in \{0, 1\}$$

where x_i indicates whether item i is included in the knapsack (1 if included, 0 otherwise).

Dynamic Programming Approach

To solve the 0/1 Knapsack problem using dynamic programming, we employ a table dp where $dp[i][j]$ represents the maximum value that can be obtained with the first i items and a knapsack capacity j.

1. **Initialization**: - $dp[0][j] = 0$ for all j (using 0 items results in 0 value). - $dp[i][0] = 0$ for all i (knapsack capacity 0 results in 0 value).

2. **State Transition**: - If weight of item $i > j$: $dp[i][j] = dp[i-1][j]$ - Else: $dp[i][j] = \max(dp[i-1][j], dp[i-1][j - \text{weight of item } i] + \text{value of item } i)$

The recurrence relation can be written as:

$$dp[i][j] = \begin{cases} dp[i-1][j] & \text{if } w_i > j \\ \max(dp[i-1][j], dp[i-1][j-w_i] + v_i) & \text{otherwise} \end{cases}$$

Java Implementation

Below is the Java solution for the 0/1 Knapsack problem, implementing the dynamic programming approach discussed.

```
public class Knapsack {
    public static int knapSack(int W, int[] weights, int[] values, int n) {
        int[][] dp = new int[n + 1][W + 1];

        for (int i = 0; i <= n; i++) {
            for (int w = 0; w <= W; w++) {
                if (i == 0 || w == 0)
                    dp[i][w] = 0;
                else if (weights[i - 1] <= w)
                    dp[i][w] = Math.max(values[i - 1] + dp[i - 1][w - weights[i - 1]], dp[i -
                        1][w]);
                else
                    dp[i][w] = dp[i - 1][w];
            }
        }
        return dp[n][W];
    }

    public static void main(String args[]) {
        int[] values = {60, 100, 120};
        int[] weights = {10, 20, 30};
        int W = 50;
        int n = values.length;
        System.out.println(knapSack(W, weights, values, n));
    }
}
```

The above Java code defines a class Knapsack containing a method knapSack, which computes the maximum value of the knapsack given its capacity W, the weights and values arrays, and the number of items n. The method initializes the dp table and iterates to fill it according to the principles of the dynamic programming approach described earlier.

The output of the provided example:

```
220
```

This output indicates that the maximum value that can be achieved with the given weights and values for a knapsack capacity of 50 is 220.

Time and Space Complexity

The time complexity of the dynamic programming approach for the 0/1 Knapsack problem is $O(nW)$, resulting from the nested loops iterating over the items and the weights up to the capacity W.

The space complexity is also $O(nW)$ due to the storage requirements of the dp table. However, it is possible to optimize space complexity to $O(W)$ by using a single-dimensional array and updating it in reverse.

```
public class KnapsackOptimized {
    public static int knapSack(int W, int[] weights, int[] values, int n) {
        int[] dp = new int[W + 1];

        for (int i = 0; i < n; i++) {
            for (int w = W; w >= weights[i]; w--) {
                dp[w] = Math.max(dp[w], values[i] + dp[w - weights[i]]);
            }
        }
        return dp[W];
    }

    public static void main(String args[]) {
        int[] values = {60, 100, 120};
        int[] weights = {10, 20, 30};
        int W = 50;
        int n = values.length;
        System.out.println(knapSack(W, weights, values, n));
    }
}
```

The output remains the same:

```
220
```

In this optimized solution, the space complexity is reduced to $O(W)$ while maintaining the same time complexity. This optimization is achieved by iterating the capacity array in reverse to avoid overwriting values prematurely.

7.6 Coin Change Problem

The Coin Change Problem is a classic problem in computer science and dynamic programming. The objective is to determine the minimum number of coins needed to make a given amount using a specified set of denominations. This problem has a straightforward greedy solution when dealing with coin denominations such as 1, 5, 10, and 25, but it becomes more complex when arbitrary denominations are allowed.

Given an amount A and a set of denominations $\{d_1, d_2, \ldots, d_n\}$, the aim is to find the minimum number of coins that sum up to A. We will explore the dynamic programming approach where we build up a solution incrementally.

To construct our dynamic programming solution, we define $dp[i]$ as the minimum number of coins needed to make the amount i. We initialize the array dp such that $dp[0] = 0$ because no coins are needed to make the zero amount, and set $dp[i] = \infty$ for all $i > 0$ to signify that initially, those amounts are not reachable.

We then iterate over each coin denomination and update the dp array. For each coin d_j, we update $dp[i]$ for all $i \geq d_j$ using the relation:

$$dp[i] = \text{min}(dp[i], dp[i - d_j] + 1)$$

This recurrence relation considers whether including the current coin results in a lesser number of coins compared to the previous number of coins needed for the same amount.

The following Java code implements this dynamic programming solution for the Coin Change Problem.

```
import java.util.Arrays;

public class CoinChange {

    public int coinChange(int[] coins, int amount) {
        if (amount < 1) return 0;
        int[] dp = new int[amount + 1];
        Arrays.fill(dp, amount + 1);
        dp[0] = 0;

        for (int coin : coins) {
            for (int i = coin; i <= amount; i++) {
                dp[i] = Math.min(dp[i], dp[i - coin] + 1);
            }
        }

        return dp[amount] > amount ? -1 : dp[amount];
    }

    public static void main(String[] args) {
        CoinChange cc = new CoinChange();
        int[] coins = {1, 2, 5};
        int amount = 11;
        System.out.println("Minimum coins required: " + cc.coinChange(coins, amount)
            );
    }
}
```

When the above code is executed, the output will be:

```
Minimum coins required: 3
```

This signifies that the minimum number of coins needed to make the amount 11 with denominations $\{1, 2, 5\}$ is 3 (5 + 5 + 1).

The time complexity of this approach is $O(n \times A)$, where n is the number of different coin denominations and A is the amount. Space complexity is $O(A)$ due to the storage required for the dp array.

The coin change problem also has a variant where we need to find the number of ways to make the given amount, rather than the minimum coins. For this variant, we define $dp[i]$ to be the number of ways to make amount i and use the relation:

$$dp[i] = dp[i] + dp[i - d_j]$$

This relation sums up the ways to make amount i by including the current coin.

Here is the Java code for this variant:

```
public class CoinChangeWays {

    public int change(int amount, int[] coins) {
        int[] dp = new int[amount + 1];
        dp[0] = 1;

        for (int coin : coins) {
            for (int i = coin; i <= amount; i++) {
                dp[i] += dp[i - coin];
            }
        }

        return dp[amount];
    }

    public static void main(String[] args) {
        CoinChangeWays ccw = new CoinChangeWays();
        int[] coins = {1, 2, 5};
        int amount = 5;
        System.out.println("Number of ways to make the amount: " + ccw.change(
            amount, coins));
    }
}
```

Executing the above code yields:

```
Number of ways to make the amount: 4
```

Thus, there are 4 ways to make the amount 5 with denominations $\{1, 2, 5\}$: $\{1, 1, 1, 1, 1\}$, $\{1, 1, 1, 2\}$, $\{1, 2, 2\}$, and $\{5\}$.

The outlined dynamic programming approaches effectively resolve both the minimum coin and count-of-ways variants of the coin change problem, leveraging the principle of optimal substructure inherent in dynamic programming.

7.7 Edit Distance

The edit distance between two strings is a measure of the minimum number of operations required to convert one string into another. These operations typically include insertion, deletion, and substitution of characters. This problem is also known as the Levenshtein distance and is highly relevant in fields such as bioinformatics, spell checking, and text comparison, where finding similarities between sequences is crucial.

The dynamic programming approach efficiently solves the edit distance problem by breaking it down into simpler subproblems. We define a two-dimensional table, where each entry *dp[i][j]* represents the edit distance between the first *i* characters of the first string and the first *j* characters of the second string.

Consider two strings, *s1* and *s2*, with lengths *m* and *n*, respectively. The recursive relation for the problem can be defined as follows:

$$dp[i][j] = \begin{cases} 0 & \text{if } i = 0 \text{ and } j = 0 \\ i & \text{if } j = 0 \\ j & \text{if } i = 0 \\ dp[i-1][j-1] & \text{if } s1[i-1] = s2[j-1] \\ 1 + \min(dp[i-1][j], & \\ dp[i][j-1], dp[i-1][j-1]) & \text{otherwise} \end{cases}$$

The meaning of these cases is clarified as follows: - If both strings are empty (*dp[0][0]*), no operations are needed. - If one string is empty (*dp[i][0]* or *dp[0][j]*), the only option is to perform *i* or *j* insertions (or deletions), respectively. - If the characters at the current positions in both strings are the same, the edit distance is the same as for the previous characters without them (*dp[i-1][j-1]*). - Otherwise, we consider the minimum cost among inserting a character (*dp[i][j-1]*), deleting a character (*dp[i-1][j]*), or substituting a character (*dp[i-1][j-1]*) and add one to it.

The following Java implementation elucidates this approach:

```
public class EditDistance {
    public int minDistance(String s1, String s2) {
```

```
        int m = s1.length();
        int n = s2.length();
        int[][] dp = new int[m + 1][n + 1];

        for (int i = 0; i <= m; i++) {
            for (int j = 0; j <= n; j++) {
                if (i == 0) {
                    dp[i][j] = j; // If s1 is empty, then we need to insert j characters of s2
                } else if (j == 0) {
                    dp[i][j] = i; // If s2 is empty, then we need to delete i characters of s1
                } else if (s1.charAt(i - 1) == s2.charAt(j - 1)) {
                    dp[i][j] = dp[i - 1][j - 1]; // If characters are the same, no new
                        operation is needed
                } else {
                    dp[i][j] = 1 + Math.min(Math.min(dp[i - 1][j], dp[i][j - 1]), dp[i - 1][j -
                        1]); // Minimum of insertion, deletion, or substitution
                }
            }
        }
        return dp[m][n];
    }
}
```

When the above code is executed with the strings *"kitten"* and *"sitting"*, the result is:

```
Output: 3
```

This means that three operations are necessary to convert *"kitten"* into *"sitting"*: one substitution (k → s), one insertion (e → i), and one insertion (n → g).

To optimize the space complexity, we can notice that we only need the previous row and the current row of the table to compute the result. Thus, instead of maintaining the entire *dp* table, we can use two one-dimensional arrays to reduce space complexity from $O(m \times n)$ to $O(\min(m, n))$. This transformation is particularly useful for long strings.

The above implementation serves as an efficient and comprehensible means to calculate the edit distance, employing dynamic programming principles to handle complexity and ensure accurate results.

7.8 Minimum Path Sum

The *Minimum Path Sum* problem involves finding the path from the top-left corner to the bottom-right corner of a grid that minimizes the sum of the values along the path. The movement is restricted to either rightward or downward movement at any point in time. This problem is a classic example of using dynamic programming to efficiently find an optimal solution.

Problem Statement:

Given a $m \times n$ grid filled with non-negative integers, find a path from the top-left to the bottom-right, which minimizes the sum of the numbers along its path.

Example:

Given the grid:

1 3 1
1 5 1
4 2 1

The minimum path sum is 7. The path is $1 \to 3 \to 1 \to 1 \to 1$.

Dynamic Programming Approach:

Define a 2D array dp where $\mathrm{dp[i][j]}$ represents the minimum path sum to reach the cell $(\mathrm{i, j})$. The solution can be approached by recursively filling this array based on the following relations: - $\mathrm{dp[0][0] = grid[0][0]}$ - For the first row ($\mathrm{dp[0][j]}$), one can only move right:

$$dp[0][j] = dp[0][j-1] + grid[0][j]$$

- For the first column ($\mathrm{dp[i][0]}$), one can only move down:

$$dp[i][0] = dp[i-1][0] + grid[i][0]$$

- For other cells ($\mathrm{dp[i][j]}$), one can move from either the left cell or the top cell:

$$dp[i][j] = \text{min}(dp[i-1][j], dp[i][j-1]) + grid[i][j]$$

Java Implementation:

The following Java code demonstrates the implementation of the dynamic programming solution to the minimum path sum problem:

```
public class MinimumPathSum {
    public int minPathSum(int[][] grid) {
        int m = grid.length;
        int n = grid[0].length;
        int[][] dp = new int[m][n];

        dp[0][0] = grid[0][0];

        // Initialize the first row
        for (int j = 1; j < n; j++) {
            dp[0][j] = dp[0][j-1] + grid[0][j];
        }

        // Initialize the first column
        for (int i = 1; i < m; i++) {
```

```
            dp[i][0] = dp[i-1][0] + grid[i][0];
        }

        // Fill up the dp array
        for (int i = 1; i < m; i++) {
            for (int j = 1; j < n; j++) {
                dp[i][j] = Math.min(dp[i-1][j], dp[i][j-1]) + grid[i][j];
            }
        }

        return dp[m-1][n-1];
    }
}
```

Explanation of Code:

1. The dimensions of the grid, m and n, are determined. 2. A 2D array dp of the same dimensions is initialized, where each element represents the minimum path sum to reach that cell. 3. The starting point $\mathrm{dp}[0][0]$ is initialized to $\mathrm{grid}[0][0]$. 4. The first row is initialized by accumulating values from the left. 5. The first column is initialized by accumulating values from above. 6. The rest of the grid is filled using the minimum sum from either the top cell or the left cell. 7. The final value, $\mathrm{dp}[\mathrm{m}\text{-}1][\mathrm{n}\text{-}1]$, gives the minimum path sum to reach the bottom-right corner of the grid.

Optimization:

The space complexity of the above solution is $O(m \times n)$. It can be optimized to $O(n)$ by using a single-dimensional array to hold the minimum path sums for the current row being processed.

```
public class MinimumPathSumOptimized {
    public int minPathSum(int[][] grid) {
        int m = grid.length;
        int n = grid[0].length;
        int[] dp = new int[n];

        dp[0] = grid[0][0];

        // Initialize the first row
        for (int j = 1; j < n; j++) {
            dp[j] = dp[j-1] + grid[0][j];
        }

        // Update the dp array for each subsequent row
        for (int i = 1; i < m; i++) {
            dp[0] += grid[i][0];
            for (int j = 1; j < n; j++) {
                dp[j] = Math.min(dp[j], dp[j-1]) + grid[i][j];
            }
        }

        return dp[n-1];
    }
}
```

In this optimized approach, the dp array is updated row by row, reusing the values from the previous row and ensuring the space complexity is reduced to $O(n)$ while maintaining the time complexity of $O(m \times n)$. The algorithm is efficient and scalable, capable of handling larger grids within feasible computational limits.

7.9 Partition Problem

The Partition Problem belongs to the class of NP-complete problems in computer science. It can be described as follows: given a set of integers, is it possible to partition this set into two subsets such that the sum of elements in both subsets is the same? Mathematically, if given a set S of n integers, we aim to determine whether there exists a subset $S_1 \subseteq S$ such that $\sum_{x \in S_1} x = \sum_{x \in S \setminus S_1} x$.

To address this using dynamic programming, we break down the problem into subproblems that can be solved optimally by leveraging computed solutions to smaller instances of the problem.

Consider the example where $S = \{1, 5, 11, 5\}$. The goal is to determine if there exists a subset of these integers whose sum equals to $\frac{1+5+11+5}{2} = 11$. Here, the problem reduces to checking if there exists a subset with a sum of 11.

We define a boolean dynamic programming table $dp[\cdot][\cdot]$, such that $dp[i][j]$ indicates whether a subset of the first i elements in S has a sum j. The recursive formulation of the problem can be expressed as follows:

$$dp[i][j] = \begin{cases} \text{True} & \text{if } j = 0 \\ \text{False} & \text{if } i = 0 \text{ and } j > 0 \\ dp[i-1][j] & \text{if } j < S[i-1] \\ dp[i-1][j] \vee dp[i-1][j - S[i-1]] & \text{if } j \geq S[i-1] \end{cases}$$

The dynamic programming algorithm can be implemented as follows:

```
public class PartitionProblem {
    public boolean canPartition(int[] nums) {
        int totalSum = 0;
        for (int num : nums) {
            totalSum += num;
        }
        if (totalSum % 2 != 0) {
```

```
            return false;
        }
        int subsetSum = totalSum / 2;
        boolean[][] dp = new boolean[nums.length + 1][subsetSum + 1];
        for (int i = 0; i <= nums.length; i++) {
            dp[i][0] = true;
        }
        for (int i = 1; i <= nums.length; i++) {
            for (int j = 1; j <= subsetSum; j++) {
                if (j < nums[i - 1]) {
                    dp[i][j] = dp[i - 1][j];
                } else {
                    dp[i][j] = dp[i - 1][j] || dp[i - 1][j - nums[i - 1]];
                }
            }
        }
        return dp[nums.length][subsetSum];
    }
}
```

In this Java implementation, the 'canPartition' method first checks if the total sum of the array 'nums' is even. If not, it immediately returns 'false' since it cannot be split into two equal subsets. If the sum is even, the algorithm proceeds by determining a target 'subsetSum', which is half of the total sum.

The boolean table 'dp' is initialized with dimensions $(n+1) \times (\text{subsetSum} + 1)$, where n is the number of elements in the array. The base case where a sum of 0 is always achievable by an empty subset is set to 'true'. For each element in the array and for each possible sum up to 'subsetSum', the algorithm updates the 'dp' table based on whether the current sum can be achieved either by including or excluding the current element.

This dynamic programming solution efficiently decides if there is a subset that sums to the desired 'subsetSum'. If so, it implies the original set can be partitioned into two equal-sum subsets.

Consider the set $S = \{1, 5, 11, 5\}$. The execution of this algorithm can be illustrated with an output table showing the 'dp' table as follows:

	0	1	2	3	4	5	6	7	8	9	10	11
[]	True	False	False	False	False	False	False	False	False	False	False	False
[1]	True	True	False	False	False	False	False	False	False	False	False	False
[1, 5]	True	True	False	False	False	True	True	False	False	False	False	False
[1, 5, 11]	True	True	False	False	False	True	True	False	False	False	False	True
[1, 5, 11, 5]	True	True	False	False	False	True	True	False	False	False	True	True

This shows that the 'dp[4][11]' is 'True', which indicates that there exists a subset of the given set that sums up to 11, hence confirming that the set can be partitioned into two subsets with equal sums.

7.10 Rod Cutting Problem

The Rod Cutting Problem is a classic optimization problem where the goal is to determine the best possible way to cut a given rod of length n into smaller pieces such that the total revenue is maximized. Given a rod of length n and an array of prices that contains prices of all pieces of size smaller than n, the Rod Cutting Problem can be formulated as follows:

Let p_i represent the price of a piece of length i. The objective is to find the maximum revenue R_n obtainable by cutting up the rod and selling the pieces. The solution can be approached using dynamic programming.

The dynamic programming solution to this problem involves defining an array R where $R[i]$ represents the maximum revenue obtainable for a rod of length i. Initially, we set $R[0] = 0$, since a rod of length zero has zero revenue.

The recursive relation for the Rod Cutting Problem can be defined as:

$$R[i] = \max_{1 \leq j \leq i} (p_j + R[i - j])$$

This means that for each length i of the rod, we compute the maximum revenue by considering all possible ways to cut the rod into two pieces: one of length j and the other of length $i - j$, and then add the corresponding prices.

Here is the Java implementation of the Rod Cutting Problem using dynamic programming:

```
public class RodCutting {

    // Function to find the maximum revenue obtainable by cutting up the rod and
        selling the pieces
    public static int cutRod(int[] price, int n) {
        int[] revenue = new int[n + 1];
        revenue[0] = 0; // No revenue for rod of length 0

        for (int i = 1; i <= n; i++) {
            int maxRevenue = Integer.MIN_VALUE;
            for (int j = 1; j <= i; j++) {
                maxRevenue = Math.max(maxRevenue, price[j - 1] + revenue[i - j]);
            }
            revenue[i] = maxRevenue;
        }

        return revenue[n];
    }

    public static void main(String[] args) {
```

```
        int[] price = {1, 5, 8, 9, 10, 17, 17, 20};
        int n = price.length;
        System.out.println("Maximum Obtainable Value is " + cutRod(price, n));
    }
}
```

The above code defines a method 'cutRod' that takes an array 'price' and an integer 'n' representing the length of the rod and returns the maximum obtainable revenue. The main function demonstrates its usage with a sample array of prices.

When this program is executed, the output will be:

```
Maximum Obtainable Value is 22
```

The function 'cutRod' dynamically builds up the solution by computing the maximum revenue for all lengths from 1 to n. The inner loop iterates through all possible first cut positions, updating the maximum revenue if a better cut is found.

Key Points of the Dynamic Programming Solution

1. **Table Construction**: We create a table 'revenue' to store the maximum revenue obtainable for each length of the rod from 0 to n. 2. **Initialization**: The base case 'revenue[0] = 0' ensures that a rod of length zero has zero revenue. 3. **Optimization Step**: For each length 'i', we examine all possible first cuts 'j' and use the recursive relation to compute the maximum revenue. 4. **Iterative Approach**: The solution is built iteratively from the bottom-up, ensuring the subproblems are solved only once.

Complexity Analysis

The time complexity of the above solution is $O(n^2)$. This is due to the nested loops where the outer loop runs n times, and the inner loop also runs up to n times for each iteration of the outer loop. The space complexity is $O(n)$ due to the storage required for the 'revenue' array.

The Rod Cutting Problem exemplifies the power of dynamic programming in solving optimization problems by breaking them down into simpler subproblems and using their solutions to construct the solution to the original problem. This approach not only efficiently computes the result but also avoids redundant computations.

7.11 Palindromic Substrings

A palindrome is a string that reads the same forward and backward. In the context of dynamic programming, one of the common problems is to find all palindromic substrings in a given string. This section will delve into the nuances of identifying palindromic substrings and present a dynamic programming solution implemented in Java.

Given a string s, our goal is to find all substrings of s that are palindromes. This problem requires us to check every possible substring of s and determine if it is a palindrome. We will explore an efficient dynamic programming approach to achieve this.

Our first task is to define a 2D boolean array dp where $dp[i][j]$ will be true if the substring $s[i \ldots j]$ is a palindrome and false otherwise. The substrings are examined in increasing order of length, ensuring that all smaller substrings are resolved before larger ones. This method allows us to utilize previously calculated results.

To build the solution, we initialize the diagonal of the dp array, since any single character is a palindrome by definition. For larger substrings, we check the characters at the start and end; if they match and the inner substring is also a palindrome, the current substring is confirmed as a palindrome.

```
public class PalindromicSubstrings {
    public int countSubstrings(String s) {
        int n = s.length();
        boolean[][] dp = new boolean[n][n];

        // Initialize the diagonal (single character palindromes)
        for (int i = 0; i < n; i++) {
            dp[i][i] = true;
        }

        // Store the count of palindromic substrings
        int count = n;

        // Fill the DP table
        for (int length = 2; length <= n; length++) {
            for (int i = 0; i <= n - length; i++) {
                int j = i + length - 1;
                if (s.charAt(i) == s.charAt(j)) {
                    if (length == 2) {
                        dp[i][j] = true; // Two characters and they are the same
                    } else {
                        dp[i][j] = dp[i + 1][j - 1]; // Check inner substring
                    }
                } else {
                    dp[i][j] = false;
                }
                if (dp[i][j]) {
                    count++;
```

```
                }
            }
        }

        return count;
    }

    public static void main(String[] args) {
        PalindromicSubstrings ps = new PalindromicSubstrings();
        String s = "abba";
        System.out.println("Total palindromic substrings: " + ps.countSubstrings(s));
    }
}
```

In this code, we first initialize the DP table to keep track of palindrome status for each substring. We set all single-character substrings as palindromes. Then, for substrings of length 2 and higher, we evaluate whether the substrings are palindromic considering the values already computed for smaller substrings.

The $count$ variable keeps track of the total number of palindromic substrings. Each time $dp[i][j]$ is set to true, the count is incremented.

The output of the above program for the string "abba" would be:

```
Total palindromic substrings: 6
```

This indicates that the string "abba" has six palindromic substrings, which include "a", "b", "b", "a", "bb", and "abba".

Understanding the efficiency of this algorithm is essential. The time complexity of this solution is $O(n^2)$, where n is the length of the input string. Each entry in the dp table is computed in constant time, leading to the quadratic time complexity.

Conclusively, dynamic programming provides a structured approach to solving the problem of finding all palindromic substrings, ensuring both efficiency and clarity in the solution. This method can be extended or modified to handle variations of the problem, demonstrating the versatility and power of dynamic programming in algorithmic problem-solving.

7.12 Practice Problems and Solutions

This section presents a collection of practice problems designed to reinforce the concepts introduced in the preceding sections. Each problem is accompanied by a detailed Java implementation, as well as a breakdown of the dynamic programming approach used to solve it. By working through these examples, readers will gain a deeper understanding of dynamic programming techniques and their applications.

Problem 1: House Robber Problem

Given an array of non-negative integers representing the amount of money of each house, determine the maximum amount of money you can rob tonight without alerting the police (i.e., you cannot rob two adjacent houses).

Dynamic Programming Solution: The core idea is to use a dynamic programming table where each entry $dp[i]$ represents the maximum amount of money that can be robbed from the first i houses. The relation can be formulated as follows: for each house i, we have the option to either rob it or skip it.

$$dp[i] = \mathsf{max}(dp[i-1], \mathsf{nums}[i] + dp[i-2])$$

where $dp[i-1]$ represents skipping the i-th house, and $\mathsf{nums}[i]+dp[i-2]$ represents robbing the i-th house after skipping one house.

Implementation in Java:

```
public class HouseRobber {
    public int rob(int[] nums) {
        if (nums == null || nums.length == 0)
            return 0;
        if (nums.length == 1)
            return nums[0];

        int[] dp = new int[nums.length];
        dp[0] = nums[0];
        dp[1] = Math.max(nums[0], nums[1]);

        for (int i = 2; i < nums.length; i++) {
            dp[i] = Math.max(dp[i-1], nums[i] + dp[i-2]);
        }

        return dp[nums.length - 1];
    }

    public static void main(String[] args) {
        HouseRobber hr = new HouseRobber();
        int[] nums = {2, 7, 9, 3, 1};
        System.out.println(hr.rob(nums)); // Outputs: 12
    }
}
```

Problem 2: Unique Paths

A robot is located at the top-left corner of a $m \times n$ grid. The robot can only move either down or right at any point in time. The robot is trying to reach the bottom-right corner of the grid. How many possible unique paths are there?

Dynamic Programming Solution: We can use a 2D table dp where $dp[i][j]$ represents the number of unique paths to cell (i, j).

$$dp[i][j] = dp[i-1][j] + dp[i][j-1]$$

i.e., the number of ways to get to (i, j) is the sum of the number of ways to get to the cell directly above it and the cell directly to the left of it.

Implementation in Java:

```
public class UniquePaths {
    public int uniquePaths(int m, int n) {
        if (m <= 0 || n <= 0)
            return 0;

        int[][] dp = new int[m][n];

        // Initializing the first row and first column
        for (int i = 0; i < m; i++)
            dp[i][0] = 1;
        for (int j = 0; j < n; j++)
            dp[0][j] = 1;

        for (int i = 1; i < m; i++) {
            for (int j = 1; j < n; j++) {
                dp[i][j] = dp[i-1][j] + dp[i][j-1];
            }
        }

        return dp[m-1][n-1];
    }

    public static void main(String[] args) {
        UniquePaths up = new UniquePaths();
        System.out.println(up.uniquePaths(3, 7)); // Outputs: 28
    }
}
```

Problem 3: Climbing Stairs

You are climbing a staircase. It takes n steps to reach the top. Each time you can either climb 1 or 2 steps. In how many distinct ways can you climb to the top?

Dynamic Programming Solution: This problem is analogous to the Fibonacci sequence. Let $dp[i]$ represent the number of ways to reach the i-th step. Then:

$$dp[i] = dp[i-1] + dp[i-2]$$

where $dp[i-1]$ is the number of ways to reach the $i-1$-th step and $dp[i-2]$ is the number of ways to reach the $i-2$-th step.

Implementation in Java:

```
public class ClimbingStairs {
    public int climbStairs(int n) {
        if (n <= 1)
            return n;

        int[] dp = new int[n+1];
        dp[0] = 1;
        dp[1] = 1;

        for (int i = 2; i <= n; i++) {
            dp[i] = dp[i-1] + dp[i-2];
        }

        return dp[n];
    }

    public static void main(String[] args) {
        ClimbingStairs cs = new ClimbingStairs();
        System.out.println(cs.climbStairs(5)); // Outputs: 8
    }
}
```

Problem 4: Best Time to Buy and Sell Stock

You are given an array where each element represents the price of a stock on a given day. You can only buy and sell the stock once. Write a function to find the maximum profit.

Dynamic Programming Solution: We can use a single pass to keep track of the minimum price seen so far and calculate the maximum profit that can be achieved by selling on each day.

$$\text{profit} = \max(\text{profit}, \text{price}[i] - \text{min\_price})$$

where min_price is the minimum price encountered so far.

Implementation in Java:

```
public class BestTimeToBuyAndSellStock {
    public int maxProfit(int[] prices) {
        if (prices == null || prices.length == 0)
            return 0;

        int min_price = Integer.MAX_VALUE;
        int max_profit = 0;

        for (int i = 0; i < prices.length; i++) {
            if (prices[i] < min_price)
                min_price = prices[i];
            else if (prices[i] - min_price > max_profit)
```

```
                max_profit = prices[i] - min_price;
            }
        }
        return max_profit;
    }

    public static void main(String[] args) {
        BestTimeToBuyAndSellStock bs = new BestTimeToBuyAndSellStock();
        int[] prices = {7, 1, 5, 3, 6, 4};
        System.out.println(bs.maxProfit(prices)); // Outputs: 5
    }
}
```

Each of these problems exemplifies different aspects of dynamic programming, from simple state transitions to more complex scenarios requiring careful consideration of previous states. Readers are encouraged to explore additional variations and extensions to deepen their understanding and proficiency.

Chapter 8

Advanced Dynamic Programming Techniques

This chapter delves into advanced dynamic programming techniques, including state compression, bitmasking, and divide and conquer DP. It covers dynamic programming on trees, range queries, and graph algorithms, alongside matrix exponentiation and bitwise operations. The chapter also discusses memory optimization and applications in competitive programming. Advanced practice problems and solutions are provided to illustrate these sophisticated methods, helping readers tackle complex scenarios and larger datasets more efficiently.

8.1 Introduction to Advanced Techniques

The foundation laid in preceding chapters has prepared us for a deeper exploration into dynamic programming (DP). Advanced dynamic programming techniques not only involve refining existing methods but also introduce entirely new paradigms that drastically improve both time and space efficiency. These techniques are instrumental in solving complex problems that are computationally intensive when approached with straightforward methods.

To start, we move beyond conventional DP table filling and look at more sophisticated approaches like state compression and bitmasking.

State compression is an optimization technique used to reduce the memory requirements of a DP algorithm. This is particularly useful when the problem's state space is vast, making direct tabulation infeasible. The key concept here is to represent multiple states in a compact form, making it easier to store and retrieve them efficiently.

Bitmasking, in the context of dynamic programming, leverages the binary representation of numbers to efficiently handle subsets. Many problems, especially combinatorial ones like the Traveling Salesman Problem or the subset sum problem, can be significantly optimized using bitmasking techniques. It reduces the complexity by encoding the state of subsets in a single integer.

Another advanced technique is divide and conquer DP, which merges the divide-and-conquer strategy with traditional dynamic programming. This method is particularly effective in scenarios where the straightforward approach of filling DP tables leads to redundant computations. By recursively dividing the problem and solving smaller subproblems more efficiently, one can achieve optimal results without the overhead of recomputing previously solved states.

We also delve into dynamic programming on trees, which extends the concept to data structures beyond linear arrays. Trees, which are hierarchical and non-linear, present unique challenges and opportunities for DP. Techniques like heavy-light decomposition and centroid decomposition are employed here, allowing us to solve complex tree problems with efficient algorithms.

Range queries play a vital role in various computational problems. Combining them with DP offers a powerful toolkit for solving diverse problems, from basic arithmetic queries to complex ones involving segment trees and Fenwick trees (binary indexed trees). This combination is particularly useful in competitive programming and scenarios requiring efficient preprocessing and query handling.

Graph algorithms, when integrated with dynamic programming, unlock potential for solving problems related to shortest paths, maximum flows, and other graph-related queries. Techniques like Dijkstra's algorithm, Floyd-Warshall algorithm, and Bellman-Ford algorithm, when combined with DP concepts, provide robust solutions to graph problems.

Matrix exponentiation is an essential technique for solving linear recurrences efficiently. Problems that involve repeated calculations of matrix powers can reap significant performance gains using this approach. By leveraging properties of matrices and their operations, complex recursive relations can be solved in logarithmic time.

Bitwise operations in dynamic programming, another advanced technique, harness the power of bit-level operations to achieve performance gains. This is particularly applicable in pattern matching, encryption algorithms, and low-level bit manipulation problems.

Memory optimization techniques, including the use of rolling arrays and space-efficient data structures, help mitigate the high space complexity typically associated with dynamic programming. These techniques ensure that the algorithm remains feasible even under stringent memory constraints.

Dynamic programming finds extensive applications in competitive programming, where time and space efficiency are paramount. The quick thinking and meticulous optimizations required to excel in competitive arenas underscore the importance of mastering these advanced techniques.

To solidify understanding, advanced practice problems and solutions are included. They illustrate the application of these sophisticated methods in tackling complex scenarios and handling larger datasets efficiently. Each problem is designed to reinforce the concepts discussed and push the reader towards expert proficiency in dynamic programming.

This progressive journey equips learners with the ability to apply advanced dynamic programming techniques effectively, transforming them into adept problem solvers capable of handling a wide array of computational challenges. The sophistication of these techniques not only enhances problem-solving skills but also opens the door to tackling real-world problems with innovation and precision.

8.2 State Compression

State compression in dynamic programming is a powerful technique used to reduce the state space of a problem, thereby optimizing both memory and time complexity. The fundamental idea is to encode multiple states into a single state representation, typically through bit manipulation or other data structure transformations. This is especially useful when dealing with combinatorial problems where the state space could otherwise be exponentially large.

To better understand state compression, we will explore its application through a detailed example and illustrate the implementation using Java.

Consider a classical problem where you're given a set of integers and you need to count the number of subsets that sum up to a target value. Normally, for each subset, you would track its sum and whether or not it includes a particular integer. This results in a large state space. Using state compression, we can encode the inclusion of elements in a subset using bitmasks.

A bitmask is a binary sequence where each bit represents whether the corresponding integer is included in the subset (1) or not (0). For example, if you have a set of four integers {1, 2, 3, 4}, the bitmask 0101 represents the subset {1, 3}.

Let us now define the state and transition more formally. Let $\mathrm{dp}[\mathrm{mask}]$ represent the number of subsets represented by the bitmask mask that sum up to the target value. Here, mask is an integer where the k-th bit indicates whether the k-th integer in the set is included in the subset.

The recursive relation can be defined as:

$$dp[\text{mask}] = dp[\text{mask} \setminus \{i\}] + dp[\text{mask}]$$

Where i is an index (integer) being considered and mask$\setminus \{i\}$ indicates flipping the ith bit from 1 to 0.

Below is the Java implementation demonstrating the use of bit masking for state compression in this problem:

```
import java.util.Scanner;

public class SubsetSumStateCompression {
    public static void main(String[] args) {
        Scanner sc = new Scanner(System.in);
        int n = sc.nextInt();
        int target = sc.nextInt();
        int[] arr = new int[n];

        for (int i = 0; i < n; i++) {
            arr[i] = sc.nextInt();
        }

        int[] dp = new int[1 << n];
        dp[0] = 1; // There's one subset (the empty subset) summing up to 0

        for (int mask = 0; mask < (1 << n); mask++) {
            if (sum(mask, arr) == target) {
                dp[mask]++;
            }
```

```
            for (int i = 0; i < n; i++) {
                if ((mask & (1 << i)) == 0) {
                    dp[mask | (1 << i)] += dp[mask];
                }
            }
        }

        int result = 0;
        for (int mask = 0; mask < (1 << n); mask++) {
            if (sum(mask, arr) == target) {
                result += dp[mask];
            }
        }

        System.out.println(result);
    }

    private static int sum(int mask, int[] arr) {
        int total = 0;
        for (int i = 0; i < arr.length; i++) {
            if ((mask & (1 << i)) != 0) {
                total += arr[i];
            }
        }
        return total;
    }
}
```

Executing the above code with input:

```
4 5
1 2 3 4
```

will result in an output of:

```
3
```

This indicates that there are three subsets of {1, 2, 3, 4} that sum up to 5 (i.e., {1, 4}, {2, 3}, and {1, 2, 3-1}).

In this implementation, dp is an array where each index represents a bitmask of the subset, and each value at $\mathrm{dp[mask]}$ represents the count of subsets corresponding to that bitmask. The operation $(\text{mask}\&(1 \ll i))$ checks whether the bit corresponding to the integer i is set in mask.

State compression using bitmasks allows a more feasible time and space complexity by reducing the problem size from potentially $O(2^n)$ states to $2^{\text{number of elements considered}}$, making it manageable even for larger datasets. This approach is particularly useful in problems involving sets, subsets, or any scenario where combinatorial inclusion-exclusion principles can be applied.

8.3 Bitmasking in Dynamic Programming

Bitmasking is a technique used in dynamic programming to efficiently represent and manipulate subsets of a set using binary numbers. This approach is particularly useful when dealing with problems that require tracking multiple states or combinations simultaneously. By representing the state of each element using a bit in an integer, we reduce the memory usage and computational complexity.

Concept of Bitmasking

In bitmasking, a set with n elements can be represented by an integer with n bits. Each bit in the integer indicates whether a corresponding element is present (bit set to 1) or absent (bit set to 0) in the subset. For example, for a set {0, 1, 2}, the subset {1, 2} can be represented by the binary number 110, which corresponds to the integer 6.

Common Operations

Several operations are commonly performed on these bitmasks to manipulate and query the subsets:

- **Check if an element is in a subset**: To check if the i-th element is in the subset represented by the bitmask mask, we use the operation

  $$(\text{mask} \ \& \ (1 << \text{i})) \ != 0$$

  This operation shifts 1 to the left by i positions and performs a bitwise AND with mask. If the i-th bit is set, the result is non-zero.

- **Add an element to a subset**: To add the i-th element to the subset, we can perform a bitwise OR operation:

  $$\text{mask} \mid (1 << \text{i})$$

- **Remove an element from a subset**: To remove the i-th element, we use the bitwise AND operation with the negation of the bitmask:

  $$\text{mask} \ \& \ \neg(1 << \text{i})$$

- **Toggle the presence of an element**: To toggle the i-th element (i.e., switch from 1 to 0 or from 0 to 1), we use the bitwise XOR operation:

  $$\text{mask} \ \hat{} \ (1 << \text{i})$$

Example Problem: Traveling Salesperson Problem (TSP)

Consider the classic Traveling Salesperson Problem (TSP), where a salesperson needs to visit n cities, each exactly once, minimizing the total traveling distance. This can be solved using bitmasking in combination with dynamic programming.

Problem Definition

Given a set of n cities and a distance matrix $dist[i][j]$ that gives the distance from city i to city j, find the shortest possible route that visits each city exactly once and returns to the starting city.

Solution Using Bitmasking and Dynamic Programming

Let $dp[mask][i]$ represent the minimum cost to visit all cities in the subset $mask$, ending at city i. The mask is a bitmask of size n, where the i-th bit indicates whether city i has been visited.

The transition equation can be derived as follows:

$$dp[\text{mask}][i] = \text{min}(dp[\text{mask} \setminus \{i\}][j] + dist[j][i])$$

where j is any city already included in the subset mask $\setminus \{i\}$.

Initialization and Base Cases

We initialize dp such that $dp[mask][i] = \infty$ for all mask and i except $dp[1 << i][i] = 0$, which corresponds to starting the tour at city i with only that city visited.

```
int n; // number of cities
vector<vector<int>> dist; // distance matrix
vector<vector<int>> dp(1 << n, vector<int>(n, INT_MAX));

for (int i = 0; i < n; ++i) {
    dp[1 << i][i] = 0;
}
```

Transition

We iterate over all possible subsets of cities and update the dp array based on the transition equation:

```
for (int mask = 1; mask < (1 << n); ++mask) {
    for (int i = 0; i < n; ++i) {
        if (mask & (1 << i)) {
            for (int j = 0; j < n; ++j) {
                if (i != j && (mask & (1 << j))) {
                    dp[mask][i] = min(dp[mask][i], dp[mask ^ (1 << i)][j] + dist[j][i]);
                }
            }
        }
```

```
    }
}
```

Final Calculation

To retrieve the minimum cost to complete the tour starting and ending at city 0, we consider all possible cities as the final stop before returning to the starting city:

```
int answer = INT_MAX;
for (int i = 1; i < n; ++i) {
    answer = min(answer, dp[(1 << n) - 1][i] + dist[i][0]);
}
```

Complexity Analysis

The time complexity of this solution is $O(2^n \times n^2)$, which is feasible for $n \leq 20$. The space complexity is $O(2^n \times n)$.

Bitmasking in dynamic programming efficiently addresses a variety of combinatorial optimization problems by compactly representing states and transitions in a manner that leverages binary operations for fast computation and memory conservation.

8.4 Divide and Conquer DP

Divide and Conquer Dynamic Programming is a technique used to optimize the computation of certain types of dynamic programming problems. Typically, this technique applies to problems with a costly transition function, where recalculating the same transitions repeatedly yields inefficiency. The Divide and Conquer DP technique aims to reduce the complexity by breaking the problem into smaller sub-problems, solving each efficiently while preserving the optimal solution.

This method often takes advantage of the "Monotonicity" and "Convexity" properties of the dynamic programming's cost function. To illustrate its application, let us consider the optimization of a specific class of DP problems known as "Knuth-Yao Quadrangle Inequality Optimization." This involves using a divide-and-conquer strategy with dynamic programming.

Knuth-Yao Quadrangle Inequality Optimization

Consider a cost function $C(i, j)$ defined on intervals $[i, j]$, where our goal is to minimize the DP relation:

$$dp[i][j] = \min_{i \leq k \leq j} (dp[i][k] + dp[k+1][j] + C(i,j))$$

Using the naive approach, solving the above DP relation requires $O(n^3)$ time complexity due to the triple nested loop. However, if the cost function $C(i,j)$ satisfies specific properties, we can optimize this to $O(n^2 \log n)$ using the divide and conquer strategy.

Criteria for Optimization

For the optimization technique to be applicable, the cost function $C(i,j)$ must satisfy the quadrangle inequality:

$$C(a,c) + C(b,d) \leq C(a,d) + C(b,c) \quad \text{where} \quad a \leq b \leq c \leq d$$

Additionally, the Knuth-Yao optimization is valid if the following monotonicity condition holds:

$$opt(i,j-1) \leq opt(i,j) \leq opt(i+1,j)$$

Here, $opt(i,j)$ is the value of k that minimizes the DP transition for $dp[i][j]$.

Implementation of Divide and Conquer DP

The recursive implementation of divide and conquer DP uses these principles. Consider an example implementation in Java:

```
public class DivideAndConquerDP {
    static int[][] dp;
    static int[][] C;

    // Initialize your dp and other relevant arrays based on problem constraints
    public static void initialize(int n) {
        dp = new int[n][n];
        C = new int[n][n];
        // Fill C[i][j] appropriately based on the problem's cost function
    }

    // Recursive function to compute dp using divide and conquer
    public static void compute(int l, int r, int optL, int optR) {
        if (l > r) {
            return;
        }
        int mid = (l + r) / 2;
        dp[mid][mid] = Integer.MAX_VALUE;
        int bestK = -1;

        for (int k = optL; k <= Math.min(mid, optR); k++) {
            int cost = dp[l][k] + dp[k+1][r] + C[l][r];
            if (cost < dp[mid][mid]) {
```

```
                dp[mid][mid] = cost;
                bestK = k;
            }
        }

        compute(l, mid - 1, optL, bestK);
        compute(mid + 1, r, bestK, optR);
    }

    public static void main(String[] args) {
        int n = 10; // Example size
        initialize(n);
        compute(0, n-1, 0, n-1);

        // Output result
        for (int i = 0; i < n; i++) {
            for (int j = 0; j < n; j++) {
                System.out.print(dp[i][j] + " ");
            }
            System.out.println();
        }
    }
}
```

Explanation of the Code

1. **Initialization**: The method 'initialize(int n)' sets up the DP table and the cost matrix C. The cost matrix should be filled according to the specific problem being solved.

2. **Recursive Compute Function**: The core of the divide and conquer approach is implemented in the 'compute(int l, int r, int optL, int optR)' method. This method divides the problem into smaller subproblems around the midpoint mid of the current range $[l, r]$.

3. **Best Partition Point**: In the loop, we evaluate the cost for different partition points k within the current range. The transition $dp[mid][mid]$ gets updated whenever a lower cost configuration is found, ensuring the solution remains optimal.

4. **Recursion**: After determining the optimal partition for mid, the function recurses to solve the left and right halves, progressively reducing the problem's size.

5. **Output**: The main method initializes the problem parameters, invokes the 'compute' method, and displays the final DP table.

This approach efficiently narrows the search space using the divide and conquer paradigm, leveraging the quadrangle and monotonicity properties to assure optimal substructures are combined efficiently. Therefore, the time complexity significantly improves from $O(n^3)$ to $O(n^2 \log n)$, making it feasible to solve larger instances of the problem within practical constraints.

8.5 Dynamic Programming on Trees

Dynamic programming (DP) on trees is an advanced and specialized technique where the principles of dynamic programming are applied to tree data structures. Trees, being acyclic connected graphs, have unique properties that necessitate specific strategies to effectively utilize dynamic programming.

Consider a rooted tree T with N nodes, where each node u has an associated value or weight. Trees are particularly useful for hierarchical data and can represent problems such as computing properties based on hierarchical relationships, optimizing subtree sums, or solving network-based problems like finding the diameter of a tree.

To effectively apply dynamic programming on trees, we commonly utilize a depth-first search (DFS) strategy. This approach involves computing values for subproblems (subtrees) and then combining these results to solve larger problems.

Example Problem: Sum of Subtree Weights

One fundamental example is computing the sum of weights of all nodes in each subtree of T. Let $subtree\_sum[u]$ represent the sum of weights in the subtree rooted at node u.

To accomplish this, we define the recursive relation for $subtree\_sum[u]$ as follows:

$$\text{subtree\_sum}[u] = w[u] + \sum_{v \in children(u)} \text{subtree\_sum}[v]$$

Here, $w[u]$ is the weight of node u, and $children(u)$ denotes the set of children of node u. We use a DFS traversal to compute this recursively.

```
import java.util.ArrayList;
import java.util.List;

public class TreeDP {
    static class TreeNode {
        int weight;
        List<Integer> children;

        TreeNode(int weight) {
            this.weight = weight;
            this.children = new ArrayList<>();
        }
    }

    static TreeNode[] tree;
```

```
    static int[] subtreeSum;

    public static void main(String[] args) {
        int N = 5;
        tree = new TreeNode[N];
        subtreeSum = new int[N];

        // For simplicity, we are assuming nodes are 0-indexed and the tree is given as
            follows:
        int[] weights = {1, 2, 3, 4, 5};
        int[][] edges = {{0, 1}, {0, 2}, {1, 3}, {1, 4}};

        for (int i = 0; i < N; i++) {
            tree[i] = new TreeNode(weights[i]);
        }

        for (int[] edge : edges) {
            tree[edge[0]].children.add(edge[1]);
        }

        // Assuming root is node 0
        dfs(0);

        // Output subtree sums
        for (int i = 0; i < N; i++) {
            System.out.println("Subtree sum of node " + i + ": " + subtreeSum[i]);
        }
    }

    static void dfs(int node) {
        subtreeSum[node] = tree[node].weight;
        for (int child : tree[node].children) {
            dfs(child);
            subtreeSum[node] += subtreeSum[child];
        }
    }
}
```

The execution of the above code yields:

```
Subtree sum of node 0: 15
Subtree sum of node 1: 14
Subtree sum of node 2: 3
Subtree sum of node 3: 4
Subtree sum of node 4: 5
```

Tree Diameter and Path Queries

Another common problem solved using DP on trees involves finding the diameter of a tree, which is the longest path between any two nodes. The diameter of a tree can be efficiently computed using two passes of DFS.

1. **First DFS:** Find the farthest node u from an arbitrary start node.
2. **Second DFS:** Perform another DFS starting from u to find the farthest node from u, which gives the length of the diameter.

This method leverages the properties of tree structures where the farthest node from a random start node u is guaranteed to be one of the endpoints of the tree's diameter.

```
import java.util.ArrayList;
import java.util.List;

public class TreeDiameter {
    static class TreeNode {
        List<Integer> neighbors;

        TreeNode() {
            this.neighbors = new ArrayList<>();
        }
    }

    static TreeNode[] tree;
    static boolean[] visited;
    static int farthestNode, maxDistance;

    public static void main(String[] args) {
        int N = 5;
        tree = new TreeNode[N];
        visited = new boolean[N];

        for (int i = 0; i < N; i++) {
            tree[i] = new TreeNode();
        }

        int[][] edges = {{0, 1}, {0, 2}, {1, 3}, {1, 4}};
        for (int[] edge : edges) {
            tree[edge[0]].neighbors.add(edge[1]);
            tree[edge[1]].neighbors.add(edge[0]);
        }

        // First DFS from node 0
        dfsDiameter(0, 0);

        // Reset visited array and maxDistance for the second DFS
        visited = new boolean[N];
        maxDistance = 0;

        // Second DFS from the farthest node found in the first DFS
        dfsDiameter(farthestNode, 0);

        // Output the diameter
        System.out.println("Diameter of the tree: " + maxDistance);
    }

    static void dfsDiameter(int node, int distance) {
        visited[node] = true;

        if (distance > maxDistance) {
            maxDistance = distance;
            farthestNode = node;
        }

        for (int neighbor : tree[node].neighbors) {
            if (!visited[neighbor]) {
                dfsDiameter(neighbor, distance + 1);
            }
        }
    }
```

```
}
```

Executing the above code will output:

```
Diameter of the tree: 3
```

Tree Decomposition and Heavy-Light Decomposition (HLD)

Heavy-Light Decomposition (HLD) is a technique that decomposes a tree into "heavy" and "light" paths. This segmentation allows efficient range queries and updates within the tree. The main idea is to decompose the tree so that the heavy path includes the most significant portion of the tree's nodes.

1. **Heavy Path:** Choose the child subtree with the largest size. 2. **Light Path:** Rest of the paths aside from the heavy path.

HLD is particularly advantageous in operations requiring frequent updates and queries on paths between nodes because it reduces the problem's complexity by simplifying the path structure.

Applying HLD requires several steps including initial preprocessing to find subtree sizes, decomposing the tree electing heavy paths, and defining segment trees for range queries.

The advanced dynamic programming techniques discussed in this section demonstrate the power of incorporating algorithmic strategies with data structures like trees. These methods prove indispensable in optimizing complex computations and solving real-world problems characterized by hierarchical relationships and dependencies.

8.6 Range Queries and DP

Range Queries are essential operations frequently encountered in numerous computational problems. These operations involve preprocessing a dataset for efficiently answering queries about subarray, sublist, or submatrix segments. Integrating Dynamic Programming (DP) with Range Queries offers versatile and robust solutions, optimizing both preprocessing and query-response times.

Consider a straightforward problem: given an array of integers, efficiently compute the sum of elements within any contiguous subarray. Direct computation requires iterating through the subarray elements, yielding a time complexity of $O(n)$ for each query. Precomputing data using a dynamic programming approach can significantly reduce the query time.

Prefix Sum Array

One effective technique involves the prefix sum array, where each entry at index i stores the cumulative sum of the array elements up to index $i-1$. The prefix sums allow for constant-time sum computation of any subarray.

Given an array A of length n, the prefix sum array P can be defined as:

$$P[i] = \sum_{j=0}^{i-1} A[j]$$

The construction of the prefix sum array has a time complexity of $O(n)$:

```
public class PrefixSum {
    private int[] prefix;

    public PrefixSum(int[] array) {
        prefix = new int[array.length + 1];
        for (int i = 0; i < array.length; i++) {
            prefix[i + 1] = prefix[i] + array[i];
        }
    }

    public int rangeSum(int left, int right) {
        return prefix[right + 1] - prefix[left];
    }
}
```

In the given implementation, the constructor $PrefixSum$ initializes the prefix sum array. The function $rangeSum$ computes the sum of the elements between indices $left$ and $right$ in constant time, $O(1)$.

Range Minimum Query (RMQ)

For more complex queries, such as finding the minimum element within a subarray, a straightforward prefix sum approach is insufficient. Instead, employing a segment tree or a sparse table is ideal.

Sparse Table

A sparse table is a data structure designed for efficient range minimum or maximum queries, allowing $O(1)$ query times following an $O(n \log n)$ preprocessing phase. Constructing a sparse table involves filling in an $n \times \log n$ table where $ST[i][j]$ stores the minimum value in the subarray from index i to $i + 2^j - 1$.

Construction and querying of a sparse table:

```
public class SparseTable {
```

```
    private int[][] st;
    private int[] log;

    public SparseTable(int[] array) {
        int n = array.length;
        int k = (int) Math.ceil(Math.log(n) / Math.log(2));
        st = new int[n][k + 1];
        log = new int[n + 1];

        for (int i = 2; i <= n; i++) {
            log[i] = log[i / 2] + 1;
        }

        for (int i = 0; i < n; i++) {
            st[i][0] = array[i];
        }

        for (int j = 1; j <= k; j++) {
            for (int i = 0; i + (1 << j) <= n; i++) {
                st[i][j] = Math.min(st[i][j - 1], st[i + (1 << (j - 1))][j - 1]);
            }
        }
    }

    public int rangeMinQuery(int left, int right) {
        int j = log[right - left + 1];
        return Math.min(st[left][j], st[right - (1 << j) + 1][j]);
    }
}
```

The constructor initializes necessary arrays and precomputes the logarithmic values in log. Then, the sparse table is constructed. The $rangeMinQuery$ function allows for constant-time query of the minimum element within any subarray defined by $left$ and $right$.

Segment Tree

Another common data structure for range queries is the segment tree, which supports both range queries and point updates efficiently. Constructing a segment tree involves a preprocessing step of $O(n \log n)$, allowing subsequent updates and queries to be handled in $O(\log n)$.

The implementation of a segment tree for range sum queries:

```
public class SegmentTree {
    private int[] tree;
    private int n;

    public SegmentTree(int[] array) {
        n = array.length;
        tree = new int[2 * n];
        buildTree(array);
    }

    private void buildTree(int[] array) {
        System.arraycopy(array, 0, tree, n, n);
        for (int i = n - 1; i > 0; --i) {
            tree[i] = tree[i * 2] + tree[i * 2 + 1];
```

```
        }
    }

    public void update(int index, int value) {
        index += n;
        tree[index] = value;
        for (; index > 1; index /= 2) {
            tree[index / 2] = tree[index] + tree[index ^ 1];
        }
    }

    public int rangeSum(int left, int right) {
        int sum = 0;
        left += n;
        right += n;
        for (; left < right; left /= 2, right /= 2) {
            if ((left & 1) == 1) sum += tree[left++];
            if ((right & 1) == 1) sum += tree[--right];
        }
        return sum;
    }
}
```

The constructor initializes the segment tree, and the *buildTree* method constructs it from the input array. The *update* method modifies a specific array element, updating necessary segment tree nodes. The *rangeSum* method calculates the sum of elements within the subarray using the segment tree efficiently.

Integrating range queries with dynamic programming enriches our toolkit, balancing preprocessing with swift query responses, essential for handling large datasets and numerous queries effectively.

8.7 Graph Algorithms and Dynamic Programming

The seamless integration of graph algorithms with dynamic programming paradigms can enhance the efficiency and capability of solving complex problems. These hybrid approaches utilize the strengths of both fields to solve problems that involve structured data, such as networks, trees, and general graphs, exhibiting multi-stage decision-making characteristics.

Graph algorithms are traditionally used to solve connectivity-related questions (e.g., shortest path, minimum spanning tree, network flows), while dynamic programming is effective for problems where subproblems overlap and exhibit optimal substructure. The intersection of these domains provides a powerful toolkit for addressing a variety of intricate problems.

Shortest Path Algorithms: Dynamic programming is fundamentally embedded in certain shortest path algorithms, such as the Bellman-Ford algorithm. Consider a directed graph $G = (V, E)$ with edge weights. The task is to compute the shortest path from a source vertex s to all other vertices. The Bellman-Ford algorithm uses a DP-based relaxation technique iteratively, processing each edge to update the shortest known distances.

The algorithm can be summarized as follows:

```
void bellmanFord(int graph[][], int V, int E, int src) {
    int dist[] = new int[V];
    for (int i = 0; i < V; i++)
        dist[i] = Integer.MAX_VALUE;
    dist[src] = 0;

    for (int i = 1; i < V; i++) {
        for (int j = 0; j < E; j++) {
            int u = graph[j][0];
            int v = graph[j][1];
            int weight = graph[j][2];
            if (dist[u] != Integer.MAX_VALUE && dist[u] + weight < dist[v])
                dist[v] = dist[u] + weight;
        }
    }

    for (int j = 0; j < E; j++) {
        int u = graph[j][0];
        int v = graph[j][1];
        int weight = graph[j][2];
        if (dist[u] != Integer.MAX_VALUE && dist[u] + weight < dist[v])
            System.out.println("Graph contains negative weight cycle");
    }

    printArr(dist, V);
}
```

The relaxation step, performed inside the inner loop, updates the distance to each vertex based on the shortest known path found so far.

```
0 -1 2 1
```

All-Pairs Shortest Path: Floyd-Warshall algorithm solves the problem of finding shortest paths between all pairs of vertices. It uses the concept of dynamic programming to iteratively improve the solution. Initially, we assume that the shortest path between any two vertices is the direct edge between them, if it exists. The core DP relation of the Floyd-Warshall algorithm updates the shortest paths:

$$dist[i][j] = \min(dist[i][j], dist[i][k] + dist[k][j])$$

The implementation can be expressed as:

```
void floydWarshall(int graph[][]) {
    int V = graph.length;
    int dist[][] = new int[V][V];

    for (int i = 0; i < V; i++)
        for (int j = 0; j < V; j++)
            dist[i][j] = graph[i][j];

    for (int k = 0; k < V; k++) {
        for (int i = 0; i < V; i++) {
            for (int j = 0; j < V; j++) {
                if (dist[i][k] + dist[k][j] < dist[i][j])
                    dist[i][j] = dist[i][k] + dist[k][j];
            }
        }
    }

    printSolution(dist);
}
```

0 5 8 9

Dynamic programming enables efficient computation by leveraging previously computed shortest paths when considering new paths that go through intermediate vertices.

Travelling Salesman Problem (TSP): The Travelling Salesman Problem (TSP) is another classic problem that can be effectively tackled via dynamic programming, particularly using a bitmasking approach. We denote the state of the DP as $dp[mask][i]$, where $mask$ represents the set of cities visited so far, and i represents the current city. The recursive relation is:

$$dp[mask][i] = \text{min}(dp[mask \setminus (1 << i)][j] + cost[j][i]) \quad \forall j$$

The goal is to find the minimum cost to visit all cities and return to the starting point.

```
int TSP(int mask, int pos, int[][] dist, int[][] dp, int n) {
    if (mask == (1 << n) - 1)
        return dist[pos][0];
    if (dp[mask][pos] != -1)
        return dp[mask][pos];

    int ans = Integer.MAX_VALUE;

    for (int city = 0; city < n; city++) {
        if ((mask & (1 << city)) == 0) {
            int newAns = dist[pos][city] + TSP(mask | (1 << city), city, dist, dp, n);
            ans = Math.min(ans, newAns);
        }
    }
```

```
    return dp[mask][pos] = ans;
}
```

By expressing the problem recursively and using memoization to store intermediate results, the TSP problem, which is NP-hard, becomes feasible for moderately sized instances.

Tree DP: We utilize dynamic programming on trees for solving optimization problems where the structure is hierarchical. Consider the problem of finding the maximum weight independent set of a tree. Let $dp[u][0]$ represent the maximum weight of the subset when node u is not included, and $dp[u][1]$ when u is included. The recursive relations are:

$$dp[u][0] = \sum_{v \in \text{children}(u)} \max(dp[v][0], dp[v][1])$$

$$dp[u][1] = w_u + \sum_{v \in \text{children}(u)} dp[v][0]$$

```
void treeDP(int u, int p, List<Integer>[] tree, int[] weight, int[][] dp) {
    dp[u][0] = 0;
    dp[u][1] = weight[u];

    for (int v : tree[u]) {
        if (v == p) continue;
        treeDP(v, u, tree, weight, dp);
        dp[u][0] += Math.max(dp[v][0], dp[v][1]);
        dp[u][1] += dp[v][0];
    }
}
```

These dynamic programming techniques, when applied in graph contexts, exploit the inherent properties of the graph and problem constraints to derive efficient solutions. Understanding these methods and their implementations provides a robust foundation for tackling a wider range of algorithmic challenges in the realm of graphs and dynamic programming.

8.8 Matrix Exponentiation

Matrix exponentiation is a powerful technique in dynamic programming used to solve recurrence relations more efficiently. This method can dramatically reduce the time complexity of problems commonly solved by traditional dynamic programming methods. Matrix exponentiation allows us to handle linear recurrences, typically through optimized computation leveraging properties of matrices.

Consider a standard linear recurrence relation of the form:

$$F(n) = a_1 F(n-1) + a_2 F(n-2) + \ldots + a_k F(n-k)$$

where $a_1, a_2, \ldots, a_k$ are constants, and the sequence F follows this relationship for $n > k$. The goal is to compute $F(n)$ efficiently for large n.

By converting the linear recurrence into a matrix form, we can significantly reduce the computational complexity. We start by modeling our recurrence relation as a matrix multiplication problem.

Transition Matrix

For the linear recurrence:

$$F(n) = 2F(n-1) + 3F(n-2)$$

we can represent it in a matrix form with a transition matrix T:

$$\begin{bmatrix} F(n) \\ F(n-1) \end{bmatrix} = \begin{bmatrix} 2 & 3 \\ 1 & 0 \end{bmatrix} \begin{bmatrix} F(n-1) \\ F(n-2) \end{bmatrix}$$

In a generalized form for a k-term recurrence:

$$\begin{bmatrix} F(n) \\ F(n-1) \\ \vdots \\ F(n-k+1) \end{bmatrix} = T \cdot \begin{bmatrix} F(n-1) \\ F(n-2) \\ \vdots \\ F(n-k) \end{bmatrix}$$

where the transition matrix T is defined as:

$$T = \begin{bmatrix} a_1 & a_2 & \cdots & a_k \\ 1 & 0 & \cdots & 0 \\ 0 & 1 & \cdots & 0 \\ \vdots & \vdots & \ddots & \vdots \\ 0 & 0 & \cdots & 1 \end{bmatrix}$$

Matrix Exponentiation by Squaring

To find $F(n)$, the nth term of the sequence, we raise the transition matrix to the power of $(n-k)$ using matrix exponentiation by squaring, an O(log

n) method. This is analogous to the fast exponentiation technique for scalars and greatly improves efficiency.

Given a matrix A, the algorithm for matrix exponentiation by squaring is:

```
public class MatrixExponentiation {
    static int MOD = 1000000007;

    public static int[][] multiply(int[][] A, int[][] B) {
        int n = A.length;
        int[][] C = new int[n][n];
        for (int i = 0; i < n; i++) {
            for (int j = 0; j < n; j++) {
                C[i][j] = 0;
                for (int k = 0; k < n; k++) {
                    C[i][j] = (C[i][j] + (int)((long)A[i][k] * B[k][j] % MOD)) % MOD;
                }
            }
        }
        return C;
    }

    public static int[][] power(int[][] A, int exp) {
        int n = A.length;
        int[][] result = new int[n][n];
        for (int i = 0; i < n; i++) {
            result[i][i] = 1;
        }

        while (exp > 0) {
            if ((exp & 1) == 1) {
                result = multiply(result, A);
            }
            A = multiply(A, A);
            exp >>= 1;
        }
        return result;
    }

    public static int fibonacci(int n) {
        if (n == 0) return 0;
        if (n == 1) return 1;

        int[][] T = {
            {1, 1},
            {1, 0}
        };

        T = power(T, n - 1);

        return T[0][0];
    }

    public static void main(String[] args) {
        System.out.println(fibonacci(10)); // Output: 55
    }
}
```

Explanation

1. **Initialization**: We initialize the identity matrix in the 'power' function to facilitate multiplication. 2. **Fast Exponentiation**: By checking whether the current exponent (exp) is odd and updating the matrix as required, we efficiently compute the exponentiation. 3. **Multiplication**: The 'multiply' function handles matrix multiplication while ensuring that each entry in the resulting matrix is modulo $10^9 + 7$ to prevent overflow and adhere to common competitive programming constraints.

Application

Matrix exponentiation is widely used in solving problems with linear recurrences, including those found in computational biology, economics, and complex systems modeling. This method is also prevalent in competitive programming, where reducing complexity can be the difference between a solution being feasible or not.

Given the above techniques and understanding, one can extend the concept to more complex state representations and transition models, fostering an appreciation of the efficiency and elegance that matrix exponentiation brings to dynamic programming. Through the interplay of linear algebra and algorithmic optimization, matrix exponentiation exemplifies the synergy of mathematical theory and computational practice.

8.9 DP with Bitwise Operations

Dynamic programming (DP) frequently intersects with bitwise operations to solve problems that include subsets, states, or configurations that align well with a binary representation. Utilizing bitwise operations can make the manipulation and evaluation of states significantly more efficient. This section explicates the integration of DP with bitwise operations and explores algorithms and practical implementations that leverage these combined techniques.

To understand DP with bitwise operations, consider the manner in which bit manipulation aids in representing sets or states. A subset of a set can be naturally represented using a binary number where each bit indicates the presence (1) or absence (0) of an element. This representation aligns well with problems requiring enumeration of subsets, combinations of items, or configurations.

```
import java.util.Arrays;

public class SubsetSum {
```

```
    public static boolean subsetSum(int[] nums, int target) {
        int n = nums.length;
        boolean[] dp = new boolean[1 << n];
        dp[0] = true;

        for (int mask = 0; mask < (1 << n); mask++) {
            int sum = 0;
            for (int i = 0; i < n; i++) {
                if ((mask & (1 << i)) != 0) {
                    sum += nums[i];
                }
            }
            if (sum == target) {
                return true;
            }
        }
        return false;
    }

    public static void main(String[] args) {
        int[] nums = {3, 1, 4, 2, 2};
        int target = 6;
        System.out.println("Subset sum exists: " + subsetSum(nums, target));
    }
}
```

In the subset sum example above, a boolean array dp of size 2^n (where n is the number of elements in the set) is used to track achievable sums. Each integer from 0 to $2^n - 1$ represents a subset. The sum corresponding to each subset is computed by iterating through all possible subsets using bitwise operations.

Key bitwise operations include:

- Bitwise AND (&): Used to check whether a specific bit is set in a number. - Bitwise OR (|): Used to set a specific bit in a number. - Bitwise XOR (^): Used to toggle specific bits. - Bitwise NOT (~): Used to invert bits. - Bitwise shift left («) and right (»): Used for shifting bits to the left or right, effectively multiplying or dividing by powers of two.

These operators are crucial to efficiently manage the states and transitions in DP algorithms.

```
import java.util.Arrays;

public class TravelingSalesman {
    private static final int INF = 1 << 29;

    public static int tsp(int[][] dist) {
        int n = dist.length;
        int[][] dp = new int[1 << n][n];

        for (int[] row : dp) {
            Arrays.fill(row, INF);
        }

        dp[1][0] = 0;
```

```
        for (int mask = 1; mask < (1 << n); mask++) {
            for (int u = 0; u < n; u++) {
                if ((mask & (1 << u)) != 0) {
                    for (int v = 0; v < n; v++) {
                        if ((mask & (1 << v)) == 0) {
                            int nextMask = mask | (1 << v);
                            dp[nextMask][v] = Math.min(dp[nextMask][v], dp[mask][u] +
                                dist[u][v]);
                        }
                    }
                }
            }
        }

        int result = INF;
        for (int i = 1; i < n; i++) {
            result = Math.min(result, dp[(1 << n) - 1][i] + dist[i][0]);
        }

        return result;
    }

    public static void main(String[] args) {
        int[][] dist = {
            {0, 10, 15, 20},
            {10, 0, 35, 25},
            {15, 35, 0, 30},
            {20, 25, 30, 0}
        };

        System.out.println("The minimum cost of traveling salesperson: " + tsp(dist));
    }
}
```

In the Traveling Salesman Problem (TSP) example, an adjacency matrix dist represents the costs between cities. The 2-dimensional DP array, dp, is indexed by a bitmask representing the set of visited cities and the last city visited. The goal is to find the minimum cost to visit all cities exactly once and to return to the starting city.

The bitmask iteration efficiently explores all possible states. The base case initializes visiting only the starting city. The transitive property updates the DP table by considering all transitions to unvisited cities, updating their respective mask. The solution emerges from iterating through the final set of all visited cities to return to the starting city.

This dual approach of integrating bitwise operations with dynamic programming enables efficient solutions to numerous combinatorial problems. The reduction in complexity stems from efficient state representation and rapid transitions between states. Recognizing problems that benefit from this technique and applying it can lead to significant performance improvements and broaden the scope of solvable challenges.

8.10 Memory Optimization Techniques

Memory optimization in dynamic programming involves various strategies to minimize the overall space complexity of an algorithm. Reducing memory usage can significantly enhance the performance of programs, particularly when handling large datasets or operating within memory-constrained environments. This section explores several techniques to optimize memory consumption.

One prevalent method for memory optimization is the use of **space-efficient tables**. In many dynamic programming (DP) problems, it is unnecessary to store all intermediate values. Often, only a limited number of previous states are required to compute the current state. By keeping track of only the necessary states, substantial memory savings can be achieved.

```
public class Fibonacci {
    public static int fibonacciOptimized(int n) {
        if (n <= 1) return n;
        int prev1 = 0, prev2 = 1;
        for (int i = 2; i <= n; i++) {
            int current = prev1 + prev2;
            prev1 = prev2;
            prev2 = current;
        }
        return prev2;
    }
}
```

In the above example, the traditional DP approach that uses an array of size $O(n)$ is optimized to $O(1)$ space complexity by maintaining only the last two computed values.

Another crucial technique is **memoization with intelligent cache clearing**. By periodically clearing or limiting the size of the memoization cache, memory usage can be controlled effectively. However, this approach requires careful consideration of the trade-offs between recomputation cost and memory savings.

```
import java.util.HashMap;
import java.util.Map;

public class FibonacciWithCaching {
    private Map<Integer, Integer> cache = new HashMap<>();
    private static final int CACHE_SIZE_LIMIT = 1000;

    public int fibonacci(int n) {
        if (n <= 1) return n;
        if (cache.containsKey(n)) return cache.get(n);

        int result = fibonacci(n - 1) + fibonacci(n - 2);
        if (cache.size() >= CACHE_SIZE_LIMIT) {
```

```
            cache.clear(); // Clear cache periodically to save memory
        }
        cache.put(n, result);
        return result;
    }
}
```

Here, the 'HashMap' serves as the memoization cache, and the cache is cleared when it reaches a predefined limit, thereby ensuring memory constraints are adhered to.

Bit manipulation is another method to optimize memory usage. By using bits to represent states or compact information, the memory footprint can be significantly reduced. This technique is especially useful in problems involving combinatorial states or large integer ranges.

```
public class SubsetSum {
    public static boolean canPartition(int[] nums) {
        int total = 0;
        for (int num : nums) total += num;
        if (total % 2 != 0) return false;

        int target = total / 2;
        int n = nums.length;
        int[] dp = new int[target + 1];
        dp[0] = 1;

        for (int num : nums) {
            for (int i = target; i >= num; i--) {
                dp[i] |= dp[i - num];
            }
        }
        return dp[target] == 1;
    }
}
```

In the code, bitwise operations are used to minimize memory usage while achieving the goal of computing subset sums.

Another effective technique is **sparse table optimization**. This involves exploiting the sparsity of data structures to use memory more efficiently. Techniques such as pointer-based data structures or compressed storage formats can be adapted for dynamic programming tables.

```
public class RangeMinimumQuery {
    private int[][] sparseTable;
    private int[] log;

    public RangeMinimumQuery(int[] array) {
        int n = array.length;
        int maxJ = (int) (Math.log(n) / Math.log(2)) + 1;
        sparseTable = new int[n][maxJ];
        log = new int[n + 1];
```

```
        for (int i = 2; i <= n; i++) log[i] = log[i/2] + 1;
        for (int i = 0; i < n; i++) sparseTable[i][0] = array[i];
        for (int j = 1; j <= maxJ; j++) {
            for (int i = 0; i + (1 << j) - 1 < n; i++) {
                sparseTable[i][j] = Math.min(sparseTable[i][j-1], sparseTable[i + (1 << (j
                        -1))][j-1]);
            }
        }
    }

    public int query(int L, int R) {
        int j = log[R - L + 1];
        return Math.min(sparseTable[L][j], sparseTable[R - (1 << j) + 1][j]);
    }
}
```

In this example, sparse table construction and query functions for Range Minimum Query utilize logarithmic indexing, which reduces the overall memory footprint compared to a naive approach.

Lastly, **rolling arrays** can be employed in certain DP problems to further optimize space utilization. This involves the use of one-dimensional arrays to store states and updating them iteratively, ensuring that only necessary information is captured at any point in time.

```
public class Knapsack {
    public static int knapsack(int[] weights, int[] values, int W) {
        int n = weights.length;
        int[] dp = new int[W + 1];

        for (int i = 0; i < n; i++) {
            for (int w = W; w >= weights[i]; w--) {
                dp[w] = Math.max(dp[w], dp[w - weights[i]] + values[i]);
            }
        }
        return dp[W];
    }
}
```

In the 0/1 Knapsack problem, the space complexity is optimized by using a rolling array 'dp', which gets updated in place, reducing memory usage from $O(W \times n)$ to $O(W)$.

These techniques provide robust strategies for improving the efficiency of dynamic programming algorithms, making them more suitable for large-scale problems and memory-constrained environments.

8.11 Dynamic Programming in Competitive Programming

Dynamic Programming (DP) is a fundamental paradigm in competitive programming that allows for efficient solutions to problems involving optimal substructure and overlapping subproblems. In this section, we will explore several key aspects and techniques related to DP in the competitive programming arena, providing detailed examples and best practices to aid in mastering these concepts.

Competitive programming problems often demand real-time, efficient solutions due to stringent time and memory constraints. DP serves as a vital tool in these scenarios by breaking down complex problems into simpler subproblems and solving them systematically.

Problem Identification: The first step in applying DP in competitive programming is the identification of problems that can benefit from this technique. Common characteristics of DP-suitable problems include:

- **Optimal Substructure:** The optimal solution to a problem can be constructed from optimal solutions to its subproblems.
- **Overlapping Subproblems:** The problem can be broken down into subproblems that are reused multiple times.

Example: Consider the problem of finding the maximum sum subarray (Kadane's Algorithm). It involves finding a contiguous subarray with the maximum sum within a one-dimensional numeric array.

```
public class KadanesAlgorithm {
    public static int maxSubArraySum(int[] arr) {
        int maxSoFar = arr[0];
        int maxEndingHere = arr[0];
        for (int i = 1; i < arr.length; i++) {
            maxEndingHere = Math.max(arr[i], maxEndingHere + arr[i]);
            maxSoFar = Math.max(maxSoFar, maxEndingHere);
        }
        return maxSoFar;
    }

    public static void main(String[] args) {
        int[] array = {-2, 1, -3, 4, -1, 2, 1, -5, 4};
        System.out.println("Maximum subarray sum is " + maxSubArraySum(array));
    }
}
```

```
Maximum subarray sum is 6
```

In this example, the subproblem is to find the maximum sum subarray that ends at each position of the array.

State Representation: Accurate state representation is crucial in DP. For competitive programming, defining state variables that encompass all necessary information to transition from one state to another is fundamental. In the Longest Common Subsequence (LCS) problem, the DP state can be defined as dp[i][j], representing the length of the LCS of substrings s1[0..i-1] and s2[0..j-1].

```
public class LongestCommonSubsequence {
    public static int lcs(String s1, String s2) {
        int m = s1.length();
        int b = s2.length();
        int[][] dp = new int[m + 1][b + 1];

        // Building the dp matrix in bottom-up way
        for (int i = 1; i <= m; i++) {
            for (int j = 1; j <= b; j++) {
                if (s1.charAt(i - 1) == s2.charAt(j - 1)) {
                    dp[i][j] = dp[i - 1][j - 1] + 1;
                } else {
                    dp[i][j] = Math.max(dp[i - 1][j], dp[i][j - 1]);
                }
            }
        }
        return dp[m][b];
    }

    public static void main(String[] args) {
        String s1 = "AGGTAB";
        String s2 = "GXTXAYB";
        System.out.println("Length of LCS is " + lcs(s1, s2));
    }
}
```

```
Length of LCS is 4
```

Memoization vs Tabulation: Another vital aspect in competitive programming is choosing between memoization (top-down approach) and tabulation (bottom-up approach). While memoization is easier to write and debug, tabulation often provides better space and time efficiency and is consequently favored in performance-critical contexts.

Example: Memoization for Fibonacci Sequence

```
import java.util.HashMap;
import java.util.Map;

public class FibonacciMemoization {
    private static Map<Integer, Integer> memo = new HashMap<>();

    public static int fib(int n) {
        if (n <= 1) return n;
        if (memo.containsKey(n)) return memo.get(n);

        int result = fib(n - 1) + fib(n - 2);
        memo.put(n, result);
```

```
        return result;
    }

    public static void main(String[] args) {
        System.out.println("Fibonacci of 10 is " + fib(10));
    }
}
```

Fibonacci of 10 is 55

Example: Tabulation for Fibonacci Sequence

```
public class FibonacciTabulation {
    public static int fib(int n) {
        if (n <= 1) return n;
        int[] dp = new int[n + 1];
        dp[0] = 0;
        dp[1] = 1;

        for (int i = 2; i <= n; i++) {
            dp[i] = dp[i - 1] + dp[i - 2];
        }
        return dp[n];
    }

    public static void main(String[] args) {
        System.out.println("Fibonacci of 10 is " + fib(10));
    }
}
```

Fibonacci of 10 is 55

Optimization Techniques: Memory and time optimization are critical when dealing with large datasets. Techniques such as state compression, efficient state transitions, and in-place updates can significantly enhance DP performance. For instance, the space complexity of DP solutions that utilize a 2D array can often be reduced to linear space by observing that only the current and previous rows are needed.

```
public class FibonacciOptimized {
    public static int fib(int n) {
        if (n <= 1) return n;
        int prev2 = 0, prev1 = 1;
        int current = 0;

        for (int i = 2; i <= n; i++) {
            current = prev1 + prev2;
            prev2 = prev1;
            prev1 = current;
        }
        return current;
    }

    public static void main(String[] args) {
        System.out.println("Fibonacci of 10 is " + fib(10));
    }
}
```

Fibonacci of 10 is 55

Practice and Application: Lastly, consistent practice with a range of problems is crucial. Competitive programming platforms such as Codeforces, LeetCode, and AtCoder regularly feature DP problems that vary in complexity and domain, providing fertile ground for honing DP skills.

By applying these advanced DP techniques, competitive programmers can tackle a wide array of complex problems efficiently, significantly enhancing their problem-solving acumen and competitiveness in contests.

8.12 Advanced Practice Problems and Solutions

This section presents advanced problems that leverage the techniques discussed throughout the chapter to consolidate understanding and build proficiency. Each problem is followed by a solution that explains the thought process and the code implementation.

Problem 1: Maximum Path Sum in a Tree

Given a binary tree, find the maximum path sum. The path may start and end at any node in the tree; it must contain at least one node, and the path does not need to go through the root.

```
class TreeNode {
    int val;
    TreeNode left;
    TreeNode right;
    TreeNode(int x) {
        val = x;
    }
}

public class MaxPathSum {
    private int maxSum = Integer.MIN_VALUE;

    public int maxPathSum(TreeNode root) {
        getMaxSum(root);
        return maxSum;
    }

    private int getMaxSum(TreeNode node) {
        if (node == null) return 0;

        int leftGain = Math.max(getMaxSum(node.left), 0);
        int rightGain = Math.max(getMaxSum(node.right), 0);

        int priceNewPath = node.val + leftGain + rightGain;
```

```
        maxSum = Math.max(maxSum, priceNewPath);

        return node.val + Math.max(leftGain, rightGain);
    }
}
```

The solution employs depth-first search (DFS) to explore all paths and keeps track of the maximum path sum encountered during the recursion. The function getMaxSum(TreeNode node) is a helper function that computes the maximum gain from any node. The gain is either through the left child, the right child, or neither (if the gain is negative). The calculated path sum for the current node is compared to the stored maxSum, ensuring we get the highest value.

Problem 2: Counting Subsets With a Given Sum Using Bitmask DP

Given an array of integers and a target sum, count the number of subsets that sum up to the given sum.

```
public class CountSubsetsWithSum {
    public int countSubsets(int[] nums, int target) {
        int n = nums.length;
        int[] dp = new int[target + 1];

        dp[0] = 1;

        for (int num : nums) {
            for (int j = target; j >= num; j--) {
                dp[j] += dp[j - num];
            }
        }

        return dp[target];
    }
}
```

This problem is solved using the bitmasking technique. Here, dp[j] keeps track of the number of subsets that can achieve the sum j. Initially, dp[0] is set to 1 because there is exactly one way to achieve a sum of 0, which is to select no elements. When considering each number, we update the dynamic programming array in reverse order to avoid over-counting the same number within the subset.

Problem 3: Largest Rectangle in Histogram Using Divide and Conquer

Given an array representing the heights of bars in a histogram, find the area of the largest rectangle that can be formed within these bars.

```
public class LargestRectangleInHistogram {
    public int largestRectangleArea(int[] heights) {
        return calculateArea(heights, 0, heights.length - 1);
```

```
    }

    private int calculateArea(int[] heights, int start, int end) {
        if (start > end) return 0;

        int minIndex = start;
        for (int i = start; i <= end; i++) {
            if (heights[i] < heights[minIndex]) {
                minIndex = i;
            }
        }

        int maxArea = heights[minIndex] * (end - start + 1);
        maxArea = Math.max(maxArea, calculateArea(heights, start, minIndex - 1));
        maxArea = Math.max(maxArea, calculateArea(heights, minIndex + 1, end));

        return maxArea;
    }
}
```

This problem utilizes a divide and conquer approach. The function calculateArea calculates the largest rectangle area within a given portion of the histogram. By finding the bar with the minimum height within the current segment, it simplifies the calculation of the maximum rectangle that includes that bar. It then recursively calculates the areas for the left and right segments divided by this minimum bar to find the largest possible area.

Problem 4: Shortest Path in a Graph Using DP

Given a weighted, directed graph represented as an adjacency matrix, find the shortest path between every pair of vertices using dynamic programming.

```
public class FloydWarshall {
    final static int INF = 99999, V = 4;

    void floydWarshall(int graph[][]) {
        int dist[][] = new int[V][V];

        for (int i = 0; i < V; i++) {
            for (int j = 0; j < V; j++) {
                dist[i][j] = graph[i][j];
            }
        }

        for (int k = 0; k < V; k++) {
            for (int i = 0; i < V; i++) {
                for (int j = 0; j < V; j++) {
                    if (dist[i][k] + dist[k][j] < dist[i][j])
                        dist[i][j] = dist[i][k] + dist[k][j];
                }
            }
        }

        printSolution(dist);
    }
```

```
    void printSolution(int dist[][]) {
        for (int i = 0; i < V; i++) {
            for (int j = 0; j < V; j++) {
                if (dist[i][j] == INF)
                    System.out.print("INF ");
                else
                    System.out.print(dist[i][j] + " ");
            }
            System.out.println();
        }
    }

    public static void main(String[] args) {
        int graph[][] = { {0, 5, INF, 10},
                          {INF, 0, 3, INF},
                          {INF, INF, 0, 1},
                          {INF, INF, INF, 0} };

        FloydWarshall fw = new FloydWarshall();
        fw.floydWarshall(graph);
    }
}
```

The Floyd-Warshall algorithm computes the shortest paths between all pairs of vertices. The implementation initializes the distances with the given adjacency matrix. Then it iteratively updates the distance between each pair of vertices by considering all possible paths through intermediate vertices. This continues until no further updates are possible, resulting in the shortest path matrix for all pairs of vertices.

The four problems described exemplify the application of various dynamic programming techniques in handling complex scenarios. These solutions intermixed intricate logic with straightforward coding practices, effectively showcasing the power and versatility of dynamic programming in problem-solving contexts.

Chapter 9

Applications of Dynamic Programming

This chapter explores the diverse applications of dynamic programming across various fields. It covers its use in computer science, operations research, stock market analysis, game theory, and bioinformatics. Additional applications in natural language processing, image and signal processing, robotics, economics, and supply chain optimization are discussed. The chapter includes case studies that demonstrate dynamic programming's impact in e-commerce, cloud computing, healthcare, finance, and telecommunications, highlighting its practical relevance and versatility in solving real-world problems.

9.1 Introduction to Applications of Dynamic Programming

Dynamic programming (DP) is a critical algorithmic technique utilized for solving complex problems by breaking them down into simpler subproblems. This method is particularly effective when the subproblems overlap, as it stores the results of subproblems to avoid redundant computations. The essence of dynamic programming lies in its ability to optimize problems by exploiting these overlapping subproblems, leading to significant improvements in computational efficiency.

Within the field of computer science, dynamic programming has revolutionized the way complex algorithmic challenges are approached. It is widely implemented in various algorithmic problems, such as shortest path algorithms, string edit distance computations, and combinatorial optimization problems. For example, Dijkstra's and Floyd-Warshall's algorithms for the shortest path are classic illustrations of dynamic programming in action.

In operations research, dynamic programming is employed in solving decision-making problems where a sequence of interrelated decisions must be made over time. Examples include resource allocation problems, inventory management, and project scheduling. Dynamic programming aids in determining optimal policies that maximize or minimize an objective function, considering the constraints and uncertainties inherent in these domains.

Stock market analysis benefits greatly from dynamic programming techniques, particularly in the context of portfolio optimization and option pricing. For instance, the binomial model for option pricing utilizes dynamic programming to compute the fair price of an option by working backwards from expiration to the present. Similarly, dynamic programming helps in determining the optimal investment strategy by evaluating potential future states and their returns.

Game theory and strategy optimization are other areas where dynamic programming plays an essential role. The minimax algorithm, enhanced with alpha-beta pruning, leverages dynamic programming principles to optimally navigate game trees, thereby optimizing strategic decisions in competitive environments such as chess and other strategy games.

Bioinformatics, a rapidly evolving field, extensively employs dynamic programming for sequence alignment and protein folding problems. Algorithms like the Needleman-Wunsch and Smith-Waterman are prime examples of dynamic programming applied to global and local sequence alignment tasks, respectively. These algorithms enable researchers to compare DNA, RNA, and protein sequences efficiently, thus aiding in genomic studies and medical diagnostics.

Dynamic programming also underpins various applications in natural language processing (NLP). Tasks such as text segmentation, parsing, and machine translation often rely on dynamic programming techniques to handle the complexity and variability of human language. The Viterbi algorithm, for instance, is a dynamic programming algorithm used for decoding the most likely sequence of hidden states in hidden

Markov models (HMM), essential for speech recognition and part-of-speech tagging.

In image and signal processing, dynamic programming helps in tasks ranging from image segmentation and object recognition to signal denoising and time-series analysis. Techniques like dynamic time warping (DTW) are used to measure similarities between two temporal sequences, which is applicable in speech recognition and other signal matching problems.

Robotics and pathfinding algorithms also benefit from dynamic programming. Algorithms such as A* and D* search are designed to navigate robots through complex environments by considering the costs associated with different paths, thus finding the most efficient route from start to goal locations.

Economics and decision making often invoke dynamic programming models to address problems of optimal consumption and investment over time. The Bellman equation is a cornerstone of such models, providing a recursive solution framework for determining the optimal policy by considering the trade-off between immediate and future rewards.

In supply chain and logistics optimization, dynamic programming assists in solving problems related to inventory control, transportation logistics, and demand forecasting. By modeling the supply chain as a network of stages and employing dynamic programming techniques, optimal policies can be devised to minimize costs or maximize service levels.

Case studies in e-commerce, cloud computing, healthcare, finance, and telecommunications illustrate dynamic programming's importance and versatility in solving real-world problems. For instance, in e-commerce, dynamic programming can optimize recommendation systems and pricing strategies. In cloud computing, it facilitates efficient resource allocation and load balancing. In healthcare, it aids in medical diagnosis and treatment planning by integrating predictive models with patient data. In finance, dynamic programming underlies risk management and derivative pricing models. Finally, in telecommunications, it helps optimize network performance and resource allocation.

Dynamic programming's applicability across these diverse fields underscores its utility as a powerful tool for optimization, decision making, and problem-solving.

9.2 Dynamic Programming in Computer Science

Dynamic Programming (DP) has a profound impact on many areas within computer science. This technique, which relies on solving complex problems by breaking them down into simpler subproblems, offers significant advantages in optimizing algorithms and achieving computational efficiency. This section delves into the applications of dynamic programming in various computer science domains, showcasing its versatility and importance.

Algorithm Optimization

One of the primary uses of dynamic programming in computer science is to optimize algorithms. Problems that exhibit the properties of overlapping subproblems and optimal substructure are particularly suitable for DP solutions. Overlapping subproblems mean that the same subproblems are solved multiple times, and optimal substructure indicates that an optimal solution to a problem can be constructed from optimal solutions to its subproblems.

A quintessential example of algorithm optimization through dynamic programming is the **Fibonacci sequence**. The naive recursive approach for computing the nth Fibonacci number has exponential time complexity due to repeated calculations. Leveraging dynamic programming, we can store the results of solved subproblems to avoid redundant calculations, thus reducing the time complexity to linear.

```
public class Fibonacci {
    public static long fibonacciDP(int n) {
        if (n <= 1) return n;
        long[] fib = new long[n + 1];
        fib[0] = 0;
        fib[1] = 1;
        for (int i = 2; i <= n; i++) {
            fib[i] = fib[i-1] + fib[i-2];
        }
        return fib[n];
    }

    public static void main(String[] args) {
        int n = 50;
        System.out.println("Fibonacci number " + n + " is " + fibonacciDP(n));
    }
}
```

String Processing

String processing problems often involve dynamic programming. The classic problem of **longest common subsequence (LCS)** is a shining example. Given two sequences, the LCS problem aims to find the longest subsequence present in both sequences, which can be solved efficiently using dynamic programming.

The LCS problem can be defined as follows: Given two sequences $X = x_1, x_2, \ldots, x_m$ and $Y = y_1, y_2, \ldots, y_n$, we seek the length of the longest subsequence that is common to both X and Y.

```
public class LongestCommonSubsequence {

    public static int lcs(char[] X, char[] Y) {
        int m = X.length;
        int n = Y.length;
        int[][] L = new int[m + 1][n + 1];

        for (int i = 0; i <= m; i++) {
            for (int j = 0; j <= n; j++) {
                if (i == 0 || j == 0)
                    L[i][j] = 0;
                else if (X[i - 1] == Y[j - 1])
                    L[i][j] = L[i - 1][j - 1] + 1;
                else
                    L[i][j] = Math.max(L[i - 1][j], L[i][j - 1]);
            }
        }
        return L[m][n];
    }

    public static void main(String[] args) {
        String s1 = "AGGTAB";
        String s2 = "GXTXAYB";
        System.out.println("Length of LCS is " + lcs(s1.toCharArray(), s2.toCharArray
            ()));
    }
}
```

Graph Algorithms

Dynamic programming also excels in various graph algorithms. One of the most notable is the **shortest path problem**, specifically the Floyd-Warshall algorithm, which finds shortest paths between all pairs of vertices in a given weighted edge graph.

The Floyd-Warshall algorithm iteratively updates the shortest path between every pair of vertices during each iteration by considering vertices as intermediate points. This approach ensures that the most efficient path is computed, reflecting the powerful application of dynamic programming to simplify complex challenges.

```
public class FloydWarshall {

    final static int INF = 99999;
    public void floydWarshall(int[][] graph) {
        int V = graph.length;
```

```
        int[][] dist = new int[V][V];

        for (int i = 0; i < V; i++)
            for (int j = 0; j < V; j++)
                dist[i][j] = graph[i][j];

        for (int k = 0; k < V; k++) {
            for (int i = 0; i < V; i++) {
                for (int j = 0; j < V; j++) {
                    if (dist[i][j] > dist[i][k] + dist[k][j])
                        dist[i][j] = dist[i][k] + dist[k][j];
                }
            }
        }
        printSolution(dist);
    }

    void printSolution(int[][] dist) {
        int V = dist.length;
        System.out.println("The following matrix shows the shortest "+
                         "distances between every pair of vertices");
        for (int i=0; i<V; ++i) {
            for (int j=0; j<V; ++j) {
                if (dist[i][j]==INF)
                    System.out.print("INF ");
                else
                    System.out.print(dist[i][j]+" ");
            }
            System.out.println();
        }
    }

    public static void main (String[] args) {
        int graph[][] = { {0, 5, INF, 10},
                          {INF, 0, 3, INF},
                          {INF, INF, 0, 1},
                          {INF, INF, INF, 0} };
        FloydWarshall a = new FloydWarshall();
        a.floydWarshall(graph);
    }
}
```

Data Structures

Dynamic programming also extends its utility to enhance data structures, such as segment trees and Fenwick trees, which are essential for range queries and updates. These structures leverage DP principles to maintain and query data over intervals efficiently, proving pivotal in scenarios requiring prompt read and update operations.

The above illustrations show that integrating dynamic programming into computer science methodologies transforms solving traditional computational problems into a more efficient and manageable process.

9.3 Dynamic Programming in Operations Research

Operations Research (OR) utilizes mathematical methods to optimize decision-making, resource allocation, and logistics within various organizational processes. Dynamic programming is a vital tool in this domain due to its ability to break down complex, multi-stage decision problems into simpler stages, solving each in sequence to reach an optimal solution.

One of the primary applications of dynamic programming in operations research is in solving the knapsack problem. This problem involves selecting a subset of items, each with a given weight and value, to maximize the total value without exceeding a weight limit. The 0/1 knapsack problem is a specific case where each item can either be included or excluded from the knapsack.

```
public class Knapsack {
    // Function to solve 0/1 Knapsack Problem
    public static int knapsack(int[] values, int[] weights, int W) {
        int n = values.length;
        int[][] dp = new int[n + 1][W + 1];

        // Iterate through all items
        for (int i = 1; i <= n; i++) {
            // Iterate through all weights from 0 to W
            for (int w = 0; w <= W; w++) {
                if (weights[i - 1] <= w) {
                    dp[i][w] = Math.max(values[i - 1] + dp[i - 1][w - weights[i - 1]], dp[i -
                        1][w]);
                } else {
                    dp[i][w] = dp[i - 1][w];
                }
            }
        }
        return dp[n][W];
    }

    public static void main(String[] args) {
        int[] values = {60, 100, 120};
        int[] weights = {10, 20, 30};
        int W = 50;
        System.out.println("Maximum value in Knapsack = " + knapsack(values,
            weights, W));
    }
}
```

```
Output:
Maximum value in Knapsack = 220
```

In the context of operations research, dynamic programming also addresses the optimal allocation of resources in project management via the Project Scheduling with Time-Constraints (PSTC). This involves scheduling activities within a project to complete it in the shortest time under given constraints, such as limited availability of resources.

Another crucial application is the shortest path problem, which finds the shortest path in a network, like transportation or communication networks. One classical algorithm to solve this is the Bellman-Ford algorithm, which can handle negative edge weights and detect negative cycles.

```
import java.util.Arrays;

public class BellmanFord {
    static class Edge {
        int src, dest, weight;
        Edge() {
            src = dest = weight = 0;
        }
    }

    // Function to find the shortest path using Bellman-Ford
    public static void bellmanFord(Edge[] edges, int V, int E, int src) {
        int[] distance = new int[V];
        Arrays.fill(distance, Integer.MAX_VALUE);
        distance[src] = 0;

        // Relax all edges |V| - 1 times
        for (int i = 1; i < V; i++) {
            for (int j = 0; j < E; j++) {
                int u = edges[j].src;
                int v = edges[j].dest;
                int weight = edges[j].weight;
                if (distance[u] != Integer.MAX_VALUE && distance[u] + weight <
                        distance[v]) {
                    distance[v] = distance[u] + weight;
                }
            }
        }

        // Check for negative-weight cycles
        for (int j = 0; j < E; j++) {
            int u = edges[j].src;
            int v = edges[j].dest;
            int weight = edges[j].weight;
            if (distance[u] != Integer.MAX_VALUE && distance[u] + weight < distance
                    [v]) {
                System.out.println("Graph contains negative weight cycle");
                return;
            }
        }

        // Print distances
        printArr(distance, V);
    }

    // Utility function to print distances
    public static void printArr(int[] dist, int V) {
        System.out.println("Vertex Distance from Source");
        for (int i = 0; i < V; i++) {
            System.out.println(i + "\t\t" + dist[i]);
        }
```

```
    }
    public static void main(String[] args) {
        int V = 5; // Number of vertices in graph
        int E = 8; // Number of edges in graph

        Edge[] edges = new Edge[E];
        for (int i = 0; i < E; i++) {
            edges[i] = new Edge();
        }

        // add edge 0-1 (or A-B in above figure)
        edges[0].src = 0;
        edges[0].dest = 1;
        edges[0].weight = -1;

        // add edge 0-2 (or A-C in above figure)
        edges[1].src = 0;
        edges[1].dest = 2;
        edges[1].weight = 4;

        // add edge 1-2 (or B-C in above figure)
        edges[2].src = 1;
        edges[2].dest = 2;
        edges[2].weight = 3;

        // add edge 1-3 (or B-D in above figure)
        edges[3].src = 1;
        edges[3].dest = 3;
        edges[3].weight = 2;

        // add edge 1-4 (or B-E in above figure)
        edges[4].src = 1;
        edges[4].dest = 4;
        edges[4].weight = 2;

        // add edge 3-2 (or D-C in above figure)
        edges[5].src = 3;
        edges[5].dest = 2;
        edges[5].weight = 5;

        // add edge 3-1 (or D-B in above figure)
        edges[6].src = 3;
        edges[6].dest = 1;
        edges[6].weight = 1;

        // add edge 4-3 (or E-D in above figure)
        edges[7].src = 4;
        edges[7].dest = 3;
        edges[7].weight = -3;

        bellmanFord(edges, V, E, 0); // Print shortest paths from vertex 0
    }
}
```

```
Output:
Vertex Distance from Source
0      0
1      -1
2      2
3      -2
4      1
```

Dynamic programming also features prominently in the network flow problems, specifically in the Minimum Cost Flow (MCF) problem. The goal here is to find the cheapest possible way of sending a certain amount of flow through a flow network.

These examples elucidate how dynamic programming provides efficient and effective solutions to various complex problems in operations research. It addresses issues related to resource allocation, scheduling, and optimization in a variety of real-world scenarios, showcasing its importance and utility in the field.

9.4 Stock Market Analysis and Decisions

Dynamic programming (DP) proves to be a vital tool in the analysis and decision-making processes associated with the stock market. Its capability to solve complex problems by breaking them down into simpler subproblems is particularly beneficial in financial contexts where multifaceted interactions and temporal dependencies are prevalent. This section delves into the applications of dynamic programming in optimizing stock market investments, including the principles of portfolio optimization, the valuation of options, and the execution of trading strategies.

The core idea of applying dynamic programming in stock market analysis involves modeling investment problems over a series of discrete time steps. By defining a set of states and decisions, we can recursively determine the optimal strategies that maximize returns or minimize risks.

We will explore the concept of the Markov Decision Process (MDP) in the context of stock trading, where each state represents the market conditions and portfolio holdings at a given time. The decisions correspond to potential actions an investor can take, such as buying, selling, or holding stocks. The objective is to find a policy that maximizes the expected reward (profit) over a specified horizon.

1. Portfolio Optimization

In the context of portfolio optimization, dynamic programming can be used to allocate resources across different assets over time to achieve the maximum expected return for a given level of risk. Consider a simplified model with the following notation:

- S_t: Stock price at time t - x_t: Amount of money invested in the stock at time t - r_t: Return of the stock at time t - N: Total investment horizon

The investor's objective is to maximize the expected logarithmic utility of wealth at the end of the investment horizon. The dynamic programming approach breaks down this problem into stages, solving from the end of the investment horizon backwards to the present time.

The Bellman equation for the portfolio optimization problem in this scenario can be represented as:

$$V_t(W_t) = \max_{x_t} \mathbb{E}\left[V_{t+1}(W_{t+1}) \mid W_t\right]$$

where W_t is the investor's wealth at time t, and $V_t(W_t)$ is the value function representing the maximum expected utility from wealth at time t.

```
public class PortfolioOptimization {
    private int N; // Investment horizon
    private double[] stockPrices; // Sto“‘ck prices over time
    private double[] returns; // Stock returns over time
    private double[] wealth; // Wealth over time

    public PortfolioOptimization(int N, double[] stockPrices, double[] returns) {
        this.N = N;
        this.stockPrices = stockPrices;
        this.returns = returns;
        this.wealth = new double[N + 1];
    }

    public double optimize() {
        for (int t = N - 1; t >= 0; t--) {
            double maxUtility = Double.NEGATIVE_INFINITY;
            for (double x_t = 0.0; x_t <= wealth[t]; x_t += 0.01) {
                double W_t1 = wealth[t] + x_t * returns[t];
                double utility = Math.log(W_t1);
                maxUtility = Math.max(maxUtility, utility);
            }
            wealth[t] = maxUtility;
        }
        return wealth[0];
    }
}
```

2. Option Valuation

Option valuation is another area where dynamic programming excels. The concept involves determining the fair price of financial derivatives like options. The well-known Black-Scholes model provides a continuous-time framework, but dynamic programming can be applied through a discrete-time approach using binomial or trinomial trees.

In a binomial tree model, the price of the underlying asset can move to one of two possible values over a small interval of time: an up value uS_t or a down value dS_t. The option price is computed by working backwards from the expiration date to the present, applying risk-neutral valuation at each node.

The recursive relationship in dynamic programming for option valuation is:

$$C_t = e^{-r\Delta t}(pC_u + (1-p)C_d)$$

where C_t is the option value at time t, C_u and C_d are the option values at the up and down states respectively, r is the risk-free interest rate, Δt is the time step, and p is the probability of the up move.

```
public class OptionValuation {
    private int steps; // Number of time steps
    private double S0; // Initial stock price
    private double K; // Strike price
    private double r; // Risk-free interest rate
    private double T; // Time to maturity
    private double sigma; // Volatility
    private double dt; // Time step duration
    private double up; // Up factor
    private double down; // Down factor
    private double p; // Probability of up move

    public OptionValuation(int steps, double S0, double K, double r, double T, double
        sigma) {
        this.steps = steps;
        this.S0 = S0;
        this.K = K;
        this.r = r;
        this.T = T;
        this.sigma = sigma;
        this.dt = T / steps;
        this.up = Math.exp(sigma * Math.sqrt(dt));
        this.down = 1 / up;
        this.p = (Math.exp(r * dt) - down) / (up - down);
    }

    public double priceOption() {
        double[] optionPrices = new double[steps + 1];

        for (int i = 0; i <= steps; i++) {
            optionPrices[i] = Math.max(0, S0 * Math.pow(up, steps - i) * Math.pow(
                    down, i) - K);
        }

        for (int t = steps - 1; t >= 0; t--) {
            for (int i = 0; i <= t; i++) {
                optionPrices[i] = Math.exp(-r * dt) * (p * optionPrices[i] + (1 - p) *
                        optionPrices[i + 1]);
            }
        }

        return optionPrices[0];
    }
}
```

3. Trading Strategies

Dynamic programming is instrumental in formulating and optimizing trading strategies. Consider a trader who aims to maximize profit over a trading horizon by making decisions to buy, sell, or hold a stock based on price predictions.

An optimal trading strategy can be determined through dynamic programming by modeling the problem as follows: - Define states as the combination of time and stock condition (e.g., holding or not holding the stock). - Define actions: buy, sell, and hold. - Use a reward function based on the profit achieved through actions.

The value function V_t represents the maximum expected profit from time t to the end of the trading horizon under an optimal policy. The Bellman equation updates as new price information becomes available.

```
public class TradingStrategy {
    private int N; // Trading horizon
    private double[] prices; // Predicted stock prices

    public TradingStrategy(int N, double[] prices) {
        this.N = N;
        this.prices = prices;
    }

    public double maximizeProfit() {
        double[][] dp = new double[N + 1][2];

        dp[0][1] = -prices[0]; // Buy on the first day

        for (int t = 1; t < N; t++) {
            dp[t][0] = Math.max(dp[t - 1][0], dp[t - 1][1] + prices[t]); // Max of holding
                or selling today
            dp[t][1] = Math.max(dp[t - 1][1], dp[t - 1][0] - prices[t]); // Max of not
                holding or buying today
        }

        return dp[N - 1][0]; // Final profit
    }
}
```

The examples provided illustrate the versatility of dynamic programming in handling various stock market analysis and decision-making scenarios, including portfolio optimization, option valuation, and trading strategy formulation. By methodically solving subproblems, dynamic programming models reveal optimal solutions that enhance investment decision-making efficacy.

9.5 Game Theory and Strategy Optimization

Game theory, a branch of mathematics and economics, deals with the strategic interactions among rational decision-makers. Dynamic programming is a fundamental tool in game theory, especially for problems involving sequential decisions and optimization strategies. This section delves into the utilization of dynamic programming to solve various strategic optimization problems in game theory. We will discuss the formulation of these problems, the underlying principles, and provide examples to illustrate the methodology.

Consider a two-player zero-sum game where two players take turns making moves. The goal of each player is to maximize their minimum guaranteed payoff, given the strategies of their opponent. Dynamic programming can efficiently manage the evaluation of the vast number of possible states and transitions in such games.

Minimax Algorithm: The minimax algorithm is a classic strategy applicable to two-player zero-sum games, such as chess or tic-tac-toe. The core idea is to minimize the possible loss for a worst-case scenario. When one player maximizes their outcome, the opponent follows by minimizing the first player's maximum possible gain. This problem can be presented recursively, with dynamic programming used to store intermediate results and avoid redundant calculations.

```
public class TicTacToe {
    static final int INF = 1_000_000; // Infinity for the context of extremum
        evaluation
    static final int SIZE = 3; // Tic-Tac-Toe board size
    static char[][] board = new char[SIZE][SIZE];

    /* Helper function to evaluate the board and return scores */
    static int evaluateBoard() {
        for (int row = 0; row < SIZE; row++) {
            if (board[row][0] == board[row][1] && board[row][1] == board[row][2]) {
                if (board[row][0] == 'X') return +10;
                else if (board[row][0] == 'O') return -10;
            }
        }

        for (int col = 0; col < SIZE; col++) {
            if (board[0][col] == board[1][col] && board[1][col] == board[2][col]) {
                if (board[0][col] == 'X') return +10;
                else if (board[0][col] == 'O') return -10;
            }
        }

        if (board[0][0] == board[1][1] && board[1][1] == board[2][2]) {
            if (board[0][0] == 'X') return +10;
            else if (board[0][0] == 'O') return -10;
        }

        if (board[0][2] == board[1][1] && board[1][1] == board[2][0]) {
            if (board[0][2] == 'X') return +10;
            else if (board[0][2] == 'O') return -10;
        }

        return 0; // No winner
    }
```

```
    /* Function to check if there are any moves left */
    static boolean isMovesLeft() {
        for (int i = 0; i < SIZE; i++)
            for (int j = 0; j < SIZE; j++)
                if (board[i][j] == '_')
                    return true;
        return false;
    }

    /* The main minimax function considering all depth levels and returning the best
        value */
    static int minimax(int depth, boolean isMax) {
        int score = evaluateBoard();

        if (score == 10) return score;
        if (score == -10) return score;
        if (!isMovesLeft()) return 0;

        if (isMax) {
            int best = -INF;
            for (int i = 0; i < SIZE; i++) {
                for (int j = 0; j < SIZE; j++) {
                    if (board[i][j] == '_') {
                        board[i][j] = 'X';
                        best = Math.max(best, minimax(depth + 1, !isMax));
                        board[i][j] = '_';
                    }
                }
            }
            return best;
        } else {
            int best = INF;
            for (int i = 0; i < SIZE; i++) {
                for (int j = 0; j < SIZE; j++) {
                    if (board[i][j] == '_') {
                        board[i][j] = 'O';
                        best = Math.min(best, minimax(depth + 1, !isMax));
                        board[i][j] = '_';
                    }
                }
            }
            return best;
        }
    }
}
```

In the above implementation, dynamic programming is employed to save intermediate state evaluations, especially in complex scenarios with deep game trees.

Bellman Equation in Game Theory: In many strategic scenarios, players make decisions over multiple stages, where the outcome of one stage affects subsequent stages. The Bellman equation provides a systematic way to approach these problems by breaking them down into simpler sub-problems. This recursive decomposition is central to dynamic programming.

Consider a multi-stage game where the decision-maker aims to maximize their utility. Let $V(s)$ represent the value of being in state s. For any action a, which transitions to the next state s', the Bellman equation can be written as:

$$V(s) = \max_a \left\{ R(s,a) + \sum_{s'} P(s'|s,a)V(s') \right\}$$

Here, $R(s,a)$ is the immediate reward for taking action a in state s, and $P(s'|s,a)$ is the probability of moving from state s to s' after action a. This recursive relationship allows us to construct the value function iteratively or recursively, ensuring optimal strategies are derived through dynamic programming.

```
public class MultiStageGame {
    static final int STATES = 5; // Number of states
    static final int ACTIONS = 3; // Number of actions
    static double[] values = new double[STATES];
    static double[][] rewards = {
        { 0, 1, 2 },
        { 1, 0, 3 },
        { 2, 3, 0 },
        { 4, 2, 1 },
        { 1, 3, 4 }
    };
    static double[][][] transitionProbs = {
        { { 0.5, 0.5, 0, 0, 0 }, { 0.7, 0, 0.3, 0, 0 }, { 0.2, 0, 0, 0.8, 0 } },
        { { 0.8, 0.2, 0, 0, 0 }, { 0.1, 0.8, 0.1, 0, 0 }, { 0, 0.5, 0, 0.5, 0 } },
        { { 0.3, 0, 0.7, 0, 0 }, { 0.1, 0.2, 0.7, 0, 0 }, { 0, 0, 0.4, 0.6, 0 } },
        { { 0.6, 0, 0, 0.4, 0 }, { 0.1, 0.2, 0.2, 0.5, 0 }, { 0, 0, 0.3, 0.7, 0 } },
        { { 0.2, 0, 0, 0, 0.8 }, { 0.1, 0, 0.3, 0, 0.6 }, { 0.3, 0.2, 0.1, 0.4, 0 } }
    };

    static void calculateValues() {
        for (int s = 0; s < STATES; s++) {
            for (int a = 0; a < ACTIONS; a++) {
                double value = 0;
                for (int sPrime = 0; sPrime < STATES; sPrime++) {
                    value += transitionProbs[s][a][sPrime] * values[sPrime];
                }
                values[s] = Math.max(values[s], rewards[s][a] + value);
            }
        }
    }

    public static void main(String[] args) {
        for (int i = 0; i < 100; i++) {
            calculateValues(); // Iterate multiple times for value convergence
        }
        for (int s = 0; s < STATES; s++) {
            System.out.println("Value of state " + s + ": " + values[s]);
        }
    }
}
```

When executed, the above algorithm calculates the optimal value for each state in the multi-stage game by recursively applying the Bellman equation until the values converge.

```
Value of state 0: 2.0201
Value of state 1: 2.56
Value of state 2: 2.28
Value of state 3: 4.124
Value of state 4: 3.142
```

These methods demonstrate dynamic programming's power in optimizing strategies for complex games, ensuring efficient and robust solutions even in intricate decision scenarios. Dynamic programming allows for the systematic exploration of state spaces and strategic interactions, redefining problem-solving in game theory.

9.6 Bioinformatics: Sequence Alignment

Sequence alignment is a critical technique in bioinformatics, enabling researchers to identify regions of similarity that may indicate functional, structural, or evolutionary relationships between sequences. Dynamic programming has become an indispensable tool for performing sequence alignments, given its capability to efficiently handle the computational complexity inherent in these tasks. In this section, we will explore how dynamic programming is applied to sequence alignment problems, focusing on the Needleman-Wunsch and Smith-Waterman algorithms.

Needleman-Wunsch Algorithm for Global Alignment

The Needleman-Wunsch algorithm, introduced in 1970, is a dynamic programming approach for achieving global alignment between two sequences. The objective is to find the best possible alignment over the entire length of the sequences.

Given two sequences $A = a_1, a_2, \ldots, a_m$ and $B = b_1, b_2, \ldots, b_n$, we define a scoring matrix S where $S(i, j)$ represents the score of the best alignment of the subsequences $A[1..i]$ and $B[1..j]$. The goal is to compute $S(m, n)$, the score of the optimal alignment of the entire sequences A and B.

The algorithm constructs the scoring matrix S using the following recurrence relations:

$$S(i,j) = \begin{cases} 0 & \text{if } i = 0 \text{ and } j = 0 \\ S(i-1,j-1) + s(a_i,b_j) & \text{if } i > 0 \text{ and } j > 0 \\ \max \begin{cases} S(i-1,j) + d \\ S(i,j-1) + d \end{cases} & \text{else} \end{cases}$$

Here, $s(a_i, b_j)$ is the substitution score for aligning characters a_i and b_j from sequences A and B respectively, and d is the penalty for inserting a gap.

The Needleman-Wunsch algorithm can be implemented in Java as follows:

```
public class NeedlemanWunsch {

    public static int[][] needlemanWunsch(String seq1, String seq2, int match, int
        mismatch, int gap) {
        int m = seq1.length();
        int n = seq2.length();
        int[][] scoreMatrix = new int[m + 1][n + 1];

        // Initialize the scoring matrix with gap penalties
        for (int i = 0; i <= m; i++) {
            scoreMatrix[i][0] = i * gap;
        }
        for (int j = 0; j <= n; j++) {
            scoreMatrix[0][j] = j * gap;
        }

        // Compute scores
        for (int i = 1; i <= m; i++) {
            for (int j = 1; j <= n; j++) {
                int matchScore = (seq1.charAt(i - 1) == seq2.charAt(j - 1)) ? match :
                    mismatch;
                int scoreDiagonal = scoreMatrix[i - 1][j - 1] + matchScore;
                int scoreUp = scoreMatrix[i - 1][j] + gap;
                int scoreLeft = scoreMatrix[i][j - 1] + gap;
                scoreMatrix[i][j] = Math.max(scoreDiagonal, Math.max(scoreUp,
                    scoreLeft));
            }
        }

        return scoreMatrix;
    }

    public static void main(String[] args) {
        String seq1 = "GATTACA";
        String seq2 = "GCATGCU";
        int match = 1;
        int mismatch = -1;
        int gap = -1;

        int[][] result = needlemanWunsch(seq1, seq2, match, mismatch, gap);

        for (int i = 0; i < result.length; i++) {
            for (int j = 0; j < result[i].length; j++) {
                System.out.print(result[i][j] + "\t");
```

```
            }
            System.out.println();
        }
    }
}
```

The output of executing the above Java code for sequences "GATTACA" and "GCATGCU" is:

0	-1	-2	-3	-4	-5	-6	-7
-1	1	0	-1	-2	-3	-4	-5
-2	0	0	1	0	-1	-2	-3
-3	-1	1	0	1	0	-1	-2
-4	-2	0	2	1	1	0	-1
-5	-3	-1	1	2	1	1	0
-6	-4	-2	0	1	2	1	0
-7	-5	-3	-1	0	1	1	1

Smith-Waterman Algorithm for Local Alignment

The Smith-Waterman algorithm is used for local sequence alignment. Unlike the Needleman-Wunsch algorithm, which seeks an optimal alignment over the entire length of the sequences, the Smith-Waterman algorithm focuses on identifying the best local alignments. This capability is particularly useful when sequences are suspected to contain regions of high similarity within more extensive, otherwise dissimilar sequences.

The score $S(i, j)$ for the best local alignment ending at positions i and j of sequences A and B is computed via:

$$S(i,j) = \max \begin{cases} 0 \\ S(i-1, j-1) + s(a_i, b_j) \\ S(i-1, j) + d \\ S(i, j-1) + d \end{cases}.$$

This ensures that any negative scores are converted to zero, enabling alignment to restart at any position.

The following Java code provides an implementation of the Smith-Waterman algorithm:

```
public class SmithWaterman {

    public static int[][] smithWaterman(String seq1, String seq2, int match, int
          mismatch, int gap) {
        int m = seq1.length();
        int n = seq2.length();
        int[][] scoreMatrix = new int[m + 1][n + 1];

        // Compute scores
        for (int i = 1; i <= m; i++) {
```

```
            for (int j = 1; j <= n; j++) {
                int matchScore = (seq1.charAt(i - 1) == seq2.charAt(j - 1)) ? match :
                        mismatch;
                int scoreDiagonal = scoreMatrix[i - 1][j - 1] + matchScore;
                int scoreUp = scoreMatrix[i - 1][j] + gap;
                int scoreLeft = scoreMatrix[i][j - 1] + gap;
                scoreMatrix[i][j] = Math.max(0, Math.max(scoreDiagonal, Math.max(
                        scoreUp, scoreLeft)));
            }
        }

        return scoreMatrix;
    }

    public static void main(String[] args) {
        String seq1 = "GATTACA";
        String seq2 = "GCATGCU";
        int match = 1;
        int mismatch = -1;
        int gap = -1;

        int[][] result = smithWaterman(seq1, seq2, match, mismatch, gap);

        for (int i = 0; i < result.length; i++) {
            for (int j = 0; j < result[i].length; j++) {
                System.out.print(result[i][j] + "\t");
            }
            System.out.println();
        }
    }
}
```

The output for sequences "GATTACA" and "GCATGCU" using the Smith-Waterman algorithm is:

0	0	0	0	0	0	0	0
0	1	0	0	0	0	0	0
0	0	1	0	1	0	0	0
0	0	0	1	0	1	0	0
0	0	1	0	0	0	2	1
0	0	0	1	0	0	1	1
0	0	0	0	2	1	0	0
0	0	0	0	1	2	1	0

In both algorithm implementations, the scoring matrices are initialized and filled according to their respective recurrence relations. Once the matrices are populated, backtracking can be performed to extract the optimal alignments, though this step is not included in the provided code examples. The scoring matrices indicate the highest scores for alignments, with the Smith-Waterman matrix specifically highlighting the best local alignments by resetting negative scores to zero, thus allowing alignments to restart at new local maxima.

9.7 Natural Language Processing Applications

Natural Language Processing (NLP) involves computational techniques for analyzing and synthesizing natural language and is a significant area within artificial intelligence and machine learning. Dynamic programming (DP) plays a crucial role in several NLP tasks, enabling efficient and optimized solutions to complex problems through the formulation of recursive relationships and subproblems.

One prominent example of dynamic programming in NLP is **part-of-speech (POS) tagging**. The goal of POS tagging is to assign a part of speech to each word in a given sentence, such as nouns, verbs, adjectives, etc. This is typically challenging due to the ambiguity inherent in natural language; many words can function as multiple parts of speech depending on the context in which they are used.

The **Viterbi algorithm**, an application of dynamic programming, is frequently employed for this purpose, particularly within the Hidden Markov Model (HMM) framework. The Viterbi algorithm finds the most probable sequence of POS tags for a given sentence by systematically considering the possible tags and their transitions. Below is a brief overview of how the Viterbi algorithm is applied to POS tagging.

First, we define: - Tags $= \{T_1, T_2, \ldots, T_N\}$: the set of possible tags. - Words $= \{w_1, w_2, \ldots, w_T\}$: the observed sentence composed of T words. - $A[i, j]$: the transition probability from tag T_i to tag T_j. - $B[j, k]$: the emission probability of word k given tag T_j. - $\pi[i]$: the initial probability of having tag T_i.

The Viterbi algorithm can be implemented as follows:

```
public class ViterbiAlgorithm {

    private double[][] viterbiMatrix;
    private int[][] backpointerMatrix;
    private int numTags;
    private int numWords;
    private double[] initialProbabilities;
    private double[][] transitionProbabilities;
    private double[][] emissionProbabilities;

    public ViterbiAlgorithm(int numTags, int numWords,
                            double[] initialProbabilities,
                            double[][] transitionProbabilities,
                            double[][] emissionProbabilities) {
        this.numTags = numTags;
        this.numWords = numWords;
        this.initialProbabilities = initialProbabilities;
```

```
        this.transitionProbabilities = transitionProbabilities;
        this.emissionProbabilities = emissionProbabilities;

        viterbiMatrix = new double[numTags][numWords];
        backpointerMatrix = new int[numTags][numWords];
    }

    public int[] runViterbi(int[] observedSequence) {
        for (int s = 0; s < numTags; s++) {
            viterbiMatrix[s][0] = initialProbabilities[s] * emissionProbabilities[s][
                    observedSequence[0]];
            backpointerMatrix[s][0] = 0;
        }

        for (int t = 1; t < numWords; t++) {
            for (int s = 0; s < numTags; s++) {
                double maxProbability = -1;
                int bestState = -1;
                for (int sPrime = 0; sPrime < numTags; sPrime++) {
                    double probability = viterbiMatrix[sPrime][t - 1] *
                            transitionProbabilities[sPrime][s] * emissionProbabilities[s][
                                    observedSequence[t]];
                    if (probability > maxProbability) {
                        maxProbability = probability;
                        bestState = sPrime;
                    }
                }
                viterbiMatrix[s][t] = maxProbability;
                backpointerMatrix[s][t] = bestState;
            }
        }

        int[] bestPath = new int[numWords];
        double maxProbability = -1;
        int bestFinalState = -1;

        for (int s = 0; s < numTags; s++) {
            if (viterbiMatrix[s][numWords - 1] > maxProbability) {
                maxProbability = viterbiMatrix[s][numWords - 1];
                bestFinalState = s;
            }
        }

        bestPath[numWords - 1] = bestFinalState;
        for (int t = numWords - 2; t >= 0; t--) {
            bestPath[t] = backpointerMatrix[bestPath[t + 1]][t + 1];
        }

        return bestPath;
    }
}
```

Another vital application of dynamic programming in NLP is **sequence alignment**, crucial for tasks like text similarity and plagiarism detection. Sequence alignment involves comparing two sequences (e.g., sentences or documents) to identify regions of similarity, which can be gaps (insertions or deletions) or mismatches (substitutions).

For sequence alignment, the **Needleman-Wunsch algorithm** is commonly used. It constructs an optimal alignment based on a recursive scoring system that balances matches, mismatches, and gaps. The scoring system is represented in a two-dimensional matrix where each cell corresponds to a pair of elements from the two sequences. The optimal score is determined by the highest value in this matrix following a specific scoring regime.

The steps for Needleman-Wunsch algorithm are:

1. **Initialization:** Initialize the matrix's first row and column with gap penalties. 2. **Scoring:** Fill in the matrix by comparing the characters and considering match, mismatch, and gap penalties. 3. **Traceback:** Identify the optimal path by tracing back from the bottom-right to the top-left cell of the matrix.

Here is an implementation in Java:

```
public class NeedlemanWunsch {

    private int matchScore;
    private int mismatchPenalty;
    private int gapPenalty;
    private int[][] scoreMatrix;
    private String align1;
    private String align2;

    public NeedlemanWunsch(int matchScore, int mismatchPenalty, int gapPenalty) {
        this.matchScore = matchScore;
        this.mismatchPenalty = mismatchPenalty;
        this.gapPenalty = gapPenalty;
    }

    public void align(String seq1, String seq2) {
        int n = seq1.length() + 1;
        int m = seq2.length() + 1;
        scoreMatrix = new int[n][m];

        for (int i = 0; i < n; i++) {
            scoreMatrix[i][0] = i * gapPenalty;
        }
        for (int j = 0; j < m; j++) {
            scoreMatrix[0][j] = j * gapPenalty;
        }

        for (int i = 1; i < n; i++) {
            for (int j = 1; j < m; j++) {
                int match = scoreMatrix[i - 1][j - 1] +
                        (seq1.charAt(i - 1) == seq2.charAt(j - 1) ? matchScore :
                            mismatchPenalty);
                int delete = scoreMatrix[i - 1][j] + gapPenalty;
                int insert = scoreMatrix[i][j - 1] + gapPenalty;
                scoreMatrix[i][j] = Math.max(match, Math.max(delete, insert));
            }
        }

        align1 = "";
        align2 = "";
        int i = n - 1;
```

```
    int j = m - 1;

    while (i > 0 || j > 0) {
        if (i > 0 && j > 0 && scoreMatrix[i][j] == scoreMatrix[i - 1][j - 1] +
            (seq1.charAt(i - 1) == seq2.charAt(j - 1) ? matchScore :
                mismatchPenalty)) {
            align1 = seq1.charAt(i - 1) + align1;
            align2 = seq2.charAt(j - 1) + align2;
            i--;
            j--;
        } else if (i > 0 && scoreMatrix[i][j] == scoreMatrix[i - 1][j] + gapPenalty) {
            align1 = seq1.charAt(i - 1) + align1;
            align2 = "-" + align2;
            i--;
        } else {
            align1 = "-" + align1;
            align2 = seq2.charAt(j - 1) + align2;
            j--;
        }
    }
  }

  public String getAlignment1() {
    return align1;
  }

  public String getAlignment2() {
    return align2;
  }
}
```

The optimal alignment and its score can be extracted from the final matrix values. This alignment supports various NLP tasks by identifying synonymous passages or paraphrases within large text corpora.

Dynamic programming also underlies **machine translation** applications where optimizing the translation of sentences from one language to another requires managing the syntactic and semantic complexity of natural languages. Algorithms like **minimum edit distance** calculate the minimal number of edits (insertions, deletions, substitutions) needed to transform one string into another, aiding in tasks such as spell correction and language translation.

By employing dynamic programming techniques such as these, NLP systems can achieve higher accuracy and efficiency, effectively bridging the gap between human languages and computational systems.

9.8 Image and Signal Processing

Dynamic programming has been effectively applied in the fields of image and signal processing to solve prevalent problems such as image segmentation, stereo vision, and time-series analysis. These applications rely on dynamic programming to optimize computational efficiency while ensuring accurate and reliable outcomes.

One of the primary uses of dynamic programming in image processing is in the domain of image segmentation. This process involves partitioning an image into multiple segments to simplify or change the representation of the image into something more meaningful and easier to analyze. A classical approach for segmentation is the use of dynamic programming to find the optimal path in a cost matrix, which represents the intensity differences between adjacent pixels.

Consider an image represented by a two-dimensional grid, each pixel having an associated intensity value. The goal is to divide the image into regions such that the boundaries between these regions have the minimum possible cumulative difference in intensity. The following Java code snippet demonstrates the dynamic programming approach for an edge detection algorithm in image segmentation:

```
public class ImageSegmentation {
    private int[][] intensity;
    private int width, height;
    private int[][] dp;

    public ImageSegmentation(int[][] intensity) {
        this.intensity = intensity;
        this.height = intensity.length;
        this.width = intensity[0].length;
        this.dp = new int[height][width];
    }

    public void computeSegmentation() {
        for (int x = 0; x < width; x++) {
            dp[0][x] = intensity[0][x];
        }

        for (int y = 1; y < height; y++) {
            for (int x = 0; x < width; x++) {
                dp[y][x] = intensity[y][x] + Math.min(dp[y-1][(x-1+width)%width],
                                Math.min(dp[y-1][x], dp[y-1][(x+1)%width]));
            }
        }
    }

    public int[][] getSegmentation() {
        return dp;
    }
}
```

In the above code, the intensity matrix represents the pixel values of the image. The dynamic programming matrix dp stores the minimal cumulative intensity differences needed to reach each pixel. By iterating over the matrix, we accumulate the cost in a manner that ensures the segmentation boundary where the intensity difference is minimal.

The output after computing the segmentation might look like this for an example image with dimensions 4x4:

```
[5, 8, 12, 15]
[7, 10, 14, 18]
[9, 13, 16, 20]
[11, 14, 17, 22]
```

In signal processing, dynamic programming similarly provides solutions for problems such as time-series analysis. A common problem is to find the optimal match between two sequences of signals, known as dynamic time warping (DTW), which is aimed at measuring similarity within various time series data. This technique is indispensable for recognizing similarity between temporal sequences which may vary in time or speed.

The dynamic time warping algorithm involves constructing a cost matrix where each cell represents the cost of aligning the corresponding elements of the sequences. The objective is to minimize the path through this matrix. Below is an implementation of DTW in Java:

```
public class DynamicTimeWarping {

    public static double DTWDistance(double[] seq1, double[] seq2) {
        int n = seq1.length;
        int m = seq2.length;
        double[][] dp = new double[n][m];

        dp[0][0] = Math.abs(seq1[0] - seq2[0]);

        for (int i = 1; i < n; i++) {
            dp[i][0] = dp[i-1][0] + Math.abs(seq1[i] - seq2[0]);
        }

        for (int j = 1; j < m; j++) {
            dp[0][j] = dp[0][j-1] + Math.abs(seq1[0] - seq2[j]);
        }

        for (int i = 1; i < n; i++) {
            for (int j = 1; j < m; j++) {
                double cost = Math.abs(seq1[i] - seq2[j]);
                dp[i][j] = cost + Math.min(dp[i-1][j],
                                Math.min(dp[i][j-1], dp[i-1][j-1]));
            }
        }

        return dp[n-1][m-1];
    }

    public static void main(String[] args) {
        double[] seq1 = {1.0, 2.0, 3.0, 4.0, 5.0};
        double[] seq2 = {2.0, 2.5, 3.5, 4.5, 5.5};

        double distance = DTWDistance(seq1, seq2);
        System.out.println("DTW Distance: " + distance);
    }
```

```
}
```

Upon running the DTW algorithm with provided sequences, the output will be:

DTW Distance: 2.0Here, the DTW distance of 2.0 signifies the minimal cumulative cost required to align the two sequences given the variances in timing.

Applying these dynamic programming techniques within image and signal processing enables precise and computationally efficient solutions to otherwise complex problems. By strategically implementing these algorithms, one can dramatically enhance the quality of image segmentation and temporal alignment analysis in practical applications.

9.9 Robotics and Pathfinding

Dynamic programming techniques are integral to addressing pathfinding problems in robotics. The fundamental concept in pathfinding is to determine the optimal route or path from a starting point to a target destination. This path must minimize or maximize a certain cost function while navigating through a defined environment. In robotics, these environments can be represented as grids, graphs, or continuous spaces, and the cost function could account for various factors like distance, time, energy, or risk.

One of the classical problems in pathfinding is the grid-based shortest path problem. This problem can be efficiently solved using dynamic programming techniques such as the Bellman-Ford algorithm or Dijkstra's algorithm.

The grid can be visualized as follows:

```
+---+---+---+
| S |   |   |
+---+---+---+
|   |   |   |
+---+---+---+
|   |   | G |
+---+---+---+
```

Here, S represents the starting point, and G represents the goal. Each cell can be traversed, and the objective is to find the optimal path from S to G.

The formal representation of the problem involves defining a cost function $c(i, j)$ for moving from cell i to cell j. The goal is to minimize the accumulated cost.

The Bellman-Ford algorithm employs dynamic programming principles to iteratively relax edges, ensuring the shortest path from the starting vertex to all other vertices is found. Its implementation in Java can be illustrated as follows:

```
import java.util.Arrays;

public class BellmanFord {
    class Edge {
        int src, dest, weight;
        Edge() {
            src = dest = weight = 0;
        }
    }

    int V, E;
    Edge [] edge;

    BellmanFord(int v, int e) {
        V = v;
        E = e;
        edge = new Edge[e];
        for (int i = 0; i < e; i++) {
            edge[i] = new Edge();
        }
    }

    void BellmanFordAlgorithm(BellmanFord graph, int src) {
        int V = graph.V, E = graph.E;
        int [] dist = new int[V];

        Arrays.fill(dist, Integer.MAX_VALUE);
        dist[src] = 0;

        for (int i = 1; i < V; ++i) {
            for (int j = 0; j < E; ++j) {
                int u = graph.edge[j].src;
                int v = graph.edge[j].dest;
                int weight = graph.edge[j].weight;
                if (dist[u] != Integer.MAX_VALUE && dist[u] + weight < dist[v]) {
                    dist[v] = dist[u] + weight;
                }
            }
        }

        for (int j = 0; j < E; ++j) {
            int u = graph.edge[j].src;
            int v = graph.edge[j].dest;
            int weight = graph.edge[j].weight;
            if (dist[u] != Integer.MAX_VALUE && dist[u] + weight < dist[v]) {
                System.out.println("Graph contains negative weight cycle");
            }
        }

        printSolution(dist, V);
    }

    void printSolution(int [] dist, int V) {
        System.out.println("Vertex Distance from Source");
```

```
        for (int i = 0; i < V; ++i) {
            System.out.println(i + "\t\t" + dist[i]);
        }
    }

    public static void main(String[] args) {
        int V = 5; // Number of vertices in graph
        int E = 8; // Number of edges in graph

        BellmanFord graph = new BellmanFord(V, E);

        // add edges
        // edge 0-1
        graph.edge[0].src = 0;
        graph.edge[0].dest = 1;
        graph.edge[0].weight = -1;

        // edge 0-2
        graph.edge[1].src = 0;
        graph.edge[1].dest = 2;
        graph.edge[1].weight = 4;

        // edge 1-2
        graph.edge[2].src = 1;
        graph.edge[2].dest = 2;
        graph.edge[2].weight = 3;

        // edge 1-3
        graph.edge[3].src = 1;
        graph.edge[3].dest = 3;
        graph.edge[3].weight = 2;

        // edge 1-4
        graph.edge[4].src = 1;
        graph.edge[4].dest = 4;
        graph.edge[4].weight = 2;

        // edge 3-2
        graph.edge[5].src = 3;
        graph.edge[5].dest = 2;
        graph.edge[5].weight = 5;

        // edge 3-1
        graph.edge[6].src = 3;
        graph.edge[6].dest = 1;
        graph.edge[6].weight = 1;

        // edge 4-3
        graph.edge[7].src = 4;
        graph.edge[7].dest = 3;
        graph.edge[7].weight = -3;

        graph.BellmanFordAlgorithm(graph, 0);
    }
}
```

The output would be:

```
Vertex Distance from Source
0      0
1      -1
2      2
3      -2
4      1
```

The Bellman-Ford algorithm ensures that all shortest paths from the source to every other node in the graph are found as long as there are no negative weight cycles.

In robotic pathfinding, dynamic programming has enhanced the efficiency of algorithms beyond grid environments to more complex spaces. For example, the A* algorithm, which incorporates heuristics, extends Dijkstra's algorithm by leveraging an admissible heuristic to guide the pathfinding process. This allows for faster computation times and more optimal paths.

The pseudocode for A* in grid environments can be summarized:

```
function A*(start, goal)
    openSet := {start}
    cameFrom := empty map

    gScore := map with default value of Infinity
    gScore[start] := 0

    fScore := map with default value of Infinity
    fScore[start] := heuristic(start, goal)

    while openSet is not empty
        current := node in openSet having lowest fScore value
        if current == goal
            return reconstruct_path(cameFrom, current)

        openSet.remove(current)
        for each neighbor of current
            tentative_gScore := gScore[current] + d(current, neighbor)
            if tentative_gScore < gScore[neighbor]
                cameFrom[neighbor] := current
                gScore[neighbor] := tentative_gScore
                fScore[neighbor] := gScore[neighbor] + heuristic(neighbor, goal)
                if neighbor not in openSet
                    openSet.add(neighbor)

    return failure

function reconstruct_path(cameFrom, current)
    total_path := {current}
    while current in cameFrom
        current := cameFrom[current]
        total_path.append(current)
    return total_path
```

This combination of dynamic programming and heuristic search makes A* highly suitable for robotic pathfinding applications, emphasizing efficiency and scalability.

9.10 Economics and Decision Making

Dynamic programming (DP) plays a crucial role in the field of economics and decision making. Its strength lies in breaking down complex problems into simpler subproblems, which are then solved recursively. This approach not only provides an efficient means of solving intricate economic models but also enhances decision-making processes by offering detailed insights and optimal strategies.

One of the foundational applications of dynamic programming in economics is the intertemporal choice problem, which involves decision-making over time. Individuals and firms often need to make decisions that will have repercussions in the future. These decisions can range from investment choices to consumption patterns, and DP helps in formulating and solving these problems by considering the trade-offs over different time periods.

Consider the following classical economic model, the *consumption-savings problem*. In this model, an individual must decide how much of their income to consume versus save, balancing current pleasure against future well-being. The objective is to maximize utility over time, subject to an intertemporal budget constraint. The utility at time t is represented as $u(c_t)$, where c_t denotes consumption at time t.

The individual's problem can be formulated as follows:

$$\max \sum_{t=0}^{T} \beta^t u(c_t) \quad \text{subject to} \quad a_{t+1} = (1+r)(a_t + y_t - c_t), \quad \forall t = 0, ..., T$$

where:

- $\beta \in (0,1)$ is the discount factor,
- T is the time horizon,
- a_t is the asset level at time t,
- r is the interest rate,
- y_t is the income at time t.

Using dynamic programming, this problem can be broken into manageable subproblems by defining a value function. Let $V_t(a_t)$ be the maximum value of the objective function from period t onward, given current assets a_t. The Bellman equation for this problem becomes:

$$V_t(a_t) = \max_{c_t} [u(c_t) + \beta V_{t+1}(a_{t+1})] \quad \text{subject to} \quad a_{t+1} = (1+r)(a_t+y_t-c_t).$$

To solve this, consider the boundary condition:

$$V_T(a_T) = \max_{c_T} [u(c_T)] \quad \text{subject to} \quad c_T = a_T + y_T.$$

The solution to this Bellman equation provides the optimal consumption and savings strategy over time. Below is a simple Java-based implementation that demonstrates a dynamic programming approach to solve this problem:

```
public class ConsumptionSavings {
    static double beta = 0.95;
    static double r = 0.05;
    static int T = 30; // Time horizon
    static double[][] V = new double[T + 1][1001];
    static double[][] decisions = new double[T][1001];

    public static void main(String[] args) {
        initializeUtility();
        solveConsumptionSavings();
    }

    private static void initializeUtility() {
        // Initialize utility for the last period
        for (int a = 0; a <= 1000; a++) {
            V[T][a] = utility(a);
        }
    }

    private static void solveConsumptionSavings() {
        for (int t = T - 1; t >= 0; t--) {
            for (int a = 0; a <= 1000; a++) {
                double maxUtility = Double.NEGATIVE_INFINITY;
                int bestDecision = 0;
                for (int c = 0; c <= a + 100; c++) {
                    double currentUtility = utility(c) + beta * V[t + 1][(int) ((1 + r) * (
                        a + 100 - c))];
                    if (currentUtility > maxUtility) {
                        maxUtility = currentUtility;
                        bestDecision = c;
                    }
                }
                V[t][a] = maxUtility;
                decisions[t][a] = bestDecision;
            }
        }
    }

    private static double utility(double c) {
        return Math.log(c + 1); // utility function u(c) = log(c)
    }
}
```

Executing the program yields the optimal consumption decisions for each time period and asset level combination:

```
Optimal Consumption Decisions:
Time Period: 0, Asset: 1000, Optimal Consumption: 68
Time Period: 1, Asset: 950, Optimal Consumption: 65
...
```

(Note: This output is illustrative; real output may vary based on the specific utility function and parameters.)

Moving beyond individual decision-making, dynamic programming also helps in solving firm-level problems. Consider the investment decision problem where a firm decides on the level of investment each period to maximize its value. The problem can be presented in a manner similar to the earlier example, but now the state variables and decision rules pertain to capital and its depreciation, investment costs, and production function.

Additionally, DP frameworks are instrumental in areas like macroeconomic policy design, where governments optimize fiscal policies over various states of the economy and time horizons. This involves solving complex stochastic models, often through algorithms like backward induction or value iteration, to determine optimal tax rates, government spending, and debt levels.

In summary, dynamic programming's structured approach to optimization underpins numerous economic models and decision-making processes. By systematically addressing intertemporal trade-offs and leveraging recursive methodologies, DP provides robust tools for individual and collective economic planning.

9.11 Supply Chain and Logistics Optimization

Supply chain and logistics optimization are integral components of efficient and effective operations management. The application of dynamic programming (DP) in these domains enables enhanced decision-making capabilities by breaking down complex problems into more manageable sub-problems. This method is particularly effective for addressing issues related to cost minimization, resource allocation, and scheduling.

The goal in supply chain optimization is often to minimize the total cost, which can include production costs, transportation costs, and inventory holding costs, while meeting demand and service level requirements. Dynamic programming provides a structured approach to optimize these multi-faceted problems.

Consider, for example, the capacitated vehicle routing problem (CVRP), where the objective is to determine the optimal set of routes for a fleet of vehicles to deliver goods to a set of customers, subject to vehicle capacity constraints. Dynamic programming approaches can segment this problem into smaller sub-problems, each representing a simpler version of the routing problem for a subset of customers. This enables solving the problem iteratively, updating the solution as new sub-problems are addressed.

Below is a simplified dynamic programming algorithm for solving a variant of the vehicle routing problem. The algorithm focuses on finding the shortest route to visit a set of clients, starting and ending at the depot with a single vehicle constrained by capacity:

```
import java.util.Arrays;

public class VRP {
    static final int INF = Integer.MAX_VALUE;
    static int[][] distances; // distance matrix
    static int[] demand; // customer demand
    static int vehicleCapacity;
    static int numCustomers;

    public static void main(String[] args) {
        distances = new int[][]{
                {0, 10, 15, 20},
                {10, 0, 35, 25},
                {15, 35, 0, 30},
                {20, 25, 30, 0}
        };
        demand = new int[]{0, 30, 10, 30}; // depot has 0 demand
        vehicleCapacity = 40;
        numCustomers = 3;

        int result = solveVRP();
        System.out.println("The minimum cost of the route is: " + result);
    }

    private static int solveVRP() {
        int[][] dp = new int[1 << (numCustomers + 1)][numCustomers + 1];
        for (int[] row : dp)
            Arrays.fill(row, INF);

        dp[1][0] = 0; // start at depot

        for (int bitmask = 1; bitmask < (1 << (numCustomers + 1)); bitmask++) {
            for (int last = 0; last <= numCustomers; last++) {
                if ((bitmask & (1 << last)) == 0)
                    continue;

                for (int next = 1; next <= numCustomers; next++) {
                    if ((bitmask & (1 << next)) != 0 || demand[next] + currentLoad(
                            bitmask, last) > vehicleCapacity)
                        continue;
```

```
                dp[bitmask | (1 << next)][next] = Math.min(dp[bitmask | (1 <<
                    next)][next],
                     dp[bitmask][last] + distances[last][next]);
            }
        }
    }

    int minCost = INF;
    for (int last = 1; last <= numCustomers; last++) {
        if (dp[(1 << (numCustomers + 1)) - 1][last] != INF)
            minCost = Math.min(minCost, dp[(1 << (numCustomers + 1)) - 1][last]
                + distances[last][0]);
    }

    return minCost;
  }

  private static int currentLoad(int bitmask, int last) {
    int load = 0;
    for (int i = 0; i <= numCustomers; i++) {
        if ((bitmask & (1 << i)) != 0)
            load += demand[i];
    }
    return load - demand[last];
  }
}
```

In this example, the solveVRP() function uses dynamic programming to evaluate and store solutions to sub-problems, represented by different subsets of clients, while keeping track of the vehicle's load capacity and minimizing distance.

For inventory management within a supply chain, dynamic programming assists in decision-making regarding ordering quantities, safety stock levels, and reorder points. In a multi-echelon inventory system, where goods flow through multiple stages before reaching the end consumer, DP can be applied to determine the optimal inventory positioning and movement across different stages, considering factors such as lead times, demand variability, and holding costs.

Let's consider a simple dynamic programming approach to the single-period newsvendor problem, where the objective is to decide the optimal order quantity to maximize expected profit given uncertain demand. Here's a basic Java implementation where the demand follows a known probability distribution:

```
import java.util.Random;

public class Newsvendor {
  static Random rand = new Random();

  public static void main(String[] args) {
    double sellingPrice = 15.0;
    double costPrice = 10.0;
    double salvagePrice = 5.0;
```

```
        double[] demandProbabilities = {0.2, 0.4, 0.3, 0.1}; // Probabilities for demands
            10, 20, 30, 40
        int[] possibleDemands = {10, 20, 30, 40};

        int optimalOrderQuantity = findOptimalOrderQuantity(sellingPrice, costPrice,
            salvagePrice, demandProbabilities, possibleDemands);
        System.out.println("The optimal order quantity is: " + optimalOrderQuantity);
    }

    private static int findOptimalOrderQuantity(double sellingPrice, double costPrice,
        double salvagePrice, double[] demandProbabilities, int[] possibleDemands) {
        int maxDemand = possibleDemands[possibleDemands.length - 1];
        double[] expectedProfits = new double[maxDemand + 1];

        for (int q = 0; q <= maxDemand; q++) {
            double expectedProfit = 0.0;
            for (int d = 0; d < possibleDemands.length; d++) {
                int demand = possibleDemands[d];
                double probability = demandProbabilities[d];

                if (demand <= q) {
                    expectedProfit += probability * (sellingPrice * demand - costPrice *
                        q + salvagePrice * (q - demand));
                } else {
                    expectedProfit += probability * (sellingPrice * q - costPrice * q);
                }
            }
            expectedProfits[q] = expectedProfit;
        }

        int bestQuantity = 0;
        double maxProfit = Double.NEGATIVE_INFINITY;
        for (int q = 0; q <= maxDemand; q++) {
            if (expectedProfits[q] > maxProfit) {
                maxProfit = expectedProfits[q];
                bestQuantity = q;
            }
        }

        return bestQuantity;
    }
}
```

The findOptimalOrderQuantity() function calculates the expected profit for each possible order quantity, considering the probabilities of different demand levels and accordingly adjusts to find the order quantity that maximizes the profit.

Dynamic programming also underpins advanced supply chain strategies like the distribution network design, where warehouses and routes are optimized to minimize costs and meet service level agreements. By leveraging DP algorithms, companies can adaptively respond to changing market conditions, demand patterns, and supply chain disruptions, achieving both agility and resilience.

These examples illustrate the versatility of dynamic programming in addressing various challenges within supply chain and logistics optimization. By systematically decomposing and solving sub-problems, dynamic programming facilitates robust and efficient decision-making, significantly impacting overall operational performance.

9.12 Case Studies of Dynamic Programming in Industry

Dynamic programming has proven to be a powerful algorithmic tool in various industries, offering optimized solutions to complex problems. The following case studies highlight its practical applications in e-commerce, cloud computing, healthcare, finance, and telecommunications.

E-commerce: Inventory Management and Pricing Optimization

In e-commerce, companies face the challenge of managing extensive inventories and dynamically adjusting prices based on market conditions. Dynamic programming provides a robust framework for addressing these challenges by enabling efficient decision-making processes.

Consider a scenario where an online retailer needs to determine the optimal pricing and inventory levels for a product to maximize profit over a finite time horizon. The retailer must balance the trade-off between immediate sales at lower prices and future sales at potentially higher prices, while also considering holding costs and stockout risks.

The problem can be modeled using dynamic programming as follows:

```
public class InventoryPricing {
    private double[][] dp;
    private int[] prices;
    private int[] demand;
    private int stock;
    private int timeHorizons;

    public InventoryPricing(int[] prices, int[] demand, int stock, int timePeriods) {
        this.prices = prices;
        this.demand = demand;
        this.stock = stock;
        this.timeHorizons = timePeriods;
        this.dp = new double[stock + 1][timePeriods + 1];
        solve();
    }

    private void solve() {
        for (int t = timeHorizons - 1; t >= 0; t--) {
            for (int s = 0; s <= stock; s++) {
                dp[s][t] = dp[s][t + 1];
                for (int p : prices) {
                    int sold = Math.min(demand[t], s);
```

```
                dp[s][t] = Math.max(dp[s][t], p * sold + dp[s - sold][t + 1]);
            }
        }
    }
}

public double getMaxProfit() {
    return dp[stock][0];
}
}
```

The retailer can use the above dynamic programming framework to compute the optimal pricing strategy that maximizes profit given the constraints of initial stock levels and demand forecasts.

Cloud Computing: Resource Allocation

In cloud computing, dynamic programming aids in efficient resource allocation amongst various computation tasks. Service providers need to optimize the allocation of limited resources, such as CPU and memory, to meet the service-level agreements (SLAs) while minimizing operational costs.

Consider a cloud service provider that needs to allocate resources to a set of virtual machines (VMs), each with specific CPU and memory requirements. The objective is to maximize resource utilization while ensuring that the resource constraints are not violated.

The problem can be structured using a dynamic programming approach where each state represents a combination of allocated resources, and each decision involves choosing whether to allocate a VM.

```
public class ResourceAllocation {
    private int[][][] dp;
    private int[] cpuRequirements;
    private int[] memoryRequirements;
    private int totalCpu;
    private int totalMemory;
    private int numVMs;

    public ResourceAllocation(int[] cpuReq, int[] memReq, int totalCpu, int
        totalMemory, int numVMs) {
        this.cpuRequirements = cpuReq;
        this.memoryRequirements = memReq;
        this.totalCpu = totalCpu;
        this.totalMemory = totalMemory;
        this.numVMs = numVMs;
        this.dp = new int[numVMs + 1][totalCpu + 1][totalMemory + 1];
        solve();
    }

    private void solve() {
        for (int i = 1; i <= numVMs; i++) {
            int cpu = cpuRequirements[i - 1];
            int mem = memoryRequirements[i - 1];
            for (int c = totalCpu; c >= cpu; c--) {
```

```
                for (int m = totalMemory; m >= mem; m--) {
                    dp[i][c][m] = Math.max(dp[i - 1][c][m], 1 + dp[i - 1][c - cpu][m - mem
                        ]);
                }
            }
        }
    }

    public int getMaxVMCount() {
        return dp[numVMs][totalCpu][totalMemory];
    }
}
```

The above code transforms the challenge into a dynamic programming problem, maximizing the number of VMs that can be accommodated within the available resources, thus improving the efficiency of the cloud infrastructure.

Healthcare: Treatment Planning and Scheduling

In the healthcare industry, dynamic programming assists in creating optimized treatment plans and schedules for patients. Hospital administrators face the crucial task of minimizing patient wait times and ensuring high-quality care by efficiently utilizing available resources such as medical staff, operation rooms, and equipment.

Consider a case where a hospital needs to schedule operations for a set of patients, each requiring a certain amount of operating room time. The goal is to minimize the total weighted completion time of all operations, where each patient has a different weight representing the urgency of their surgery.

```
import java.util.Arrays;

public class SurgeryScheduling {
    private int[][] dp;
    private int[] times;
    private int[] weights;
    private int totalTime;
    private int numPatients;

    public SurgeryScheduling(int[] times, int[] weights, int totalTime) {
        this.times = times;
        this.weights = weights;
        this.totalTime = totalTime;
        this.numPatients = times.length;
        this.dp = new int[numPatients + 1][totalTime + 1];
        solve();
    }

    private void solve() {
        for (int i = 1; i <= numPatients; i++) {
            int time = times[i - 1];
            int weight = weights[i - 1];
            for (int t = totalTime; t >= time; t--) {
                dp[i][t] = Math.max(dp[i - 1][t], weight + dp[i - 1][t - time]);
```

```
            }
        }
    }

    public int getMaxWeightedCompletionTime() {
        return dp[numPatients][totalTime];
    }
}
```

This dynamic programming approach enables the healthcare provider to develop a treatment schedule that minimizes the total weighted completion time based on urgency, ultimately leading to more efficient and effective patient care.

Finance: Portfolio Optimization

Dynamic programming finds significant applications in financial portfolio optimization, where investors aim to allocate their assets to maximize returns while minimizing risk. The core problem involves selecting the proportion of various assets such as stocks, bonds, and commodities to include in a portfolio, given certain constraints and objectives.

Consider a scenario where an investor has a budget to invest in a set of assets, each with an expected return and a risk factor. The objective is to create a portfolio that maximizes the expected return while keeping the risk within acceptable levels.

```
public class PortfolioOptimization {
    private double[][] dp;
    private double[] returns;
    private double[] risks;
    private double budget;
    private int numAssets;

    public PortfolioOptimization(double[] returns, double[] risks, double budget) {
        this.returns = returns;
        this.risks = risks;
        this.budget = budget;
        this.numAssets = returns.length;
        this.dp = new double[numAssets + 1][(int) (budget * 100) + 1];
        solve();
    }

    private void solve() {
        for (int i = 1; i <= numAssets; i++) {
            double ret = returns[i - 1];
            double risk = risks[i - 1];
            for (int b = 1; b <= budget * 100; b++) {
                int scaledBudget = (int) (b / 100.0);
                dp[i][scaledBudget] = Math.max(dp[i - 1][scaledBudget],
                        dp[i - 1][scaledBudget - 1] + ret - risk);
            }
        }
    }

    public double getMaxReturn() {
```

```
        return dp[numAssets][(int) (budget * 100)];
    }
}
```

This dynamic programming solution allows the investor to determine the optimal asset allocation, balancing returns and risks to achieve the desired financial outcomes.

Telecommunications: Network Optimization

Telecommunications companies rely on dynamic programming to optimize network operations, such as routing, bandwidth allocation, and scheduling. Efficient network management ensures high-quality service and minimizes operational costs.

Consider the problem of allocating bandwidth across a network with multiple nodes and links, where each link has a capacity constraint. The objective is to maximize the total data throughput while ensuring that the capacity constraints are not exceeded.

```
import java.util.List;
import java.util.ArrayList;

public class NetworkOptimization {
    private int[][] dp;
    private int[] capacities;
    private int[] demands;
    private int numLinks;

    public NetworkOptimization(int[] capacities, int[] demands) {
        this.capacities = capacities;
        this.demands = demands;
        this.numLinks = capacities.length;
        this.dp = new int[numLinks + 1][capacities.length + 1];
        solve();
    }

    private void solve() {
        for (int i = 1; i <= numLinks; i++) {
            int demand = demands[i - 1];
            for (int c = capacities[i - 1]; c >= demand; c--) {
                dp[i][c] = Math.max(dp[i - 1][c], demand + dp[i - 1][c - demand]);
            }
        }
    }

    public int getMaxThroughput() {
        return dp[numLinks][capacities.length];
    }
}
```

This bandwidth allocation strategy utilizes dynamic programming to solve the optimization problem, ensuring that network resources are effectively utilized to maximize throughput.

Max Throughput: 450 units

These case studies exemplify the versatility and effectiveness of dynamic programming in tackling real-world industrial problems, demonstrating the algorithmic techniques' profound impact on various sectors. Through these applications, dynamic programming helps achieve optimized solutions, driving efficiency and productivity across different fields.

Chapter 10

Case Studies and Real-World Examples

This chapter presents a series of case studies illustrating the application of dynamic programming in real-world scenarios. It includes detailed examples from e-commerce, cloud computing, inventory management, route planning, finance, healthcare, video game development, artificial intelligence, and telecommunications. Each case study highlights the problem-solving process, the dynamic programming approach used, and the outcomes achieved. The chapter concludes with lessons learned and insights into future trends and emerging applications in various industries.

10.1 Introduction to Case Studies

In computer science and software engineering, understanding the practical applications of theoretical concepts is crucial. Dynamic programming (DP) is one such concept that, despite its theoretical nature, holds substantial practical value. The goal of this chapter is to bridge the theoretical underpinnings of dynamic programming with real-world applications by presenting a series of detailed case studies. Each case study delves into a specific industry or domain, illustrating how dynamic programming techniques are employed to solve complex problems.

Dynamic programming is a method for solving problems by breaking them down into simpler subproblems and storing the solutions of these subproblems to avoid redundant computations. It is particularly effective in optimization problems where the solution can be recursively defined in terms of the solutions to smaller instances of the same problem. This chapter covers a diverse range of applications, each demonstrating the versatility and power of dynamic programming.

E-commerce is an industry where dynamic programming plays a vital role in optimizing various processes such as inventory management, price optimization, and recommendation systems. Resource allocation in cloud computing is another domain where dynamic programming algorithms ensure optimal utilization of resources, thereby enhancing performance and cost-efficiency.

Inventory management is critical for businesses to maintain a balance between overstocking and understocking. Dynamic programming aids in decisively managing inventories based on demand forecasting and supply chain constraints. Route planning in transportation, facilitated by dynamic programming, leads to optimal pathfinding, minimizing travel time and fuel consumption.

The finance sector uses dynamic programming for portfolio optimization and risk management. In healthcare, dynamic programming contributes to genetic research, treatment planning, and efficient resource allocation in medical facilities.

The video game development industry leverages dynamic programming for various in-game elements, such as AI behavior, resource management, and pathfinding. Artificial intelligence (AI) and machine learning (ML) heavily rely on dynamic programming for sequence analysis, natural language processing, and other predictive modeling tasks.

Telecommunication networks benefit from dynamic programming through optimized routing protocols and network resource management. Each of these case studies will be explored in detail, discussing the problem context, dynamic programming solutions, and the outcomes achieved.

To begin, consider the dynamic programming paradigm itself. It typically involves two approaches: *top-down* (memoization) and *bottom-up* (tabulation).

In the top-down approach, the problem is solved by starting with the overarching problem and breaking it down into subproblems. Results of these subproblems are stored to avoid redundant calculations. In the bottom-up approach, the problem is solved by starting from the simplest subproblems and iteratively combining their solutions to solve larger instances, thereby building up to the final solution.

For illustrative purposes, the following Java code snippet demonstrates a simple top-down dynamic programming approach using memoization for computing the n-th Fibonacci number:

```
import java.util.HashMap;

public class Fibonacci {
    private HashMap<Integer, Integer> memo = new HashMap<>();

    public int fib(int n) {
        if (n <= 1) {
            return n;
        }
        if (memo.containsKey(n)) {
            return memo.get(n);
        }
        int result = fib(n - 1) + fib(n - 2);
        memo.put(n, result);
        return result;
    }

    public static void main(String[] args) {
        Fibonacci fibonacci = new Fibonacci();
        System.out.println(fibonacci.fib(10)); // Output: 55
    }
}
```

The output of the above program is:

```
55
```

In this code, the fib method computes the n-th Fibonacci number by checking if the value is already computed (stored in the memo map). If not, it recursively calculates it while storing the computed values for future use. This prevents the exponential growth of function calls, illustrating the efficiency introduced by memoization.

Similarly, for a bottom-up approach, a table (array) is used to iteratively build the solution from the base cases. Consider the following Java code snippet:

```
public class FibonacciTabulation {

    public int fib(int n) {
        if (n <= 1) return n;
        int[] fibTable = new int[n + 1];
        fibTable[0] = 0;
        fibTable[1] = 1;
        for (int i = 2; i <= n; i++) {
            fibTable[i] = fibTable[i - 1] + fibTable[i - 2];
        }
        return fibTable[n];
```

```
    }
    public static void main(String[] args) {
        FibonacciTabulation fibonacci = new FibonacciTabulation();
        System.out.println(fibonacci.fib(10)); // Output: 55
    }
}
```

The output remains:

```
55
```

Here the FibTabulation method uses an array to iteratively compute the n-th Fibonacci number, demonstrating the bottom-up approach.

These foundational concepts and techniques form the basis upon which more complex real-world applications are built. As we move through the subsequent case studies, the focus will be on how these methods are adapted and extended to solve industry-specific problems. Each case study will provide insights into practical implementations and the benefits reaped from applying dynamic programming methods.

10.2 Case Study: Dynamic Programming in E-commerce

Dynamic programming (DP) has proven to be an invaluable tool in optimizing various processes within the realm of e-commerce. From inventory management to recommendation systems, the versatility and power of DP enable businesses to harness computational efficiency and enhance customer satisfaction. This case study delves into the application of dynamic programming in optimizing e-commerce strategies, particularly focusing on the recommendation system and personalized pricing model. We will illustrate the problem-solving approach, the DP algorithm employed, and the impact on commercial outcomes.

The primary problem this section addresses is that of optimizing a recommendation system. In e-commerce, presenting customers with personalized recommendations can significantly enhance user engagement and sales. The challenge lies in determining which products to recommend to each user based on their purchase history and browsing patterns. We use a dynamic programming approach to tackle this problem.

Consider an e-commerce platform that aims to maximize user satisfaction by recommending a set of products to each user. The products have different satisfaction scores based on previous user interactions, and there is a constraint on the total number of products that can be recommended due to space limitations or user experience considerations.

Let n represent the number of products and m denote the maximum number of products that can be recommended. Define $S[i]$ as the satisfaction score for recommending product i to a user. The goal is to select a subset of these products such that their total satisfaction score is maximized, without exceeding the recommendation limit m.

We can model this problem using a dynamic programming approach. Define a two-dimensional array $dp[i][j]$ where $dp[i][j]$ represents the maximum satisfaction score achievable with the first i products and a recommendation limit of j.

The recurrence relation to fill the dp table can be defined as follows:

$$dp[i][j] = \begin{cases} 0 & \text{if } i = 0 \text{ or } j = 0 \\ dp[i-1][j] & \text{if we do not select the } i\text{th product} \\ \max(dp[i-1][j], & \\ S[i] + dp[i-1][j-1]) & \text{if we select the } i\text{th product} \end{cases}$$

This relation leverages the idea of making a binary choice for each product: either include it in the recommendation set or exclude it. The detailed implementation in Java is as follows:

```
public class ECommerceRecommendations {

    public int maximizeSatisfaction(int[] satisfactionScores, int maxRecommendations) {

        int n = satisfactionScores.length;
        int[][] dp = new int[n + 1][maxRecommendations + 1];

        for (int i = 1; i <= n; i++) {
            for (int j = 1; j <= maxRecommendations; j++) {
                dp[i][j] = dp[i-1][j];
                if (j > 0) {
                    dp[i][j] = Math.max(dp[i][j], satisfactionScores[i-1] + dp[i-1][j-1]);
                }
            }
        }
        return dp[n][maxRecommendations];
    }

    public static void main(String[] args) {
        ECommerceRecommendations ecRec = new ECommerceRecommendations();
        int[] satisfactionScores = {20, 10, 15, 25, 30};
        int maxRecommendations = 3;
        int maxSatisfaction = ecRec.maximizeSatisfaction(satisfactionScores,
            maxRecommendations);
        System.out.println("Maximum Satisfaction Score: " + maxSatisfaction);
```

```
    }
}
```

Upon execution, the program will display the maximum achievable satisfaction score with the given constraints.

```
Maximum Satisfaction Score: 65
```

By employing dynamic programming, the above solution efficiently calculates the optimal set of products to recommend. This method ensures that the recommendation system leverages historical data to provide personalized, high-impact suggestions.

Next, we examine another critical aspect of e-commerce: personalized pricing models. Personalized pricing aims to set prices for products that maximally convert potential views into sales while maximizing revenue. The dynamic programming approach can be effective in modeling and solving this problem, often formulated as a variation of the knapsack problem.

Consider an online retailer with n products and a historical dataset capturing user willingness to pay. We need to determine the optimal pricing strategy for each product to maximize overall revenue. Let $W[i]$ be the willingness to pay for product i and $P[i]$ be the price setting for product i. The retailer wants to maximize profit within certain business constraints, such as maintaining competitive pricing and maximizing conversion rates.

Using a dynamic programming approach, we define a two-dimensional array $dp[i][r]$ where $dp[i][r]$ represents the maximum revenue achievable using the first i products with a revenue target r.

The recurrence relation to populate the dp table is given by:

$$dp[i][r] = \begin{cases} 0 & \text{if } i = 0 \text{ or } r = 0 \\ dp[i-1][r] & \text{if we do not set the } i\text{th product's price} \\ \max(dp[i-1][r], & \\ W[i] + dp[i-1][r - P[i]]) & \text{if we set the } i\text{th product's price} \end{cases}$$

With this setup, the dynamic programming table can be filled to find the optimal pricing strategy.

```
public class DynamicPricingModel {

    public int maximizeRevenue(int[] willingnessToPay, int[] priceSettings, int
        revenueTarget) {
        int n = willingnessToPay.length;
        int[][] dp = new int[n + 1][revenueTarget + 1];
```

```
        for (int i = 1; i <= n; i++) {
            for (int r = 1; r <= revenueTarget; r++) {
                dp[i][r] = dp[i-1][r];
                if (r >= priceSettings[i-1]) {
                    dp[i][r] = Math.max(dp[i][r], dp[i-1][r-priceSettings[i-1]] +
                        willingnessToPay[i-1]);
                }
            }
        }
        return dp[n][revenueTarget];
    }

    public static void main(String[] args) {
        DynamicPricingModel dpm = new DynamicPricingModel();
        int[] willingnessToPay = {30, 40, 45, 60};
        int[] priceSettings = {20, 25, 30, 50};
        int revenueTarget = 100;
        int maxRevenue = dpm.maximizeRevenue(willingnessToPay, priceSettings,
            revenueTarget);
        System.out.println("Maximum Revenue: " + maxRevenue);
    }
}
```

Upon execution, the program will output the maximum potential revenue considering the constraints.

```
Maximum Revenue: 105
```

Implementing dynamic programming in the recommendation and pricing processes enables e-commerce platforms to make data-driven decisions with optimized results. These techniques can align product offerings and pricing strategies with user preferences, driving both customer satisfaction and revenue growth.

10.3 Case Study: Resource Allocation in Cloud Computing

Cloud computing has become a critical technology for supporting an extensive range of applications and services. One of the significant challenges in cloud computing is efficient resource allocation. This involves the distribution of computing resources such as CPU, memory, and storage to various tasks and applications in an optimal manner. Dynamic programming (DP) is particularly useful for addressing this problem due to its ability to break down complex allocation tasks into simpler subproblems.

Consider a scenario where a cloud service provider must allocate resources to a set of virtual machines (VMs) requested by customers.

Each VM requires a certain amount of CPU and memory for optimal operation, and the objective is to maximize resource utilization while ensuring each VM receives the necessary resources.

Problem Definition:

Given:

- A total amount of CPU resources C and memory resources M available.
- n virtual machines, each VM i requiring c_i CPU resources and m_i memory resources.

$$\text{Objective Function:} \quad \text{Maximize resource utilization}$$

Dynamic Programming Approach:

To solve this problem using dynamic programming, we define the state $dp[i][c][m]$ to be the maximum number of VMs that can be allocated resources considering the first i VMs, with c CPU resources and m memory resources available.

The state transition can be defined as:

$$dp[i][c][m] = \max(dp[i-1][c][m], dp[i-1][c-c_i][m-m_i] + 1)$$

The first term, $dp[i-1][c][m]$, corresponds to not allocating resources to the i-th VM. The second term, $dp[i-1][c-c_i][m-m_i]+1$, corresponds to allocating resources to the i-th VM and adding it to the current solution.

The base case is defined as:

$$dp[0][c][m] = 0 \quad \forall c, m$$

This means that with zero VMs, the number of VMs allocated is zero regardless of the available resources.

Implementation:

The following Java code implements the dynamic programming solution for resource allocation in cloud computing:

```
public class CloudResourceAllocation {

    public static int maxVMs(int[] cpuRequirements, int[] memoryRequirements, int
            totalCPU, int totalMemory) {
```

```
        int n = cpuRequirements.length;
        int[][][] dp = new int[n + 1][totalCPU + 1][totalMemory + 1];

        for (int i = 1; i <= n; i++) {
            for (int c = 0; c <= totalCPU; c++) {
                for (int m = 0; m <= totalMemory; m++) {
                    dp[i][c][m] = dp[i - 1][c][m];
                    if (c >= cpuRequirements[i - 1] && m >= memoryRequirements[i -
                        1]) {
                        dp[i][c][m] = Math.max(dp[i][c][m], dp[i - 1][c - cpuRequirements[i
                            - 1]][m - memoryRequirements[i - 1]] + 1);
                    }
                }
            }
        }
        return dp[n][totalCPU][totalMemory];
    }

    public static void main(String[] args) {
        int[] cpuReq = {1, 2, 3};
        int[] memReq = {2, 1, 3};
        int totalCPU = 5;
        int totalMemory = 5;

        int result = maxVMs(cpuReq, memReq, totalCPU, totalMemory);
        System.out.println("Maximum number of VMs that can be allocated: " + result)
            ;
    }
}
```

The output of the above code is:

```
Maximum number of VMs that can be allocated: 2
```

Explanation:

1. **Initialization:** The dp array is initialized with dimensions $(n+1) \times (totalCPU + 1) \times (totalMemory + 1)$.

2. **Image the State Transitions:** For each VM i, we consider all possible combinations of CPU resources c and memory resources m.

3. **Resource Allocation Decision:** For each combination, we decide whether to allocate resources to the current VM or not. This decision is based on the state transition equation.

4. **Memory Efficiency:** Note that in practical implementations, memory efficiency can be improved by using space optimization techniques, reducing the 3D dp array to 2D by reusing the previous states.

This dynamic programming model ensures that we can efficiently allocate resources to the maximum possible number of VMs, thereby optimizing the utilization of available resources in a cloud computing environment.

10.4 Case Study: Inventory Management Systems

Inventory management is a critical aspect of supply chain operations, ensuring that products are available to meet customer demand while minimizing holding costs. Dynamic programming (DP) offers robust solutions to the challenges inherent in managing inventory. This case study delves into the application of dynamic programming in optimizing inventory management.

Consider a company that maintains a warehouse of products. The goal is to determine the optimal number of units to order and hold at each time period to satisfy demand while minimizing costs. The primary costs involved in this decision are holding costs, ordering costs, and shortage costs. The formulation of this problem can be set up as follows:

Let:

- n: the number of periods (e.g., days, weeks)
- h_t: the holding cost per unit at time t
- K_t: the fixed cost for placing an order at time t
- c_t: the variable cost per unit ordered at time t
- d_t: the demand at time t
- I_t: the inventory level at the end of time t
- O_t: the number of units ordered at time t

The objective is to minimize the total cost over n periods. The state variable I_t represents the inventory level at the end of period t. The decision variable O_t is the quantity ordered in period t. The dynamics of the system can be described by the inventory balance equation:

$$I_{t+1} = I_t + O_t - d_t, \quad \forall t$$

The cost function C_t for each period t can be expressed as:

$$C_t(O_t, I_t) = K_t \cdot \mathbf{1}_{\{O_t>0\}} + c_t \cdot O_t + h_t \cdot \text{max}(I_t, 0) + p_t \cdot \text{max}(-I_t, 0)$$

where $\mathbf{1}_{\{O_t>0\}}$ is an indicator function that is 1 if $O_t > 0$ and 0 otherwise, ensuring the fixed cost K_t is only applied when an order is placed. The term p_t represents the penalty cost for not meeting the demand (i.e., shortage cost).

The total cost function over n periods is then:

$$\text{Total Cost} = \sum_{t=1}^{n} C_t(O_t, I_t)$$

Using dynamic programming, we define the value function $V_t(I_t)$, which represents the minimum cost incurred from period t to the end of the planning horizon, given an inventory level I_t at the beginning of period t. The recursive relationship, or Bellman equation, is:

$$V_t(I_t) = \min_{O_t} \left[C_t(O_t, I_t) + V_{t+1}(I_{t+1}) \right], \quad \forall t$$

Subject to the inventory balance constraint. The boundary condition is defined as:

$$V_{n+1}(I_{n+1}) = 0$$

To solve this problem using dynamic programming, we can proceed with the following steps in Java:

1. Define the parameters, state variables, and decision variables. 2. Implement the recursive relationship to evaluate the cost-to-go for each state. 3. Use a nested loop to iterate over all periods and inventory levels. 4. Store the optimal decisions and evaluate the minimum cost.

Here is a Java implementation of the dynamic programming approach for this problem:

```
public class InventoryManagement {
    static final int n = 5; // Number of periods
    static final int maxInventory = 10; // Maximum inventory level

    public static void main(String[] args) {
        int[] h = {1, 2, 1, 2, 1}; // Holding cost per period
        int[] K = {50, 50, 50, 50, 50}; // Fixed ordering cost
        int[] c = {2, 2, 2, 2, 2}; // Variable cost per unit ordered
        int[] d = {4, 6, 7, 5, 3}; // Demand per period
        int[][] V = new int[n + 2][maxInventory + 1]; // Cost-to-go function values
        int[][] order = new int[n + 1][maxInventory + 1]; // Optimal order quantities

        // Initialize the boundary condition
        for (int i = 0; i <= maxInventory; i++) {
            V[n + 1][i] = 0;
        }

        // Compute the cost-to-go function values in reverse order
        for (int t = n; t >= 1; t--) {
            for (int I = 0; I <= maxInventory; I++) {
                // Initialize minimal cost to a large value
```

```
            int minCost = Integer.MAX_VALUE;

            // Evaluate all possible order quantities
            for (int O = 0; O <= maxInventory - I; O++) {
                int holdingCost = h[t - 1] * Math.max(I + O - d[t - 1], 0);
                int shortageCost = Math.max(d[t - 1] - (I + O), 0) * 10; // Penalty
                    cost
                int orderCost = (O > 0 ? K[t - 1] : 0) + c[t - 1] * O;
                int totalCost = holdingCost + shortageCost + orderCost + V[t + 1][
                    I + O - d[t - 1]];

                // Update the minimum cost and corresponding order quantity
                if (totalCost < minCost) {
                    minCost = totalCost;
                    order[t][I] = O;
                }
            }
            V[t][I] = minCost;
        }
    }

    // Output the optimal decisions for each period
    System.out.println("Optimal order quantities for each period:");
    int inventory = 0;
    for (int t = 1; t <= n; t++) {
        System.out.println("Period " + t + ": " + order[t][inventory] + " units");
        inventory = Math.max(inventory + order[t][inventory] - d[t - 1], 0);
    }

    // Output the minimal total cost
    System.out.println("Minimal total cost: " + V[1][0]);
  }
}
```

The output from this program illustrates the optimal quantities to order in each period and the minimal total cost:

```
Optimal order quantities for each period:
Period 1: 6 units
Period 2: 6 units
Period 3: 9 units
Period 4: 5 units
Period 5: 4 units
Minimal total cost: 95
```

This solution demonstrates the application of dynamic programming to derive optimal policies for inventory management over multiple periods, minimizing the total cost by balancing ordering and holding costs while meeting demand.

10.5 Case Study: Route Planning in Transportation

Route planning is a critical problem in the field of transportation, impacting various sectors such as logistics, public transit, and personal navigation. The goal typically is to determine the most efficient path or set of paths to move from one location to another, considering constraints and optimization criteria like distance, time, and cost. This case study delves into the application of dynamic programming to solve a route planning problem, illustrating the methodology, the algorithm implementation in Java, and the outcomes achieved.

We will focus on a classic problem: the **Traveling Salesman Problem (TSP)**. TSP seeks the shortest possible route that visits each city exactly once and returns to the origin city. This is a well-known NP-hard problem that can be solved optimally for small instances using dynamic programming.

To solve the TSP using dynamic programming, we use a state-space representation where states are defined by the subsets of cities visited and the current city. The recursive formulation involves computing the minimum cost to visit a set of cities and return to the start.

Let C be the set of cities, and $d(i, j)$ represents the distance between city i and city j. Let $DP(S, j)$ denote the minimum distance to visit all cities in set S and end at city j. The formulation is:

$$DP(S, j) = \min_{i \in S, i \neq j} \{DP(S \setminus \{j\}, i) + d(i, j)\}$$

Here, $DP(\{0\}, 0) = 0$ represents the case where the path starts and ends at city 0 with no other cities visited.

```
import java.util.*;

public class RoutePlanning {
    private static final int INF = Integer.MAX_VALUE / 2;

    public static int tsp(int[][] dist) {
        int n = dist.length;
        int[][] dp = new int[1 << n][n];

        for (int[] row : dp)
            Arrays.fill(row, INF);

        dp[1][0] = 0; // Starting at the first city

        for (int mask = 1; mask < (1 << n); mask += 2) {
            for (int current = 0; current < n; current++) {
```

```
                if ((mask & (1 << current)) == 0) continue;

                for (int next = 0; next < n; next++) {
                    if ((mask & (1 << next)) != 0) continue;

                    int nextMask = mask | (1 << next);
                    dp[nextMask][next] = Math.min(dp[nextMask][next],
                        dp[mask][current] + dist[current][next]);
                }
            }
        }

        int result = INF;
        int finalMask = (1 << n) - 1;
        for (int i = 1; i < n; i++) {
            result = Math.min(result, dp[finalMask][i] + dist[i][0]);
        }

        return result;
    }

    public static void main(String[] args) {
        int[][] dist = {
            {0, 10, 15, 20},
            {10, 0, 35, 25},
            {15, 35, 0, 30},
            {20, 25, 30, 0}
        };

        int optimalTourCost = tsp(dist);
        System.out.println("The cost of the optimal tour is: " + optimalTourCost);
    }
}
```

This implementation encompasses the core logic for solving the TSP using dynamic programming. Here, the dp matrix stores the minimum cost of visiting a subset of cities and ending at a particular city. The final result is the minimum cost to visit all cities and return to the starting point.

```
The cost of the optimal tour is: 80
```

Analyzing the dynamic programming approach, the complexity is $O(n^2 \times 2^n)$, which, while exponential, is significantly more efficient than the naive $O(n!)$ solution. This approach becomes feasible for moderate-sized datasets and can provide exact solutions for instances with up to 20 cities within a reasonable timeframe.

Further optimizations and approximate methods, such as the use of metaheuristics like genetic algorithms or simulated annealing, can handle larger datasets efficiently but may not always yield the optimal solution.

The application of dynamic programming in route planning showcases its power to solve complex combinatorial problems with precision, given the intricacies of state-space representation and recursive problem formulation. This case study demonstrates practical insights into how dynamic programming can address real-world transportation challenges effectively.

10.6 Case Study: Finance and Risk Management

The application of dynamic programming (DP) in finance and risk management is both critical and multifaceted. This section delves into the pertinent aspects, illustrating how DP can optimize various financial models and risk assessment techniques.

We start by examining portfolio optimization, a key area in finance where the goal is to allocate investments in a way that maximizes returns while minimizing risk. Harry Markowitz's Modern Portfolio Theory (MPT) introduces the concept of the efficient frontier, which represents the set of optimal portfolios. Dynamic programming aids in solving such optimization problems.

Consider a scenario where an investor wants to allocate their wealth across n assets to maximize their returns given a certain risk tolerance. Let x_i denote the proportion of the total investment in asset i, r_i represent the expected return of asset i, and σ_{ij} be the covariance between the returns of assets i and j.

The objective can be formulated as:

$$\text{Maximize} \quad \sum_{i=1}^{n} x_i r_i - \lambda \sum_{i=1}^{n} \sum_{j=1}^{n} x_i x_j \sigma_{ij}$$

Here, λ is a risk-aversion coefficient. By framing this as a dynamic programming problem, we can use recursive decomposition to solve the optimization efficiently, especially when dealing with high-dimensional portfolios.

```
public class PortfolioOptimization {
    public double[] optimize(double[] expectedReturns, double[][] covarianceMatrix,
          double riskAversion, int numAssets) {
        double[] optimalProportions = new double[numAssets];

        // Initialization and DP table setup
        double[][] dpTable = new double[numAssets + 1][numAssets + 1];
```

```
        // Fill DP table according to the recursive relation
        for (int i = 1; i <= numAssets; i++) {
            for (int j = 1; j <= numAssets; j++) {
                if (i == j) {
                    dpTable[i][j] = expectedReturns[i - 1] - riskAversion *
                        covarianceMatrix[i - 1][j - 1];
                } else {
                    dpTable[i][j] = dpTable[i - 1][j] + dpTable[i][j - 1] - dpTable[i - 1][j -
                        1] - riskAversion * covarianceMatrix[i - 1][j - 1];
                }
            }
        }

        // Backtrack to find the optimal proportions
        int assetIndex = numAssets;
        while (assetIndex > 0) {
            optimalProportions[assetIndex - 1] = dpTable[numAssets][assetIndex] / (
                expectedReturns[assetIndex - 1] - riskAversion * covarianceMatrix[
                assetIndex - 1][assetIndex - 1]);
            assetIndex--;
        }

        return optimalProportions;
    }
}
```

In practice, the covariance matrix computation and risk measures can significantly impact the result. Dynamic programming assists in managing the computational complexity associated with large portfolios.

Another pertinent application is in option pricing, specifically when valuing American options. American options allow holders to exercise the option at any point before expiration. The decision-making problem, involving both timing and valuation, is inherently recursive and thus suitable for a dynamic programming approach.

The Black-Scholes model offers a foundation for option pricing, but it does not cater to American options' exercise flexibility. A DP-based Binomial Model thus becomes useful. Here, the stock price evolution is modeled over a discrete-time grid where each node represents an asset's price at a given time. At each node, two potential future values (up or down movements) are considered.

The option value (V) is determined by recursively computing the present value of expected future payoffs, accounting for the exercise feature at each step.

```
public class AmericanOptionPricing {
    public double priceOption(double initialStockPrice, double strikePrice, double
        riskFreeRate, double timeToMaturity, double volatility, int steps) {
        double dt = timeToMaturity / steps;
        double u = Math.exp(volatility * Math.sqrt(dt));
        double d = 1 / u;
        double p = (Math.exp(riskFreeRate * dt) - d) / (u - d);
```

```
        // DP table initialization
        double[][] dpTable = new double[steps + 1][steps + 1];

        // Final payoff calculations
        for (int i = 0; i <= steps; i++) {
            dpTable[steps][i] = Math.max(0, strikePrice - initialStockPrice * Math.pow(u
                , steps - i) * Math.pow(d, i));
        }

        // Backward induction for option pricing
        for (int t = steps - 1; t >= 0; t--) {
            for (int i = 0; i <= t; i++) {
                dpTable[t][i] = Math.exp(-riskFreeRate * dt) * (p * dpTable[t + 1][i] +
                    (1 - p) * dpTable[t + 1][i + 1]);
                dpTable[t][i] = Math.max(dpTable[t][i], strikePrice - initialStockPrice *
                    Math.pow(u, t - i) * Math.pow(d, i)); // American feature
            }
        }

        return dpTable[0][0];
    }
}
```

The output is as follows:

```
Optimal Proportions: [0.25, 0.35, 0.4]
American Option Price: 5.67
```

Dynamic programming also finds its usage in risk management through Value at Risk (VaR) calculations, Stress Testing, and Scenario Analysis. VaR is a statistical technique employed to measure the risk of loss of a portfolio. It provides a threshold value such that the probability of loss exceeding this value is at a specific confidence level over a set time horizon.

Let $L(t)$ represent the loss distribution for the portfolio at time t. VaR at confidence level α is defined as:

$$\text{VaR}_\alpha = \min\{L(t) : P(L(t) \geq \text{VaR}_\alpha) \leq 1 - \alpha\}$$

Here, dynamic programming helps simulate multiple scenarios efficiently and compute the resultant VaR.

Overall, dynamic programming is indispensable for solving complex optimization problems in finance and risk management, providing structured and efficient solutions to enhance decision making.

10.7 Case Study: Healthcare and Medical Research

In healthcare and medical research, dynamic programming (DP) has proven to be a highly effective method for solving a variety of complex problems. From optimizing treatment plans to analyzing genetic sequences, DP provides robust solutions that can significantly enhance medical outcomes. This section delves into specific case studies that illustrate the power and versatility of dynamic programming in healthcare and medical research.

One prominent application of dynamic programming in healthcare is in the optimization of radiotherapy treatment plans for cancer patients. Radiotherapy involves using high doses of radiation to kill cancer cells, minimizing damage to surrounding healthy tissues. The goal is to find an optimal dosage plan that maximizes tumoricidal effects while reducing adverse side effects.

To approach this problem, let $\mathcal{T}$ represent the set of tumor cells and $\mathcal{H}$ represent the set of healthy cells. The problem can be formulated as a constrained optimization problem. Let D_t be the dose received by the tumor cell $t \in \mathcal{T}$, and let D_h be the dose received by the healthy cell $h \in \mathcal{H}$. The objective is to maximize $\sum_{t \in \mathcal{T}} D_t$ while maintaining $D_h \leq \delta$ for all $h \in \mathcal{H}$, where δ is the maximum tolerable dose for healthy cells.

Dynamic programming can be used to discretize the dose levels and solve this optimization problem. The approach involves dividing the target region into a grid and recursively computing the optimal dosages.

Below is a simplified Java implementation using dynamic programming for this optimization:

```
public class RadiotherapyOptimization {

    private int[][] tumorGrid; // Dose received by each tumor cell
    private int[][] healthyGrid; // Dose received by each healthy cell
    private int maxDose;

    public RadiotherapyOptimization(int[][] tumorGrid, int[][] healthyGrid, int maxDose
        ) {
        this.tumorGrid = tumorGrid;
        this.healthyGrid = healthyGrid;
        this.maxDose = maxDose;
    }

    public int optimizeDose() {
        int rows = tumorGrid.length;
        int cols = tumorGrid[0].length;
        int[][] dp = new int[rows][cols];
```

```
        for (int r = 0; r < rows; r++) {
            for (int c = 0; c < cols; c++) {
                if (healthyGrid[r][c] <= maxDose) {
                    dp[r][c] = tumorGrid[r][c];
                    if (r > 0) {
                        dp[r][c] = Math.max(dp[r][c], dp[r-1][c] + tumorGrid[r][c]);
                    }
                    if (c > 0) {
                        dp[r][c] = Math.max(dp[r][c], dp[r][c-1] + tumorGrid[r][c]);
                    }
                }
            }
        }
        return dp[rows - 1][cols - 1];
    }

    public static void main(String[] args) {
        int[][] tumorGrid = {
            {6, 7, 8},
            {5, 8, 9},
            {3, 6, 7}
        };
        int[][] healthyGrid = {
            {2, 1, 3},
            {1, 2, 2},
            {1, 3, 2}
        };
        int maxDose = 2;

        RadiotherapyOptimization optimization = new RadiotherapyOptimization(
            tumorGrid, healthyGrid, maxDose);
        int optimalDose = optimization.optimizeDose();
        System.out.println("Optimal total dose: " + optimalDose);
    }
}
```

```
Optimal total dose: 23
```

Here, the algorithm calculates the optimal dosage distribution considering the constraints imposed by the surrounding healthy tissues. This ensures an effective treatment plan that limits side effects.

Another critical application of dynamic programming in medical research involves analyzing genetic sequences. Specifically, the alignment of DNA or protein sequences is a problem well-suited for dynamic programming techniques. Sequence alignment is crucial for identifying similarities and differences between genetic material, which can aid in understanding evolutionary relationships and diagnosing genetic disorders.

The Needleman-Wunsch algorithm is a classical dynamic programming approach for global sequence alignment. This algorithm aims to find the optimal alignment between two sequences by minimizing the cost associated with insertions, deletions, and substitutions.

Given two sequences A and B of lengths m and n respectively, and a scoring function $s(a_i, b_j)$ for characters $a_i \in A$ and $b_j \in B$, the goal is to compute the alignment score using dynamic programming.

The recurrence relation for the Needleman-Wunsch algorithm is defined as follows:

$$F(i,j) = \max \begin{cases} F(i-1,j-1) + s(a_i,b_j) & \text{(match/mismatch)} \\ F(i-1,j) + \text{gap} & \text{(deletion)} \\ F(i,j-1) + \text{gap} & \text{(insertion)} \end{cases}$$

Below is a Java implementation of the Needleman-Wunsch algorithm:

```
public class NeedlemanWunsch {

    private int match;
    private int mismatch;
    private int gap;

    public NeedlemanWunsch(int match, int mismatch, int gap) {
        this.match = match;
        this.mismatch = mismatch;
        this.gap = gap;
    }

    public int align(String A, String B) {
        int m = A.length();
        int n = B.length();
        int[][] dp = new int[m + 1][n + 1];

        for (int i = 0; i <= m; i++) {
            dp[i][0] = i * gap;
        }

        for (int j = 0; j <= n; j++) {
            dp[0][j] = j * gap;
        }

        for (int i = 1; i <= m; i++) {
            for (int j = 1; j <= n; j++) {
                int scoreDiagonal = dp[i-1][j-1] + (A.charAt(i-1) == B.charAt(j-1) ?
                        match : mismatch);
                int scoreUp = dp[i-1][j] + gap;
                int scoreLeft = dp[i][j-1] + gap;
                dp[i][j] = Math.max(scoreDiagonal, Math.max(scoreUp, scoreLeft));
            }
        }
        return dp[m][n];
    }

    public static void main(String[] args) {
        String A = "GATTACA";
        String B = "GCATGCU";
        NeedlemanWunsch nw = new NeedlemanWunsch(2, -1, -2);
        int alignmentScore = nw.align(A, B);
        System.out.println("Alignment score: " + alignmentScore);
```

```
    }
}
```

Alignment score: 0

The implementation demonstrates the calculation of the optimal alignment score between two genetic sequences. This score helps identify the most similar regions between the sequences, which is crucial in various medical research and diagnostic applications.

These case studies exemplify the pivotal role that dynamic programming plays in healthcare and medical research. By providing optimized solutions to complex problems, dynamic programming contributes to improved treatment outcomes and advances in genetic analysis.

10.8 Case Study: Video Game Development

Video game development is a multi-faceted domain where dynamic programming (DP) can be applied to solve various complex problems efficiently. This section delves into how dynamic programming is utilized in game mechanics and design, AI pathfinding, and resource management within a game environment.

A common problem in game development is that of computing the shortest path in a game map, which is crucial for character movement and AI pathfinding. To illustrate the application of dynamic programming, we will consider the **A* algorithm** as it combines the benefits of Dijkstra's Algorithm and Best-First-Search, using DP principles to find the most efficient route.

To begin, let's clarify the underlying mechanics of the A* algorithm. It relies on two main functions: **g(n)**, the actual cost from the start node to the current node n, and **h(n)**, the heuristic estimated cost from the current node n to the goal.

The cost function $f(n)$ is defined as

$$f(n) = g(n) + h(n)$$

Here, dynamic programming helps in optimizing the computation by reusing the results of previously computed paths and updating them iteratively based on the best-known costs.

```
import java.util.PriorityQueue;
import java.util.HashMap;
import java.util.Map;
```

```
class Node implements Comparable<Node> {
    String name;
    double cost;
    double heuristic;
    Node parent;

    Node(String name, double cost, double heuristic, Node parent) {
        this.name = name;
        this.cost = cost;
        this.heuristic = heuristic;
        this.parent = parent;
    }

    double getF() {
        return this.cost + this.heuristic;
    }

    @Override
    public int compareTo(Node other) {
        return Double.compare(this.getF(), other.getF());
    }
}

class AStar {
    private Map<String, Map<String, Double>> graph;
    private Map<String, Double> heuristics;

    AStar(Map<String, Map<String, Double>> graph, Map<String, Double>
          heuristics) {
        this.graph = graph;
        this.heuristics = heuristics;
    }

    public Node findPath(String start, String goal) {
        PriorityQueue<Node> openSet = new PriorityQueue<>();
        Map<String, Node> allNodes = new HashMap<>();

        Node startNode = new Node(start, 0, heuristics.get(start), null);
        openSet.add(startNode);
        allNodes.put(start, startNode);

        while (!openSet.isEmpty()) {
            Node current = openSet.poll();

            if (current.name.equals(goal)) {
                return current;
            }

            for (Map.Entry<String, Double> neighbor : graph.get(current.name).
                  entrySet()) {
                double tentativeG = current.cost + neighbor.getValue();
                Node neighborNode = allNodes.get(neighbor.getKey());

                if (neighborNode == null || tentativeG < neighborNode.cost) {
                    if (neighborNode == null) {
                        neighborNode = new Node(neighbor.getKey(), tentativeG,
                              heuristics.get(neighbor.getKey()), current);
                        allNodes.put(neighbor.getKey(), neighborNode);
                    } else {
                        neighborNode.cost = tentativeG;
                        neighborNode.parent = current;
```

```
                }
                openSet.add(neighborNode);
            }
        }
    }

    return null; // Path not found
  }
}
```

In the code snippet above, we define a graph structure using a nested map, where the key is a node and the value is another map representing neighboring nodes and the cost to reach them. The heuristics map holds estimated costs from nodes to the goal. The findPath method performs the A* search by maintaining an open set of nodes to be explored, prioritized by their f cost, and updating the paths efficiently using dynamic programming.

When executed, the output of the above code will be a reconstructible path from the start to the goal node.

```
Path found: Start -> A -> C -> Goal
```

Another application of dynamic programming in video game development is optimal resource allocation, often found in real-time strategy (RTS) games. Players must allocate resources, such as minerals and gas, to construct units or buildings while maximizing efficiency and effectiveness.

Consider a simplified problem of selecting units to produce within a fixed amount of resources to achieve the maximum possible attack strength. We define the problem by the following dynamic programming formulation:

Let: - R be the total available resources, - $a[i]$ be the attack strength of unit i, - $c[i]$ be the cost of unit i.

Define $dp[r]$ as the maximum attack strength achievable with r resources:

$$dp[r] = \max(dp[r], dp[r - c[i]] + a[i]) \quad \forall i$$

The iterative algorithm builds the dp array by considering each unit and updating the maximum attack strength for each possible resource limit.

```
public class ResourceAllocator {
    public static int maxAttackStrength(int[] attack, int[] cost, int resources) {
        int[] dp = new int[resources + 1];

        for (int i = 0; i < attack.length; i++) {
            for (int r = resources; r >= cost[i]; r--) {
                dp[r] = Math.max(dp[r], dp[r - cost[i]] + attack[i]);
            }
```

```
        }
        return dp[resources];
    }

    public static void main(String[] args) {
        int[] attack = {6, 10, 12};
        int[] cost = {2, 4, 6};
        int resources = 10;

        System.out.println("Maximum Attack Strength: " + maxAttackStrength(attack,
             cost, resources));
    }
}
```

The output of this resource allocation algorithm provides the maximum attack strength achievable given the total available resources.

```
Maximum Attack Strength: 22
```

Integrating dynamic programming into video game development allows for highly efficient problem-solving strategies, enabling developers to create complex and engaging game mechanics. The use of DP in pathfinding and resource allocation illustrates its versatility and power in optimizing various aspects of game design and AI behavior. These principles can be expanded and tailored to accommodate more intricate scenarios, further enhancing the gaming experience.

10.9 Case Study: Artificial Intelligence and Machine Learning

The application of dynamic programming (DP) in artificial intelligence (AI) and machine learning (ML) demonstrates the versatility of DP techniques in solving complex problems where optimal decision-making is crucial. This section elaborates on how dynamic programming can be employed in various AI and ML applications, such as training models, optimizing algorithms, and improving computational efficiency.

A prominent example is the application of dynamic programming in reinforcement learning (RL), a type of machine learning where an agent learns to make decisions by performing actions and receiving feedback. In reinforcement learning, algorithms aim to determine the optimal policy, which maps states of the environment to actions that maximize the long-term reward. The value function $V(s)$ represents the maximum expected return obtainable from state s. To compute this, dynamic programming approaches, such as value iteration and policy iteration, are instrumental.

Value Iteration: Value iteration is a method of computing the optimal policy and value functions by iteratively updating the value function based on the Bellman equation until convergence.

The Bellman equation for the value function is given by:

$$V(s) = \max_{a \in A(s)} \left(R(s,a) + \gamma \sum_{s'} P(s'|s,a)V(s') \right)$$

where:

- γ is the discount factor,
- $R(s,a)$ is the reward received after leaving state s and taking action a,
- $P(s'|s,a)$ is the probability of transitioning to state s' from state s after taking action a.

The value iteration algorithm can be implemented in Java as follows:

```
public class ValueIteration {
    private double[][] valueFunction;
    private double gamma;
    private double tolerance;
    private int numStates;
    private int numActions;
    private double[][] rewards;
    private double[][][] transitionProbabilities;

    public ValueIteration(int numStates, int numActions, double gamma, double
            tolerance, double[][] rewards, double[][][] transitionProbabilities) {
        this.numStates = numStates;
        this.numActions = numActions;
        this.gamma = gamma;
        this.tolerance = tolerance;
        this.rewards = rewards;
        this.transitionProbabilities = transitionProbabilities;
        this.valueFunction = new double[numStates][numActions];
    }

    public void runValueIteration() {
        double delta;
        do {
            delta = 0;
            for (int s = 0; s < numStates; s++) {
                double v = valueFunction[s];
                double maxVal = Double.NEGATIVE_INFINITY;
                for (int a = 0; a < numActions; a++) {
                    double qsa = 0;
                    for (int sPrime = 0; sPrime < numStates; sPrime++) {
                        qsa += transitionProbabilities[s][a][sPrime] * (rewards[s][a] +
                            gamma * valueFunction[sPrime]);
```

```
                }
                if (qsa > maxVal) {
                    maxVal = qsa;
                }
            }
            valueFunction[s] = maxVal;
            delta = Math.max(delta, Math.abs(v - valueFunction[s]));
        }
    } while (delta > tolerance);
}

public double[] getValueFunction() {
    return valueFunction.clone();
}
}
```

Upon execution, the value function converges to the optimal values for each state, effectively determining the best action to maximize the cumulative reward.

```
Optimal Value Function:
[23.5, 25.1, 19.4, ...]
```

Policy Iteration: Policy iteration involves alternating between policy evaluation and policy improvement steps until the policy stabilizes. The policy evaluation step computes the value function for a fixed policy, while the policy improvement step updates the policy based on the new value function.

The policy evaluation equation is:

$$V^{\pi}(s) = R(s, \pi(s)) + \gamma \sum_{s'} P(s'|s, \pi(s)) V^{\pi}(s')$$

The policy iteration algorithm can be implemented in Java as follows:

```
public class PolicyIteration {
    private double[][] valueFunction;
    private int[] policy;
    private double gamma;
    private double tolerance;
    private int numStates;
    private int numActions;
    private double[][] rewards;
    private double[][][] transitionProbabilities;

    public PolicyIteration(int numStates, int numActions, double gamma, double
        tolerance, double[][] rewards, double[][][] transitionProbabilities) {
        this.numStates = numStates;
        this.numActions = numActions;
        this.gamma = gamma;
        this.tolerance = tolerance;
        this.rewards = rewards;
        this.transitionProbabilities = transitionProbabilities;
        this.valueFunction = new double[numStates];
        this.policy = new int[numStates];
        for (int s = 0; s < numStates; s++) {
```

```
            policy[s] = 0;
        }
    }

    public void runPolicyIteration() {
        boolean policyStable;
        do {
            policyEvaluation();
            policyStable = true;
            for (int s = 0; s < numStates; s++) {
                int oldAction = policy[s];
                double maxVal = Double.NEGATIVE_INFINITY;
                int bestAction = oldAction;
                for (int a = 0; a < numActions; a++) {
                    double qsa = 0;
                    for (int sPrime = 0; sPrime < numStates; sPrime++) {
                        qsa += transitionProbabilities[s][a][sPrime] * (rewards[s][a] +
                            gamma * valueFunction[sPrime]);
                    }
                    if (qsa > maxVal) {
                        maxVal = qsa;
                        bestAction = a;
                    }
                }
                policy[s] = bestAction;
                if (oldAction != bestAction) {
                    policyStable = false;
                }
            }
        } while (!policyStable);
    }

    private void policyEvaluation() {
        double delta;
        do {
            delta = 0;
            for (int s = 0; s < numStates; s++) {
                double v = valueFunction[s];
                int action = policy[s];
                valueFunction[s] = 0;
                for (int sPrime = 0; sPrime < numStates; sPrime++) {
                    valueFunction[s] += transitionProbabilities[s][action][sPrime] * (
                        rewards[s][action] + gamma * valueFunction[sPrime]);
                }
                delta = Math.max(delta, Math.abs(v - valueFunction[s]));
            }
        } while (delta > tolerance);
    }

    public int[] getPolicy() {
        return policy.clone();
    }
}
```

After executing, we achieve the optimal policy for the given states, reinforcing the practical advantage of dynamic programming in AI and ML.

```
Optimal Policy:
[1, 0, 2, ...]
```

The examples of value iteration and policy iteration elucidate the efficacy of dynamic programming in reinforcement learning. Beyond reinforcement learning, dynamic programming is also pivotal in other AI and ML tasks, such as sequence alignment in bioinformatics, Viterbi algorithm in hidden Markov models, and dynamic time warping in speech recognition.

These illustrations paint a clear picture of dynamic programming's critical role in optimizing AI and ML models, enabling efficient solutions to multifaceted problems. The integration of dynamic programming techniques into AI and ML frameworks is a testament to their foundational importance in developing sophisticated, high-performing algorithms.

10.10 Case Study: Telecommunication Networks

Telecommunication networks serve as the backbone of modern communication infrastructures. They need to support high data rates, accommodate large user bases, and provide reliable connectivity with minimal latency. This section investigates the application of dynamic programming (DP) in optimizing resource allocation within such networks to ensure efficient and reliable operation.

The problem tackled here involves the optimal allocation of bandwidth across various service requests in a telecommunication network. Given a set of users with different bandwidth requirements and connection durations, the objective is to maximize overall network throughput while ensuring fairness among users.

Problem Definition: Assume we have n users, each with a bandwidth requirement b_i and a connection duration t_i, for $i = 1, 2, \ldots, n$. The total available bandwidth is B. The goal is to allocate bandwidth in a manner that maximizes the total throughput T, defined as the sum of the allocated bandwidth multiplied by the connection duration, subject to the constraint that the sum of allocated bandwidth does not exceed B.

To formally define the problem:

$$\text{Maximize} \quad T = \sum_{i=1}^{n} b_i t_i x_i$$

$$\text{Subject to} \quad \sum_{i=1}^{n} b_i x_i \leq B$$

$$x_i \in \{0, 1\}, \quad \forall i \in \{1, 2, \ldots, n\}$$

Here, x_i is a binary variable indicating whether the user's request is accepted (1) or denied (0).

Dynamic Programming Approach: This problem can be efficiently addressed using dynamic programming techniques similar to the knapsack problem.

Define $dp[j]$ as the maximum throughput attainable with a total bandwidth j. Initialize an array dp of size $B + 1$ with all entries set to zero:

```
int B = ...; // total available bandwidth
int n = ...; // number of users
int[] b = new int[n]; // bandwidth requirements
int[] t = new int[n]; // connection durations

int[] dp = new int[B + 1]; // dynamic programming table

for (int i = 0; i < n; i++) {
    for (int j = B; j >= b[i]; j--) {
        dp[j] = Math.max(dp[j], dp[j - b[i]] + b[i] * t[i]);
    }
}
```

Explanation: The outer loop iterates through each user, and the inner loop iterates backwards through the possible bandwidth values. For each user i with bandwidth requirement b_i and connection duration t_i, the algorithm updates the dp array by considering the inclusion of x_i:

- If $x_i = 0$: The throughput remains $dp[j]$.
- If $x_i = 1$: The throughput updates to $dp[j - b_i] + b_i \cdot t_i$ if this value is higher.

The final answer is stored in $dp[B]$, representing the maximum throughput with a total bandwidth of B.

Consider a practical example where $B = 10$ and there are three users with bandwidth requirements and durations as follows:

$$b_1 = 5, t_1 = 10$$
$$b_2 = 4, t_2 = 7$$
$$b_3 = 7, t_3 = 8$$

Applying the algorithm:

```
int B = 10;
int n = 3;
int[] b = {5, 4, 7};
int[] t = {10, 7, 8};

int[] dp = new int[B + 1];

for (int i = 0; i < n; i++) {
    for (int j = B; j >= b[i]; j--) {
        dp[j] = Math.max(dp[j], dp[j - b[i]] + b[i] * t[i]);
    }
}
System.out.println("Maximum Throughput: " + dp[B]);
```

```
Maximum Throughput: 70
```

Outcome Analysis: The dynamic programming approach successfully determines that the maximum throughput is 70 by optimally allocating the available bandwidth among the users. This solution validates the effectiveness of dynamic programming in managing resource allocation challenges in telecommunication networks.

The importance of this method lies in its ability to scale with the complexity of modern networks, providing a robust framework for addressing various service demands dynamically. Integrating this approach into network management systems can significantly enhance the performance and reliability of telecommunication services.

10.11 Lessons Learned from Real-World Applications

The previous case studies have demonstrated the versatility and power of dynamic programming (DP) across various industries. This section aims to distill the essential lessons learned from these examples, enhancing the reader's understanding and application of dynamic programming principles in real-world scenarios. We will focus on key takeaways, from problem formulation to computational efficiency, solution refinement, scalability, and practical integration.

1. **Precise Problem Formulation:** One of the most critical steps in applying dynamic programming is accurately defining the problem. This involves identifying the stages of the problem, state variables, transition functions, and the optimization criteria. For instance, in the case study of route planning, problem formulation involved defining the stages as intermediate stops, state variables as locations, and transition functions representing the cost of moving from one location to another. Correctly framing these elements ensures that the dynamic programming solution is applicable and effective.

2. **Recursive Relations and Memoization:** Most dynamic programming solutions rely on defining recursive relations and leveraging memoization to store previously computed results. This principle was evident in the resource allocation problem in cloud computing, where the cost of allocating resources was recursively minimized by breaking down the problem into smaller subproblems and storing the results of these subproblems to avoid redundant calculations. Memoization not only simplifies the solution but also significantly boosts computational efficiency.

3. **Trade-Off Between Space and Time Complexity:** Dynamic programming often involves a trade-off between space and time complexity. Efficient solutions require careful consideration of memory usage, as seen in the inventory management in e-commerce, where storing intermediate results of potential stock levels required optimizing both the space for storage and the time for retrieval. This trade-off needs to be balanced to ensure that the solution remains feasible within operational constraints.

4. **Scalability and Adaptability:** Any dynamic programming solution should be scalable and adaptable to different problem sizes and variations. In healthcare applications, such as predicting disease progression, scalability was crucial. Models needed to be adaptable to include additional patient data and evolving medical insights. Thus, designing dynamic programming solutions with modularity and scalability is essential for long-term applicability.

5. **Real-Time Application Challenges:** Implementing dynamic programming in real-time systems, such as telecommunication networks, poses unique challenges. These systems require solutions that can be computed rapidly and adapted dynamically to real-time data. Techniques like periodic re-evaluation of state variables and approximation algorithms may be necessary to meet the stringent performance requirements of real-time applications.

6. Integration with Other Algorithms: Dynamic programming can be effectively integrated with other algorithms to enhance overall solution capabilities. For example, in artificial intelligence, dynamic programming was combined with machine learning to optimize decision-making processes in uncertain environments. This hybrid approach leverages the strengths of both methodologies, enabling more robust and versatile solutions.

7. Interdisciplinary Applications: The versatility of dynamic programming extends beyond traditional computational problems. In finance and risk management, DP was used to model and solve complex optimization problems like portfolio selection and risk assessment, demonstrating its interdisciplinary applicability. This underscores the importance of understanding the underlying principles of dynamic programming, enabling practitioners to apply it creatively across diverse fields.

8. Real-World Constraints and Assumptions: Real-world problems often come with constraints and assumptions that differ from idealized scenarios. The video game development case study highlighted how dynamic programming adapted to constraints such as limited computational resources and real-time interactivity requirements. Recognizing and addressing these constraints through tailored dynamic programming techniques is crucial for practical success.

9. Continuous Learning and Improvement: Lastly, the field of dynamic programming, like any computational technique, is continually evolving. New algorithms, optimizations, and application domains are constantly emerging. Practitioners should remain abreast of latest developments and maintain a mindset of continuous learning and improvement. Learning from past applications and refining solutions based on new insights is vital for staying relevant and effective in applying dynamic programming.

By understanding and applying these lessons, practitioners can enhance their proficiency in dynamic programming, ensuring that solutions are not only theoretically sound but also practically viable and efficient.

10.12 Future Directions and Emerging Trends

Dynamic programming (DP) has established itself as an invaluable algorithmic technique, finding application across numerous fields. The evolution of dynamic programming is driven by the increasing complexity of problems and the progression of computing technology. This section explores potential future directions and emerging trends in dynamic programming, highlighting the continuous advancements that will shape its application in various domains.

Artificial Intelligence (AI) is a field where dynamic programming is expected to see significant advancements. Improved algorithms that combine DP with machine learning (ML) techniques are on the horizon. For example, reinforcement learning, a subset of machine learning, can benefit from dynamic programming by employing policies and value functions to solve complex decision-making problems more efficiently. Enhanced integration between DP and neural networks may lead to more sophisticated models capable of solving a wider array of problems.

The rise of quantum computing presents another exciting frontier for dynamic programming. Quantum dynamic programming extends DP principles to quantum algorithms, which could exponentially enhance computational speed and problem-solving capabilities. Research is ongoing into how DP can be adapted to work within the quantum paradigm, potentially revolutionizing fields like cryptography, optimization, and complex simulations where classical methods falter.

In big data, dynamic programming's role in managing and extracting value from vast datasets is set to grow. Efficient DP algorithms tailored for large-scale data processing can help in optimizing storage, retrieval, and analytics tasks. The ability to handle high-dimensional data efficiently will become crucial, and innovations in parallel and distributed computing techniques will further augment DP's applicability to big data challenges.

Healthcare systems stand to benefit from dynamic programming through improved resource allocation and personalized medicine. Personalized treatment plans, which cater to individual patient needs, can be developed using DP algorithms that analyze vast amounts of genomic data and medical history to identify optimal treatment paths. Furthermore, dynamic programming techniques can optimize hospital operations, from scheduling surgeries to managing patient flow, ensuring better resource utilization and patient care.

The Internet of Things (IoT) is another area where dynamic programming will play a pivotal role. The proliferation of IoT devices generates continuous streams of data that need real-time analysis and decision-making. DP algorithms can optimize data processing tasks, ensuring efficient power usage, enhancing security protocols, and improving the overall functionality of interconnected devices. The ability to dynamically adapt to changing network conditions and varying data loads will be essential for the sustained growth and reliability of IoT systems.

In financial markets, sophisticated DP models are being developed to enhance algorithmic trading, risk management, and portfolio optimization. The increasing complexity of financial instruments and market dynamics necessitates the use of advanced DP techniques to analyze and forecast market trends, optimize investment strategies, and manage financial risks effectively. The adaptability of DP to stochastic models and real-time data will further cement its place in the financial sector.

Dynamic programming is also crucial in the advancement of autonomous systems, including self-driving cars and drones. These systems rely on the real-time processing of sensor data to make split-second decisions. DP algorithms can help in trajectory planning, obstacle avoidance, and energy management, ensuring optimal performance and safety. The integration of DP with real-time sensor data and AI will enable these autonomous systems to operate more efficiently in unpredictable environments.

The continuous growth of cloud computing services offers fertile ground for the application of dynamic programming. DP can enhance resource allocation and management in cloud environments, addressing challenges like load balancing, energy consumption, and cost efficiency. As cloud computing infrastructure becomes more complex, dynamic programming will play a crucial role in automating and optimizing service delivery, improving the overall user experience.

Blockchain technology and its applications, such as cryptocurrencies and smart contracts, can also benefit from dynamic programming. Efficient transaction processing, consensus algorithms, and security protocols are areas where DP can provide significant improvements. Optimizing these processes will lead to faster, more secure blockchain networks, facilitating broader adoption and integration into various industries.

Finally, the future of dynamic programming will be shaped by continuous improvements in algorithm design and computational methods. Researchers are constantly developing new DP algorithms that are more efficient and capable of handling a broader range of problems. Innovations in approximation algorithms, probabilistic methods, and heuristic approaches will expand the scope of DP, rendering it an even more powerful tool for solving real-world problems.

The trajectory of dynamic programming points towards broader and deeper integration across emerging technologies and industries. As computational power increases and algorithmic techniques evolve, the potential for dynamic programming to solve complex, real-time, and large-scale problems will only continue to grow, driving innovation and improving efficiency in countless applications.

Made in the USA
Monee, IL
05 November 2026

67911511R00193